The Story of Franc

Stanley John Weyman

Alpha Editions

This edition published in 2024

ISBN : 9789362920720

Design and Setting By
Alpha Editions
www.alphaedis.com
Email - info@alphaedis.com

As per information held with us this book is in Public Domain.
This book is a reproduction of an important historical work. Alpha Editions uses the best technology to reproduce historical work in the same manner it was first published to preserve its original nature. Any marks or number seen are left intentionally to preserve its true form.

Contents

CHAPTER I. ....- 1 -

   "HÉ, SIRE ANE, HÉ!" ....- 1 -

CHAPTER II. ....- 11 -

   IN THE BISHOP'S ROOM. ....- 11 -

CHAPTER III. ....- 20 -

   "DOWN WITH PURVEYORS!" ....- 20 -

CHAPTER IV. ....- 30 -

   TWO SISTERS OF MERCY ....- 30 -

CHAPTER V. ....- 40 -

   MISTRESS BERTRAM. ....- 40 -

CHAPTER VI. ....- 50 -

   MASTER CLARENCE. ....- 50 -

CHAPTER VII. ....- 58 -

   ON BOARD THE "FRAMLINGHAM." ....- 58 -

CHAPTER VIII. ....- 69 -

   A HOUSE OF PEACE ....- 69 -

CHAPTER IX. ....- 79 -

   PLAYING WITH FIRE. ....- 79 -

CHAPTER X. ....- 91 -

   THE FACE IN THE PORCH. ....- 91 -

CHAPTER XI. ....- 101 -

   A FOUL BLOW. ....- 101 -

CHAPTER XII. ....- 112 -

   ANNE'S PETITION. ....- 112 -

CHAPTER XIII. ....- 123 -

   A WILLFUL MAN'S WAY. ....- 123 -

CHAPTER XIV. ....- 135 -

   AT BAY IN THE GATEHOUSE. ....- 135 -

CHAPTER XV ....- 147 -

   BEFORE THE COURT. ....- 147 -

CHAPTER XVI. ....- 156 -

   IN THE DUKE'S NAME. ....- 156 -

CHAPTER XVII. ....- 166 -

   A LETTER THAT HAD MANY ESCAPES. ....- 166 -

CHAPTER XVIII ....- 175 -

THE WITCH'S WARNING. ....- 175 -

CHAPTER XIX. ....- 187 -

FERDINAND CLUDDE. ....- 187 -

CHAPTER XX. ....- 198 -

THE COMING QUEEN. ....- 198 -

CHAPTER XXI. ....- 208 -

MY FATHER. ....- 208 -

CHAPTER XXII. ....- 217 -

SIR ANTHONY'S PURPOSE. ....- 217 -

CHAPTER XXIII. ....- 225 -

THE LAST MASS. ....- 225 -

CHAPTER XXIV. ....- 234 -

AWAITING THE BLOW. ....- 234 -

CHAPTER XXV. ....- 245 -

IN HARBOR AT LAST. ....- 245 -

THE END. ....- 249 -

CHAPTER I.

"HÉ, SIRE ANE, HÉ!"

On the boundary line between the two counties of Warwick and Worcester there is a road very famous in those parts, and called the Ridgeway. Father Carey used to say--and no better Latinist could be found for a score of miles round in the times of which I write--that it was made by the Romans. It runs north and south along the narrow spine of the country, which is spread out on either side like a map, or a picture. As you fare southward you see on your right hand the green orchards and pastures of Worcestershire stretching as far as the Malvern Hills. You have in front of you Bredon Hill, which is a wonderful hill, for if a man goes down the Avon by boat it goes with him--now before, and now behind--a whole day's journey--and then stands in the same place. And on the left hand you have the great Forest of Arden, and not much besides, except oak trees, which grow well in Warwickshire.

I describe this road, firstly, because it is a notable one, and forty years ago was the only Queen's highway, to call a highway, in that country. The rest were mere horse-tracks. Secondly, because the chase wall of Coton End runs along the side of it for two good miles; and the Cluddes--I am Francis Cludde--have lived at Coton End by the Ridgeway time out of mind, probably--for the name smacks of the soil--before the Romans made the road. And thirdly, because forty years ago, on a drizzling February day in 1555--second year of Mary, old religion just reestablished--a number of people were collected on this road, forming a group of a score or more, who stood in an ordered kind of disorder about my uncle's gates and looked all one way, as if expecting an arrival, and an arrival of consequence.

First, there was my uncle Sir Anthony, tall and lean. He wore his best black velvet doublet and cloak, and had put them on with an air of huge importance. This increased each time he turned, staff in hand, and surveyed his following, and as regularly gave place to a "Pshaw!" of vexation and a petulant glance when his eye rested on me. Close beside him, looking important too, but anxious and a little frightened as well, stood good Father Carey. The priest wore his silk cassock, and his lips moved from time to time without sound, as though he were trying over a Latin oration--which, indeed, was the fact. At a more respectful distance were ranged Baldwin Moor, the steward, and a dozen servants; while still farther away lounged as many ragamuffins--landless men, who swarmed about every gentleman's door in those times, and took toll of such abbey lands as the king might have given him. Against one of the stone gate-pillars I leaned myself--nineteen years and six months old, and none too wise, though well grown, and as strong as one here and there. And perched on the top of the twin post, with his chin on his knees, and his hands clasped about them, was Martin Luther, the fool.

Martin had chosen this elevated position partly out of curiosity, and partly, perhaps, under a strong sense of duty. He knew that, whether he would or no, he must needs look funny up there. His nose was red, and his eyes were running, and his teeth chattering; and he did look funny. But as he felt the cold most his patience failed first. The steady, silent drizzle, the mist creeping about the stems of the oak trees, the leaden sky proved too much for him in the end. "A watched pot never boils!" he grumbled.

"Silence, sirrah!" commanded my uncle angrily. "This is no time for your fooling. Have a care how you talk in the same breath of pots and my Lord Bishop!"

"*Sanctæ ecclesiæ*," Father Carey broke out, turning up his eyes in a kind of ecstasy, as though he were knee to knee with the prelate--"*te defensorem inclytum atque ardentem----*"

"*Pottum!*" cried I, laughing loudly at my own wit.

It was an ill-mannered word, but I was cold and peevish. I had been forced to this function against my will. I had never seen the guest whom we were expecting, and who was no other than the Queen's Chancellor, Stephen Gardiner, but I disliked him as if I had. In truth, he was related to us in a peculiar fashion, which my uncle and I naturally looked at from different standpoints. Sir Anthony viewed with complacence, if not with pride, any connection with the powerful Bishop of Winchester, for the knight knew the world, and could appreciate the value it sets on success, and the blind eyes it has for spots if they do but speckle the risen sun. I could make no such allowance, but, with the pride of youth and family, at once despised the great Bishop for his base blood, and blushed that the shame lay on our side. I hated this parade of doing honor to him, and would fain have hidden at home with Petronilla, my cousin, Sir Anthony's daughter, and awaited our guest there. The knight, however, had not permitted this, and I had been forced out, being in the worst of humors.

So I said "*Pottum!*" and laughed.

"Silence, boy!" cried Sir Anthony fiercely. He loved an orderly procession, and to arrange things decently. "Silence!" he repeated, darting an angry glance first at me and then at his followers, "or I will warm that jacket of yours, lad! And you, Martin Luther, see to your tongue for the next twenty-four hours, and keep it off my Lord Bishop! And, Father Carey, hold yourself ready----"

"For here Sir Hot-Pot cometh!" cried the undaunted Martin, skipping nimbly down from his post of vantage; "and a dozen of London saucepans with him, or may I never lick the inside of one again!"

A jest on the sauciness of London serving-men was sure to tell with the crowd, and there was a great laugh at this, especially among the landless men, who were on the skirts of the party, and well sheltered from Sir Anthony's eye. He glared about him, provoked to find at this critical moment smiles where there should have been looks of deference, and a ring round a fool where he had marshaled a procession. Unluckily, he chose to visit his displeasure upon me. "You won't behave, won't you, you puppy!" he cried. "You won't, won't you!" and stepping forward he aimed a blow at my shoulders, which would have made me rub myself if it had reached me. But I was too quick. I stepped back, the stick swung idly, and the crowd laughed.

And there the matter would have ended, for the Bishop's party were now close upon us, had not my foot slipped on the wet grass and I fallen backward. Seeing me thus at his mercy, the temptation proved too much for the knight. He forgot his love of seemliness and even that his visitors were at his elbow--and, stooping a moment to plant home a couple of shrewd cuts, cried, "Take that! Take that, my lad!" in a voice that rang as crisply as his thwacks.

I was up in an instant; not that the pain was anything, and before our own people I should have thought as little of shame, for if the old may not lay hand to the young, being related, where is to be any obedience? Now, however, my first glance met the grinning faces of strange lackeys, and while my shoulders still smarted, the laughter of a couple of soberly-clad pages stung a hundred times more sharply. I glared furiously round, and my eyes fell on one face--a face long remembered. It was that of a man who neither smiled nor laughed; a man whom I recognized immediately, not by his sleek hackney or his purple cassock, which a riding-coat partially concealed, or even by his jeweled hand, but by the keen glance of power which passed over me, took me in, and did not acknowledge me; which saw my humiliation without interest or amusement. The look hurt me beyond smarting of shoulders, for it conveyed to me in the twentieth part of a second how very small a person Francis Cludde was, and how very great a personage was Stephen Gardiner, whom in my thoughts I had presumed to belittle.

I stood irresolute a moment, shifting my feet and glowering at him, my face on fire. But when he raised his hand to give the Benediction, and the more devout, or those with mended hose, fell on their knees in the mud, I turned my back abruptly, and, climbing the wall, flung away across the chase.

"What, Sir Anthony!" I heard him say as I stalked off, his voice ringing clear and incisive amid the reverential silence which followed the Latin words; "have we a heretic here, cousin? How is this? So near home too!"

"It is my nephew, my Lord Bishop," I could hear Sir Anthony answer, apology in his tone; "and a willful boy at times. You know of him; he has queer notions of his own, put into his head long ago."

I caught no more, my angry strides carrying me out of earshot. Fuming, I hurried across the long damp grass, avoiding here and there the fallen limb of an elm or a huge round of holly. I wanted to get out of the way, and be out of the way; and made such haste that before the slowly moving cavalcade had traversed one-half of the interval between the road and the house I had reached the bridge which crossed the moat, and, pushing my way impatiently through the maids and scullions who had flocked to it to see the show, had passed into the courtyard.

The light was failing, and the place looked dark and gloomy in spite of the warm glow of burning logs which poured from the lower windows, and some show of green boughs which had been placed over the doorways in honor of the occasion. I glanced up at a lattice in one of the gables--the window of Petronilla's little parlor. There was no face at it, and I turned fretfully into the hall--and yes, there she was, perched up in one of the high window-seats. She was looking out on the chase, as the maids were doing.

Yes, as the maids were doing. She too was watching for his High Mightiness, I muttered, and that angered me afresh. I crossed the rushes in silence, and climbed up beside her.

"Well," I said ungraciously, as she started, hearing me at her shoulder, "well, have you seen enough of him yet, cousin? You will, I warrant you, before he leaves. A little of him goes far."

"A little of whom, Francis?" she asked simply.

Though her voice betrayed some wonder at my rough tone, she was so much engaged with the show that she did not look at me immediately. This of course kept my anger warm, and I began to feel that she was in the conspiracy against me.

"Of my Lord of Winchester, of course," I answered, laughing rudely; "of Sir Hot-Pot!"

"Why do you call him that?" she remonstrated in gentle wonder. And then she did turn her soft dark eyes upon me. She was a slender, willowy girl in those days, with a complexion clear yet pale--a maiden all bending and gracefulness, yet with a great store of secret firmness, as I was to learn. "He seems as handsome an old man," she continued, "as I have ever met, and stately and benevolent, too, as I see him at this distance. What is the matter with you, Francis? What has put you out?"

"Put me out!" I retorted angrily. "Who said anything had put me out?"

But I reddened under her eyes; I was longing to tell her all, and be comforted, while at the same time I shrank with a man's shame from saying to her that I had been beaten.

"I can see that something is the matter," she said sagely, with her head on one side, and that air of being the elder which she often assumed with me, though she was really the younger by two years. "Why did you not wait for the others? Why have you come home alone? Francis," [with sudden conviction] "you have vexed my father! That is it!"

"He has beaten me like a dog!" I blurted out passionately; "and before them all! Before those strangers he flogged me!"

She had her back to the window, and some faint gleam of wintry sunshine, passing through the gules of the shield blazoned behind her, cast a red stain on her dark hair and shapely head. She was silent, probably through pity or consternation; but I could not see her face, and misread her. I thought her hard, and, resenting this, bragged on with a lad's empty violence.

"He did; but I will not stand it! I give you warning, I won't stand it, Petronilla!" and I stamped, young bully that I was, until the dust sprang out of the boards, and the hounds by the distant hearth jumped up and whined. "No! not for all the base bishops in England!" I continued, taking a step this way and that. "He had better not do it again! If he does, I tell you it will be the worse for some one!"

"Francis," she exclaimed abruptly, "you must not speak in that way!"

But I was too angry to be silenced, though instinctively I changed my ground.

"Stephen Gardiner!" I cried furiously. "Who is Stephen Gardiner, I should like to know? He has no right to call himself Gardiner at all! Dr. Stephens he used to call himself, I have heard. A child with no name but his godfather's; that is what he is, for all his airs and his bishopric! Who is he to look on and see a Cludde beaten? If my uncle does not take care----"

"Francis!" she cried again, cutting me short ruthlessly. "Be silent, sir!" [and this time I was silent], "You unmanly boy," she continued, her face glowing with indignation, "to threaten my father before my face! How dare you, sir? How dare you? And who are you, you poor child," she exclaimed, with a startling change from invective to sarcasm--"who are you to talk of bishops, I should like to know?"

"One," I said sullenly, "who thinks less of cardinals and bishops than some folk, Mistress Petronilla!"

"Ay, I know," she retorted scathingly--"I know that you are a kind of half-hearted Protestant--neither fish, flesh, nor fowl!"

"I am what my father made me!" I muttered.

"At any rate," she replied, "you do not see how small you are, or you would not talk of bishops. Heaven help us! That a boy who has done nothing and seen nothing, should talk of the Queen's Chancellor! Go! Go on, you foolish boy, and rule a country, or cut off heads, and then you may talk of such men--men who could unmake you and yours with a stroke of the pen! You, to talk so of Stephen Gardiner! Fie, fie, I say! For shame!"

I looked at her, dazed and bewildered, and had long afterward in my mind a picture of her as she stood above me, in the window bay, her back to the light, her slender figure drawn to its full height, her hand extended toward me. I could scarcely understand or believe that this was my gentle cousin. I turned without a word and stole away, not looking behind me. I was cowed.

It happened that the servants came hurrying in at the moment with a clatter of dishes and knives, and the noise covered my retreat. I had a fancy afterward that, as I moved away, Petronilla called to me. But at the time, what with the confusion and my own disorder, I paid no heed to her, but got myself blindly out of the hall, and away to my own attic.

It was a sharp lesson. But my feelings when, being alone, I had time to feel, need not be set down. After events made them of no moment, for I was even then on the verge of a change so great that all the threats and misgivings, the fevers and agues, of that afternoon, real as they seemed at the time, became in a few hours as immaterial as the dew which fell before yesterday's thunderstorm.

The way the change began to come about was this. I crept in late to supper, facing the din and lights, the rows of guests and the hurrying servants, with a mixture of shame and sullenness. I was sitting down with a scowl next the Bishop's pages--my place was beside them, half-way down the table, and I was not too careful to keep my feet clear of their clothing--

when my uncle's voice, raised in a harsher tone than was usual with him, even when he was displeased, summoned me.

"Come here, sirrah!" he cried roundly. "Come here, Master Francis! I have a word to speak to you!"

I went slowly, dragging my feet, while all looked up, and there was a partial silence. I was conscious of this, and it nerved me. For a moment indeed, as I stepped on to the dais I had a vision of scores of candles and rushlights floating in mist, and of innumerable bodiless faces all turned up to me. But the vision and the mistiness passed away, and left only my uncle's long, thin face inflamed with anger, and beside it, in the same ring of light, the watchful eyes and stern, impassive features of Stephen Gardiner. The Bishop's face and his eyes were all I saw then; the same face, the same eyes, I remembered, which had looked unyielding into those of the relentless Cromwell and had scarce dropped before the frown of a Tudor. His purple cap and cassock, the lace and rich fur, the chain of office, I remembered afterward.

"Now, boy," thundered Sir Anthony, pointing out the place where I should stand, "what have you to say for yourself? why have you so misbehaved this afternoon? Let your tongue speak quickly, do you hear, or you will smart for it. And let it be to the purpose, boy!"

I was about to answer something--whether it was likely to make things worse or better, I cannot remember--when Gardiner stayed me. He laid his hand gently on Sir Anthony's sleeve, and interposed. "One moment," he said mildly, "your nephew did not stay for the Church's blessing, I remember. Perhaps he has scruples. There are people nowadays who have. Let us hear if it be so."

This time it was Sir Anthony who did not let me answer.

"No, no," he cried hastily; "no, no; it is not so. He conforms, my lord, he conforms. You conform, sir," he continued, turning fiercely upon me, "do you not? Answer, sir."

"Ah!" the Bishop put in with a sneer, "you conform, do you?"

"I attend mass--to please my uncle," I replied boldly.

"He was ill brought up as a child," Sir Anthony said hastily, speaking in a tone which those below could not hear. "But you know all that, my lord--you know all that. It is an old story to you. So I make, and I pray you to make for the sake of the house, some allowance. He conforms; he undoubtedly conforms."

"Enough!" Gardiner assented. "The rest is for the good priest here, whose ministrations will no doubt in time avail. But a word with this young gentleman, Sir Anthony, on another subject. If it was not to the holy office he objected, perhaps it was to the Queen's Chancellor, or to the Queen?" He raised his voice with the last words and bent his brows, so that I could scarcely believe it was the same man speaking. "Eh, sir, was that so?" he continued severely, putting aside Sir Anthony's remonstrance and glowering at me. "It may be that we have a rebel here instead of a heretic."

"God forbid!" cried the knight, unable to contain himself. It was clear that he repented already of his ill-timed discipline. "I will answer for it that we have no Wyatts here, my lord."

"That is well!" the Chancellor replied. "That is well!" he repeated, his eyes leaving me and roving the hall with so proud a menace in their glance that all quailed, even the fool. "That is very well," he said, drumming on the table with his fingers; "but let Master Francis speak for himself."

"I never heard," said I boldly--I had had a moment for thought--"that Sir Thomas Wyatt had any following in this country. None to my knowledge. As for the Queen's marriage with the Prince of Spain, which was the ground, as we gathered here, of Wyatt's rising with the Kentish folk, it seems a matter rather for the Queen's grace than her subjects. But if that be not so, I, for my part, would rather have seen her married to a stout Englishman--ay, or to a Frenchman."

"And why, young gentleman?"

"Because I would we kept at peace with France. We have more to gain by fighting Spain than fighting France," I answered bluntly.

My uncle held up his hands. "The boy is clean mad!" he groaned. "Who ever heard of such a thing? With all France, the rightful estate of her Majesty, waiting to be won back, he talks of fighting Spain! And his own grandmother was a Spaniard!"

"I am none the less an Englishman for that!" I said; whereon there was a slight murmur of applause in the hall below. "And for France," I continued, carried away by this, "we have been fighting it, off and on, as long as men remember; and what are we the better? We have only lost what we had to begin. Besides, I am told that France is five times stronger than it was in Henry the Fifth's time, and we should only spend our strength in winning what we could not hold. While as to Spain----"

"Ay, as to Spain?" grumbled Sir Anthony, forgetting his formidable neighbor, and staring at me with eyes of wonder. "Why, my father fought the French at Guinegate, and my grandfather at Cherbourg, and his father at Agincourt! But there! As to Spain, you popinjay?"

"Why, she is conquering here," I answered warmly, "and colonizing there among the newly-discovered countries of the world, and getting all the trade and all the seaports and all the gold and silver; and Spain after all is a nation with no greater strength of men than England. Ay, and I hear," I cried, growing more excited and raising my voice, "that now is our time or never! The Spaniards and the Portuguese have discovered a new world over seas.

"A Castilla y á Leon
Nuevo mundo dió Coton!

say they; but depend upon it, every country that is to be rich and strong in the time that is coming must have part in it. We cannot conquer either Spain or France; we have not men enough. But we have docks and sailors, and ships in London and Fowey, and Bristol and the Cinque Ports, enough to fight Spain over the great seas, and I say, 'Have at her!'"

"What next?" groaned Sir Anthony piteously. "Did man ever hear such crackbrained nonsense?"

But I think it was not nonsense, for his words were almost lost in the cry which ran through the hall as I ceased speaking--a cry of English voices. One moment my heart beat high and proudly with a new sense of power; the next, as a shadow of a cloud falls on a sunny hillside, the cold sneer on the statesman's face fell on me and chilled me. His set look had neither thawed nor altered, his color had neither come nor gone. "You speak your lesson well, lad," he said. "Who taught you statecraft?"

I grew smaller, shrinking with each word he uttered; and faltered, and was dumb.

"Come," he said, "you see but a little way; yet country lads do not talk of Fowey and Bristol! Who primed you?"

"I met a Master Sebastian Cabot," I said reluctantly at last, when he had pressed me more than once, "who stayed a while at a house not far from here, and had been Inspector of the Navy to King Edward. He had been a seaman seventy years, and he talked----"

"Too fast!" said Gardiner, with a curt nod. "But enough, I understand. I know the man. He is dead."

He was silent then, and seemed to have fallen suddenly into thought, as a man well might who had the governing of a kingdom on his shoulders.

Seemingly he had done with me. I looked at Sir Anthony. "Ay, go!" he said irritably, waving me off. "Go!"

And I went. The ordeal was over, and over so successfully that I felt the humiliation of the afternoon cheap at the price of this triumph; for, as I stepped down, there was a buzz around me, a murmur of congratulation and pride and excitement. On every Coton face I marked a flush, in every Coton eye I read a sparkle, and every flush and every sparkle was for me. Even the Chancellor's secretaries, grave, down-looking men, all secrecy and caution, cast curious glances at me, as though I were something out of the common; and the Chancellor's pages made way for me with new-born deference. "There is for country wits!" I heard Baldwin Moor cry gleefully, while the man who put food before me murmured of "the Cludde bull-pup!" If I read in Father Carey's face, as indeed I did, solicitude as well as relief and gladness, I marked the latter only, and hugged a natural pride to my breast. When Martin Luther said boldly that it was not only Bishop could fill a bowl, it was by an effort I refrained from joining in the laugh which followed.

For an hour I enjoyed this triumph, and did all but brag of it. Especially I wished Petronilla had witnessed it. At the end of that time--*Finis*, as the book says. I was crossing the courtyard, one-half of which was bathed in a cold splendor of moonlight, and was feeling the first sobering touch of the night air on my brow, when I heard some one call out my name. I turned, to find one of the Chancellor's servants, a sleek, substantial fellow, with a smug mouth, at my elbow.

"What is it?" I said.

"I am bidden to fetch you at once, Master Cludde," he answered, a gleam of sly malice peeping through the gravity of his demeanor. "The Chancellor would see you in his room, young sir."

CHAPTER II.

IN THE BISHOP'S ROOM.

Chancellor was lodged in the great chamber on the southern side of the courtyard, a room which we called the Tapestried Chamber, and in which tradition said that King Henry the Sixth had once slept. It was on the upper floor, and for this reason free from the damp air which in autumn and winter rose from the moat and hung about the lower range of rooms. It was besides, of easy access from the hall, a door in the gallery of the latter leading into an anteroom, which again opened into the Tapestried Chamber; while a winding staircase, starting from a dark nook in the main passage of the house, also led to this state apartment, but by another and more private door.

I reached the antechamber with a stout heart in my breast, though a little sobered by my summons, and feeling such a reaction from the heat of a few minutes before as follows a plunge into cold water. In the anteroom I was bidden to wait while the great man's will was taken, which seemed strange to me, then unused to the mummery of Court folk. But before I had time to feel much surprise, the inner door was opened, and I was told to enter.

The great room, which I had seldom seen in use, had now an appearance quite new to me. A dull red fire was glowing comfortably on the hearthstone, before which a posset stool was standing. Near this, seated at a table strewn with a profusion of papers and documents, was a secretary writing busily. The great oaken bedstead, with its nodding tester, lay in a background of shadows, which played about the figures broidered on the hangings, or were lost in the darkness of the corners; while near the fire, in the light cast by the sconces fixed above the hearth, lay part of the Chancellor's equipment. The fur rugs and cloak of sable, the saddle-bags, the dispatch-boxes, and the silver chafing-dish, gave an air of comfort to this part of the room. Walking up and down in the midst of these, dictating a sentence at every other turn, was Stephen Gardiner.

As I entered the clerk looked up, holding his pen suspended. His master, by a quick nod, ordered him to proceed. Then, signaling to me in a like silent fashion his command that I should stand by the hearth, the Bishop resumed his task of composition.

For some minutes my interest in the man, whom I had now an opportunity of scrutinizing unmarked and at my leisure, took up all my attention. He was at this time close on seventy, but looked, being still tall and stout, full ten years younger. His face, square and sallow, was indeed wrinkled and lined; his eyes lay deep in his head, his shoulders were beginning to bend, the nape of his neck to become prominent. He had lost an inch of his full height. But his eyes still shone brightly, nor did any trace of weakness mar the stern character of his mouth, or the crafty wisdom of his brow. The face was the face of a man austere, determined, perhaps cruel; of a man who could both think and act.

My curiosity somewhat satisfied, I had leisure, first to wonder why I had been sent for, and then to admire the prodigious number of books and papers which lay about, more, indeed, than I had ever seen together in my life. From this I passed to listening, idly at first, and with interest afterward, to the letter which the Chancellor was dictating. It seemed from its tenor to be a letter to some person in authority, and presently one passage attracted my attention, so that I could afterward recall it word for word.

"I do not think"--the Chancellor pronounced, speaking in a sonorous voice, and the measured tone of one whose thoughts lie perfectly arranged in his head--"that the Duchess Katherine will venture to take the step suggested as possible. Yet Clarence's report may be of moment. Let the house, therefore, be watched if anything savoring of flight be marked, and take notice whether there be a vessel in the Pool adapted to her purpose. A vessel trading to Dunquerque would be most likely. Leave her husband till I return, when I will deal with him roundly."

I missed what followed. It was upon another subject, and my thoughts lagged behind, being wholly taken up with the Duchess Katherine and her fortunes. I wondered who she was, young or old, and what this step could be she was said to meditate, and what the jargon about the Pool and Dunquerque meant. I was still thinking of this when I was aroused by an abrupt silence, and looking up found that the Chancellor was bending over the papers on the table. The secretary was leaving the room.

As the door closed behind him, Gardiner rose from his stooping posture and came slowly toward me, a roll of papers in his hand. "Now," he said tranquilly, seating himself in an elbow-chair which stood in front of the hearth, "I will dispose of your business, Master Cludde."

He paused, looking at me in a shrewd, masterful way, much as if--I thought at the time, little knowing how near the truth my fancy went--I were a beast he was about to buy; and then he went on. "I have sent for you, Master Francis," he said dryly, fixing his piercing eyes on mine, "because I think that this country does not suit your health. You conform, but you conform with a bad grace, and England is no longer the place for such. You incite the commonalty against the Queen's allies, and England is not the place for such. Do not contradict me; I have heard you myself. Then," he continued, grimly thrusting out his jaw in a sour smile, "you misname those whom the Queen honors; and were Dr. Stephens--you take me, Master Malapert? such a man as his predecessors, you would rue the word. For a trifle scarce weightier Wolsey threw a man to rot six years in a dungeon, boy!"

I changed color, yet not so much in fear--though it were vain to say I did not tremble--as in confusion. I had called him Dr. Stephens indeed, but it had been to Petronilla only. I stood, not knowing what to say, until he, after lingering on his last words to enjoy my misery, resumed his subject. "That is one good and sufficient reason--mind you, sufficient, boy--why England is no place for you. For another, the Cluddes have always been soldiers; and you--though readier-witted than some, which comes of your Spanish grandmother--are quicker with a word than a thought, and a blow than either. Of which afterward. Well, England is going to be no place for soldiers. Please God, we have finished with wars at home. A woman's reign should be a reign of peace."

I hardened my heart at that. A reign of peace, forsooth, when the week before we had heard of a bishop burned at Gloucester! I hardened my heart. I would not be frightened, though I knew his power, and knew how men in those days misused power. I would put a bold face on the matter.

He had not done with me yet, however. "One more reason I have," he continued, stopping me as I was about to speak, "for saying that England will not suit your health, Master Cludde. It is that I do not want you here. Abroad, you may be of use to me, and at the same time carve out your own fortune. You have courage and can use a sword, I hear. You understand-- and it is a rare gift with Englishmen--some Spanish, which I suppose your father or your uncle taught you. You can--so Father Carey says--construe a Latin sentence if it be not too difficult. You are scarcely twenty, and you will have me for your patron. Why, were I you, boy, with your age and your chances, I would die Prince or Pope! Ay, I would!" He stopped speaking, his eyes on fire. Nay, a ring of such real feeling flashed out in his last words that, though I distrusted him, though old prejudices warned me against him, and, at heart a Protestant, I shuddered at things I had heard of him, the longing to see the world and have adventures seized upon me. Yet I did not speak at once. He had told me that my tongue outran my thoughts, and I stood silent until he asked me curtly, "Well, sirrah, what do you say?"

"I say, my Lord Bishop," I replied respectfully, "that the prospect you hold out to me would tempt me were I a younger son, or without those ties of gratitude which hold me to my uncle. But, my father excepted, I am Sir Anthony's only heir."

"Ah, your father!" he said contemptuously. "You do well to remind me of him, for I see you are forgetting the first part of my speech in thinking of the last! Should I have promised first and threatened later? You would fain, I expect, stay here and woo Mistress Petronilla? Do I touch you there? You think to marry the maid and be master of Coton End in God's good time, do you? Then listen, Francis Cludde. Neither one nor the other, neither maid nor meadow will be yours should you stay here till Doomsday!"

I started, and stood glowering on him, speechless with anger and astonishment.

"You do not know who you are," he continued, leaning forward with a sudden movement, and speaking with one claw-like finger extended, and a malevolent gleam in his eyes. "You called me a nameless child a while ago, and so I was; yet have I risen to be ruler of England, Master Cludde! But you--I will tell you which of us is base-born. I will tell you who and what your father, Ferdinand Cludde, was. He was, nay, he is, my tool, spy, jackal! Do you understand, boy? Your father is one of the band of foul creatures to whom such as I, base-born though I be, fling the scraps from their table! He is the vilest of the vile men who do my dirty work, my lad."

He had raised his voice and hand in passion, real or assumed. He dropped them as I sprang forward. "You lie!" I cried, trembling all over.

"Easy! easy!" he said. He stopped me where I was by a gesture of stern command. "Think!" he continued, calmly and weightily. "Has any one ever spoken to you of your father since the day seven years ago, when you came here, a child, brought by a servant? Has Sir Anthony talked of him? Has any servant named his name to you. Think, boy. If Ferdinand Cludde be a father to be proud of, why does his brother make naught of him?"

"He is a Protestant," I said faintly. Faintly, because I had asked myself this very question not once but often. Sir Anthony so seldom mentioned my father that I had thought it strange myself. I had thought it strange, too, that the servants, who must well remember Ferdinand Cludde, never talked to me about him. Hitherto I had always been satisfied to answer, "He is a Protestant"; but face to face with this terrible old man and his pitiless charge, the words came but faintly from my lips.

"A Protestant," he replied solemnly. "Yes, this comes of schism, that villains cloak themselves in it, and parade for true men. A Protestant you call him, boy? He has been that, ay, and all things to all men; and he has betrayed all things and all men. He was in the great Cardinal's confidence, and forsook him, when he fell, for Cromwell. Thomas Cromwell, although they were of the same persuasion, he betrayed to me. I have here, here"--

and he struck the letters in his hand a scornful blow--"the offer he made to me, and his terms. Then eight years back, when the late King Edward came to the throne, I too fell on evil days, and Master Cludde abandoned me for my Lord Hertford, but did me no great harm. But he did something which blasted him--blasted him at last."

He paused. Had the fire died down, or was it only my imagination that the shadows thickened round the bed behind him, and closed in more nearly on us, leaving his pale grim face to confront me--his face, which seemed the paler and grimmer, the more saturnine and all-mastering, for the dark frame which set it off?

"He did this," he continued slowly, "which came to light and blasted him. He asked, as the price of his service in betraying me, his brother's estate."

"Impossible!" I stammered. "Why, Sir Anthony----"

"What of Sir Anthony, you would ask?" the Chancellor replied, interrupting me with savage irony. "Oh, he was a Papist! an obstinate Papist! He might go hang--or to Warwick Jail!"

"Nay, but this at least, my lord, is false!" I cried. "Palpably false! If my father had so betrayed his own flesh and blood, should I be here? Should I be at Coton End? You say this happened eight years ago. Seven years ago I came here. Would Sir Anthony----"

"There are fools everywhere," the old man sneered. "When my Lord Hertford refused your father's suit, Ferdinand began--it is his nature--to plot against him. He was found out, and execrated by all--for he had been false to all--he fled for his life. He left you behind, and a servant brought you to Coton End, where Sir Anthony took you in."

I covered my face. Alas! I believed him; I, who had always been so proud of my lineage, so proud of the brave traditions of the house and its honor, so proud of Coton End and all that belonged to it! Now, if this were true, I could never again take pleasure in one or the other. I was the son of a man branded as a turncoat and an informer, of one who was the worst of traitors! I sank down on the settle behind me and hid my face. Another might have thought less of the blow, or, with greater knowledge of the world, might have made light of it as a thing not touching himself. But on me, young as I was, and proud, and as yet tender, and having done nothing myself, it fell with crushing force.

It was years since I had seen my father, and I could not stand forth loyally and fight his battle, as a son his father's friend and familiar for years might have fought it. On the contrary, there was so much which seemed mysterious in my past life, so much that bore out the Chancellor's accusation, that I felt a dread of its truth even before I had proof. Yet I would have proof. "Show me the letters!" I said harshly; "show me the letters, my lord!"

"You know your father's handwriting?"

"I do."

I knew it, not from any correspondence my father had held with me, but because I had more than once examined with natural curiosity the wrappers of the dispatches which at intervals of many months, sometimes of a year, came from him to Sir Anthony. I had never known anything of the contents of the letters, all that fell to my share being certain formal messages, which Sir Anthony would give me, generally with a clouded brow and a testy manner that grew genial again only with the lapse of time.

Gardiner handed me the letters, and I took them and read one. One was enough. That my father! Alas! alas! No wonder that I turned my face to the wall, shivering as with the ague, and that all about me--except the red glow of the fire, which burned into my brain--seemed darkness! I had lost the thing I valued most. I had lost at a blow everything of which I was proud. The treachery that could flush that worn face opposite to me, lined as it was with statecraft, and betray the wily tongue into passion, seemed to me, young and impulsive, a thing so vile as to brand a man's children through generations.

Therefore I hid my face in the corner of the settle, while the Chancellor gazed at me a while in silence, as one who had made an experiment might watch the result.

"You see now, my friend," he said at last, almost gently, "that you may be base-born in more ways than one. But be of good cheer; you are young, and what I have done you may do. Think of Thomas Cromwell--his father was naught. Think of the old Cardinal--my master. Think of the Duke of Suffolk--Charles Brandon, I mean. He was a plain gentleman, yet he married a queen. More, the door which they had to open for themselves I will open for you--only, when you are inside, play the man, and be faithful."

"What would you have me do?" I whispered hoarsely.

"I would have you do this," he answered. "There are great things brewing in the Netherlands, boy--great changes, unless I am mistaken. I have need of an agent there, a man, stout, trusty, and, in particular, unknown, who will keep me informed of events. If you will be that agent, I can procure for you--and not appear in the matter myself--a post of pay and honor in the Regent's Guards. What say you to that, Master Cludde? A few weeks and you will be making history, and Coton End will seem a mean place to you. Now, what do you say?"

I was longing to be away and alone with my misery, but I forced myself to reply patiently.

"With your leave I will give you my answer to-morrow, my lord," I said, as steadily as I could; and I rose, still keeping my face turned from him.

"Very well," he replied, with apparent confidence. But he watched me keenly, as I fancied. "I know already what your answer will be. Yet before you go I will give you a piece of advice which in the new life you begin to-night will avail you more than silver, more than gold--ay, more than steel, Master Francis. It is this: Be prompt to think, be prompt to strike, be slow to speak! Mark it well! It is a simple recipe, yet it has made me what I am, and may make you greater. Now go!"

He pointed to the little door opening on the staircase, and I bowed and went out, closing it carefully behind me. On the stairs, moving blindly in the dark, I fell over some one who lay sleeping there, and who clutched at my leg. I shook him off, however, with an exclamation of rage, and, stumbling down the rest of the steps, gained the open air. Excited and feverish, I shrank with aversion from the confinement of my room, and, hurrying over the drawbridge, sought at random the long terrace by the fish-pools, on which the moonlight fell, a sheet of silver, broken only by the sundial and the shadows of the rose bushes. The night air, weeping chill from the forest, fanned my cheeks as I paced up and down. One way I had before me the manor-house--the steep gable-ends, the gateway tower, the low outbuildings and cornstacks and stables--and flanking these the squat tower and nave of the church. I turned. Now I saw only the water and the dark line of trees which fringed the further bank. But above these the stars were shining.

Yet in my mind there was no starlight. There all was a blur of wild passions and resolves. Shame and an angry resentment against those who had kept me so long in ignorance--even against Sir Anthony--were my uppermost feelings. I smarted under the thought that I had been living on his charity. I remembered many a time when I had taken much on myself, and he had smiled, and the remembrance stung me. I longed to assert myself and do something to wipe off the stain.

But should I accept the Bishop's offer? It never crossed my mind to do so. He had humiliated me, and I hated him for it. Longing to cut myself off from my old life, I could not support a patron who would know, and might cast in my teeth the old shame. A third reason, too, worked powerfully with me as I became cooler. This was the conviction that, apart from the glitter which the old man's craft had cast about it, the part he would have me play was that of a spy--an informer! A creature like--I dared not say like my father, yet I had him in my mind. And from this, from the barest suspicion of this, I shrank as the burned puppy from the fire--shrank with fierce twitching of nerve and sinew.

Yet if I would not accept his offer it was clear I must fend for myself. His threats meant as much as that, and I smiled sternly as I found necessity at one with inclination. I would leave Coton End at once, and henceforth I would fight for my own hand. I would have no name until I had made for myself a new one.

This resolve formed, I turned and went back to the house, and felt my way to my own chamber. The moonlight poured through the lattice and fell white on my pallet. I crossed the room and stood still. Down the middle of the coverlet--or my eyes deceived me--lay a dark line.

I stooped mechanically to see what this was and found my own sword lying there; the sword which Sir Anthony had given me on my last birthday. But how had it come there? As I took it up something soft and light brushed my hand and drooped from the hilt. Then I remembered. A week before I had begged Petronilla to make me a sword-knot of blue velvet for use on state occasions. No doubt she had done it, and had brought the sword back this evening, and laid it there in token of peace.

I sat down on my bed, and softer and kindlier thoughts came to me; thoughts of love and gratitude, in which the old man who had been a second father to me had part. I would go as I had resolved, but I would return to them when I had done a thing worth doing; something which should efface the brand that lay on me now.

With gentle fingers I disengaged the velvet knot and thrust it into my bosom. Then I tied about the hilt the old leather thong, and began to make my preparations; considering this or that route while I hunted for my dagger and changed my doublet and hose for stouter raiment and long, untanned boots. I was yet in the midst of this, when a knock at the door startled me.

"Who is there?" I asked, standing erect.

For answer Martin Luther slid in, closing the door behind him. The fool did not speak, but turning his eyes first on one thing and then on another nodded sagely.

"Well?" I growled.

"You are off, master," he said, nodding again. "I thought so."

"Why did you think so?" I retorted impatiently.

"It is time for the young birds to fly when the cuckoo begins to stir," he answered.

I understood him dimly and in part. "You have been listening," I said wrathfully, my cheeks burning.

"And been kicked in the face like a fool for my pains," he answered. "Ah, well, it is better to be kicked by the boot you love than kissed by the lips you hate. But Master Francis, Master Francis!" he continued in a whisper.

He said no more, and I looked up. The man was stooping slightly forward, his pale face thrust out. There was a strange gleam in his eyes, and his teeth grinned in the moonlight. Thrice he drew his finger across his lean knotted throat. "Shall I?" he hissed, his hot breath reaching me, "shall I?"

I recoiled from him shuddering. It was a ghastly pantomime, and it seemed to me that I saw madness in his eyes.

"In Heaven's name, no!" I cried--"No! Do you hear, Martin? No!"

He stood back on the instant, as a dog might have done being reproved. But I could hardly finish in comfort after that with him standing there, although when I next turned to him he seemed half asleep and his eyes were dull and fishy as ever.

"One thing you can do," I said brusquely. Then I hesitated, looking round me. I wished to send something to Petronilla, some word, some keepsake. But I had nothing that would serve a maid's purpose, and could think of nothing until my eye lit on a house-martin's nest, lying where I had cast it on the window-sill. I had taken it down that morning because the droppings during the last summer had fallen on the lead work, and I would not have it used when the swallows returned. It was but a bit of clay, and yet it would serve. She would guess its meaning.

I gave it into his hands. "Take this," I said, "and give it privately to Mistress Petronilla. Privately, you understand. And say nothing to any one, or the Bishop will flay your back, Martin."

CHAPTER III.

"DOWN WITH PURVEYORS!"

The first streak of daylight found me already footing it through the forest by paths known to few save the woodcutters, but with which many a boyish exploration had made me familiar. From Coton End the London road lies plain and fair through Stratford-on-Avon and Oxford. But my plan, the better to evade pursuit, was, instead, to cross the forest in a northeasterly direction, and, passing by Warwick, to strike the great north road between Coventry and Daventry, which, running thence southeastward, would take me as straight as a bird might fly through Dunstable, St. Albans, and Barnet, to London. My baggage consisted only of my cloak, sword, and dagger; and for money I had but a gold angel, and a few silver bits of doubtful value. But I trusted that this store, slender as it was, would meet my charges as far as London. Once there I must depend on my wits either for providence at home or a passage abroad.

Striding steadily up and down hill, for Arden Forest is made up of hills and dells which follow one another as do the wave and trough of the sea, only less regularly, I made my way toward Wootton Wawen. As soon as I espied its battlemented church lying in a wooded bottom below me, I kept a more easterly course, and, leaving Henley-in-Arden far to the left, passed down toward Leek Wootton. The damp, dead bracken underfoot, the leafless oaks and gray sky overhead, nay the very cry of the bittern fishing in the bottoms, seemed to be at one with my thoughts; for these were dreary and sad enough.

But hope and a fixed aim form no bad makeshifts for happiness. Striking the broad London road as I had purposed I slept that night at Ryton Dunsmoor, and the next at Towcester; and the third day, which rose bright and frosty, found me stepping gayly southward, travel-stained indeed, but dry and whole. My spirits rose with the temperature. For a time I put the past behind me, and found amusement in the sights of the road; in the heavy wagons and long trains of pack-horses, and the cheery greetings which met me with each mile. After all, I had youth and strength, and the world before me; and particularly Stony Stratford, where I meant to dine.

There was one trouble common among wayfarers which did not touch me; and that was the fear of robbers, for he would be a sturdy beggar who would rob an armed foot-passenger for the sake of an angel; and the groats were gone. So I felt no terrors on that account, and even when about noon I heard a horseman trot up behind me, and rein in his horse so as to keep pace with me at a walk, step for step--a thing which might have seemed suspicious to some--I took no heed of him. I was engaged with my first view of Stratford, and did not turn my head. We had walked on so for fifty paces or more, before it struck me as odd that the man did not pass me.

Then I turned, and shading my eyes from the sun, which stood just over his shoulder, said, "Good-day, friend."

"Good-day, master," he answered.

He was a stout fellow, looking like a citizen, although he had a sword by his side, and wore it with an air of importance which the sunshine of opportunity might have ripened into a swagger. His dress was plain; and he sat a good hackney as a miller's sack might have sat it. His face was the last thing I looked at. When I raised my eyes to it, I got an unpleasant start. The man was no stranger. I knew him in a moment for the messenger who had summoned me to the Chancellor's presence.

The remembrance did not please me; and reading in the fellow's sly look that he recognized me, and thought he had made a happy discovery on finding me, I halted abruptly. He did the same.

"It is a fine morning," he said, taken aback by my sudden movement, but affecting an indifference which the sparkle in his eye belied. "A rare day for the time of year."

"It is," I answered, gazing steadily at him.

"Going to London? Or may be only to Stratford?" he hazarded. He fidgeted uncomfortably under my eye, but still pretended ignorance of me.

"That is as may be," I answered.

"No offense, I am sure," he said.

I cast a quick glance up and down the road. There happened to be no one in sight. "Look here!" I replied, stepping forward to lay my hand on the horse's shoulder--but the man reined back and prevented me, thereby giving me a clew to his character--"you are in the service of the Bishop of Winchester?"

His face fell, and he could not conceal his disappointment at being recognized. "Well, master," he answered reluctantly, "perhaps I am, and perhaps I am not."

"That is enough," I said shortly. "And you know me. You need not lie about it, man, for I can see you do. Now, look here, Master Steward, or whatever your name may be----"

"It is Master Pritchard," he put in sulkily; "and I am not ashamed of it."

"Very well. Then let us understand one another. Do you mean to interfere with me?"

He grinned. "Well, to be plain, I do," he replied, reining his horse back another step. "I have orders to look out for you, and have you stopped if I find you. And I must do my duty, sir; I am sworn to it, Master Cludde."

"Right," said I calmly; "and I must do mine, which is to take care of my skin." And I drew my sword and advanced upon him with a flourish. "We will soon decide this little matter," I added grimly, one eye on him and one on the empty road, "if you will be good enough to defend yourself."

But there was no fight in the fellow. By good luck, too, he was so startled that he did not do what he might have done with safety; namely, retreat, and keep me in sight until some passers-by came up. He did give back, indeed, but it was against the bank. "Have a care," he cried in a fume, his eye following my sword nervously; he did not try to draw his own. "There is no call for fighting, I say."

"But I say there is," I replied bluntly. "Call and cause! Either you fight me, or I go where I please."

"You may go to Bath for me!" he spluttered, his face the color of a turkey-cock's wattles with rage.

"Do you mean it, my friend?" I said, and I played my point about his leg, half-minded to give him a little prod by way of earnest. "Make up your mind."

"Yes!" he shrieked out, suspecting my purpose, and bouncing about in his saddle like a parched pea. "Yes, I say!" he roared. "Do you hear me? You go your way, and I will go mine."

"That is a bargain," I said quietly; "and mind you keep to it."

I put up my sword with my face turned from him, lest he should see the curl of my lip and the light in my eyes. In truth, I was uncommonly well pleased with myself, and was thinking that if I came through all my adventures as well, I should do merrily. Outwardly, however, I tried to ignore my victory, and to make things as easy as I could for my friend--if one may call a man who will not fight him a friend, a thing I doubt. "Which way are you going?" I asked amicably; "to Stratford?"

He nodded, for he was too sulky to speak.

"All right!" I said cheerfully, feeling that my dignity could take care of itself now. "Then so far we may go together. Only do you remember the terms. After dinner each goes his own way."

He nodded again, and we turned, and went on in silence, eying one another askance, like two ill-matched dogs coupled together. But, luckily, our forced companionship did not last long, a quarter of a mile and a bend in the road bringing us to the first low, gray houses of Stratford; a long, straggling village it seemed, made up of inns strewn along the road, like beads threaded on a rosary. And to be sure, to complete the likeness, we came presently upon an ancient stone cross standing on the green. I pulled up in front of this with a sigh of pleasure, for on either side of it, one facing the other, was an inn of the better class.

"Well," I said, "which shall it be? The Rose and Crown, or the Crown without the Rose?"

"Choose for yourself," he answered churlishly. "I go to the other."

I shrugged my shoulders. After all, you cannot make a silk purse out of a sow's ear, and if a man has not courage he is not likely to have good-fellowship. But the words angered me, nevertheless, for a shabby, hulking fellow lounging at my elbow overheard them and grinned; a hiccoughing, blear-eyed man he was as I had ever met, with a red nose and the rags of a tattered cassock about him. I turned away in annoyance, and chose the "Crown" at hazard; and pushing my way through a knot of horses that stood tethered at the door, went in, leaving the two to their devices.

I found a roaring fire in the great room, and three or four yeomen standing about it, drinking ale. But I was hot from walking, so, after saluting them and ordering my meal, I went and sat for choice on a bench by the window away from the fire. The window was one of a kind common in Warwickshire houses; long and low and beetle-browed, the story above projecting over it. I sat here a minute looking idly out at the inn opposite, a heavy stone building with a walled courtyard attached to it; such an inn as was common enough about the time of the Wars of the Roses when wayfarers looked rather for safety than comfort. Presently I saw a boy come out of it and start up the road at a run. Then, a minute later, the ragged fellow I had seen on the green came out and lurched across the road. He seemed to be making, though uncertainly, for my inn, and, sure enough, just as my bread and bacon--the latter hot and hissing--were put before me, he staggered into the room, bringing a strong smell of ale and onions with him. "*Pax vobiscum!*" he said, leering at me with tipsy solemnity.

I guessed what he was--a monk, one of those unfortunates still to be found here and there up and down the country, whom King Henry, when he put down the monasteries, had made homeless. I did not look on the class with much favor, thinking that for most of them the cloister, even if the Queen should succeed in setting the abbeys on their legs again, would have few attractions. But I saw that the simple farmers received his scrap of Latin with respect, and I nodded civilly as I went on with my meal.

I was not to get off so easily, however. He came and planted himself opposite to me.

"*Pax vobiscum*, my son," he repeated. "The ale is cheap here, and good."

"So is the ham, good father," I replied cheerfully, not pausing in my attack on the victuals. "I will answer for so much."

"Well, well," the knave replied with ready wit, "I breakfasted early. I am content. Landlord, another plate and a full tankard. The young gentleman would have me dine with him."

I could not tell whether to be angry or to laugh at his impudence.

"The gentleman says he will answer for it!" repeated the rascal, with a twinkle in his eye, as the landlord hesitated. He was by no means so drunk as he looked.

"No, no, father," I cried, joining in the general laugh into which the farmers by the fire broke. "A cup of ale is in reason, and for that I will pay, but for no more. Drink it, and wish me Godspeed."

"I will do more than that, lad," he answered. Swaying to and fro my cup, which he had seized in his grasp, he laid his hand on the window-ledge beside me, as though to steady himself, and stooped until his coarse, puffy face was but a few inches from mine. "More than that," he whispered hoarsely; and his eyes, peering into mine, were now sober and full of meaning. "If you do not want to be put in the stocks or worse, make tracks! Make tracks, lad!" he continued. "Your friend over there--he is a niggardly oaf--has sent for the hundredman and the constable, and you are the quarry. So the word is, Go! That," he added aloud, standing erect again, with a drunken smile, "is for your cup of ale; and good coin too!"

For half a minute I sat quite still; taken aback, and wondering, while the bacon cooled on the plate before me, what I was to do. I did not doubt the monk was telling the truth. Why should he lie to me? And I cursed my folly in trusting to a coward's honor or a serving-man's good faith. But lamentations were useless. What was I to do? I had no horse, and no means of getting one. I was in a strange country, and to try to escape on foot from pursuers who knew the roads, and had the law on their side, would be a hopeless undertaking. Yet to be haled back to Coton End a prisoner--I could not face that. Mechanically I raised a morsel of bacon to my lips, and as I did so, a thought occurred to me--an idea suggested by some talk I had heard the evening before at Towcester.

Fanciful as the plan was, I snatched at it; and knowing each instant to be precious, took my courage in my hand--and my tankard. "Here," I cried, speaking suddenly and loudly, "here is bad luck to purveyors, Master Host!"

There were a couple of stablemen within hearing, lounging in the doorway, besides the landlord and his wife and the farmers. A villager or two also had dropped in, and there were two peddlers lying half asleep in the corner. All these pricked up their ears more or less at my words. But, like most country folk, they were slow to take in anything new or unexpected; and I had to drink afresh and say again, "Here is bad luck to purveyors!" before any one took it up.

Then the landlord showed he understood.

"Ay, so say I!" he cried, with an oath. "Purveyors, indeed! It is such as they give the Queen a bad name."

"God bless her!" quoth the monk loyally.

"And drown the purveyors!" a farmer exclaimed.

"They were here a year ago, and left us as bare as a shorn sheep," struck in a strapping villager, speaking at a white heat, but telling me no news; for this was what I had heard at Towcester the night before. "The Queen should lie warm if she uses all the wool they took! And the packhorses they purveyed to carry off the plunder--why, the packmen avoid Stratford ever since as though we had the Black Death! Oh, down with the purveyors, say I! The first that comes this way I will show the bottom of the Ouse. Ay, that I will, though I hang for it!"

"Easy! easy, Tom Miller!" the host interposed, affecting an air of assurance, even while he cast an eye of trouble at his flitches. "It will be another ten years before they harry us again. There is Potter's Pury! They never took a tester's worth from Potter's Pury! No, nor from Preston Gobion! But they will go to them next, depend upon it!"

"I hope they will," I said, with a world of gloomy insinuation in my words. "But I doubt it!"

And this time my hint was not wasted. The landlord changed color. "What are you driving at, master?" he asked mildly, while the others looked at me in silence and waited for more.

"What if there be one across the road now!" I said, giving way to the temptation, and speaking falsely--for which I paid dearly afterward. "A purveyor, I mean, unless I am mistaken in him, or he tells lies. He has come straight from the Chancellor, white wand, warrant, and all. He is taking his dinner now, but he has sent for the hundredman, so I guess he means business."

"For the hundredman?" repeated the landlord, his brows meeting.

"Yes; unless I am mistaken."

There was silence for a moment. Then the man they called Tom Miller dashed his cap on the floor and, folding his arms defiantly, looked round on his neighbors. "He has come, has he!" he roared, his face swollen, his eyes bloodshot. "Then I will be as good as my word! Who will help? Shall we sit down and be shorn like sheep, as we were before, so that our children lay on the bare stones, and we pulled the plow ourselves? Or shall we show that we are free Englishmen, and not slaves of Frenchmen? Shall we teach Master Purveyor not to trouble us again? Now, what say you, neighbors?"

So fierce a growl of impatience and anger rose round me as at once answered the question. A dozen red faces glared at me and at one another, and from the very motion and passion of the men as they snarled and threatened, the room seemed twice as full as it was. Their oaths and cries of encouragement, not loud, but the more dangerous for that, the fresh burst of fury which rose as the village smith and another came in and learned the news, the menacing gestures of a score of brandished fists--these sights, though they told of the very effect at which I had aimed, scared as well as pleased me. I turned red and white, and hesitated, fearing that I had gone too far.

The thing was done, however; and, what was more, I had soon to take care of myself. At the very moment when the hubbub was at its loudest I felt a chill run down my back as I met the monk's eye, and, reading in it whimsical admiration, read in it something besides, and that was an unmistakable menace. "Clever lad!" the eye said. "I will expose you," it threatened.

I had forgotten him--or, at any rate, that my acting would be transparent enough to him holding the clew in his hand--and his look was like the shock of cold water to me. But it is wonderful how keen the wits grow on the grindstone of necessity. With scarcely a second's hesitation I drew out my only piece of gold, and unnoticed by the other men, who were busy swearing at and encouraging one another, I disclosed a morsel of it. The monk's crafty eye glistened. I laid my finger on my lips.

He held up two fingers.

I shook my head and showed an empty palm. I had no more. He nodded; and the relief that nod gave me was great. Before I had time, however, to consider the narrowness of my escape, a movement of the crowd--for the news had spread with strange swiftness, and there was now a crowd assembled which more than filled the room--proclaimed that the purveyor had come out, and was in the street.

The room was nearly emptied at a rush. Though I prudently remained behind, I could, through the open window, hear as well as see what passed. The leading spirits had naturally struggled out first, and were gathered, sullen and full of dangerous possibilities, about the porch.

I suppose the Bishop's messenger saw in them nothing but a crowd of country clowns, for he came hectoring toward the door, smiting his boot with his whip, and puffing out his red cheeks mightily. He felt brave enough, now that he had dined and had at his back three stout constables sworn to keep the Queen's peace.

"Make way! Make way, there, do you hear?" he cried in a husky, pompous voice. "Make way!" he repeated, lightly touching the nearest man with his switch. "I am on the Queen's service, boobies, and must not be hindered."

The man swore at him, but did not budge, and the bully, brought up thus sharply, awoke to the lowering faces and threatening looks which confronted him. He changed color a little. But the ale was still in him, and, forgetting his natural discretion, he thought to carry matters with a high hand. "Come! come!" he exclaimed angrily. "I have a warrant, and you resist me at your peril. I have to enter this house. Clear the way, Master Hundredman, and break these fellows' heads if they withstand you."

A growl as of a dozen bulldogs answered him, and he drew back, as a child might who has trodden on an adder. "You fools!" he spluttered, glaring at them viciously. "Are you mad? Do you know what you are doing? Do you see this?" He whipped out from some pocket a short white staff and brandished it. "I come direct from the Lord Chancellor and upon his business, do you hear, and if you resist me it is treason. Treason, you dogs!" he cried, his rage getting the better of him, "and like dogs you will hang for it. Master Hundredman, I order you to take in your constables and arrest that man!"

"What man?" quoth Tom Miller, eying him fixedly.

"The stranger who came in an hour ago, and is inside the house."

"Him, he means, who told about the purveyor across the road," explained the monk with a wink.

That wink sufficed. There was a roar of execration, and in the twinkling of an eye the Jack-in-office, tripped up this way and shoved that, was struggling helplessly in the grasp of half a dozen men, who fought savagely for his body with the Hundredman and the constables.

"To the river! To the Ouse with him!" yelled the mob. "In the Queen's name!" shouted the officers. But these were to those as three to a score, and taken by surprise besides, and doubtful of the rights of the matter. Yet for an instant, as the crowd went reeling and fighting down the road, they prevailed; the constables managed to drag their leader free, and I caught a glimpse of him, wild-eyed and frantic with fear, his clothes torn from his back, standing at bay like some animal, and brandishing his staff in one hand, a packet of letters in the other.

"I have letters, letters of state!" he screamed shrilly. "Let me alone, I tell you! Let me go, you curs!"

But in vain. The next instant the mob were upon him again. The packet of letters went one way, the staff was dashed another. He was thrown down and plucked up again, and hurried, bruised and struggling, toward the river, his screams for mercy and furious threats rising shrilly above the oaths and laughter.

I felt myself growing pale as scream followed scream. "They will kill him!" I exclaimed trembling, and prepared to follow. "I cannot see this done."

But the monk, who had returned to my side, grasped my arm. "Don't be a fool," he said sharply. "I will answer for it they will not kill him. Tom Miller is not a fool, though he is angry. He will duck him, and let him go. But I will trouble you for that bit of gold, young gentleman."

I gave it to him.

"Now," he continued with a leer, "I will give you a hint in return. If you are wise, you will be out of this county in twelve hours. Tethered to the gate over there is a good horse which belongs to a certain purveyor now in the river. Take it! There is no one to say you nay. And begone!"

I looked hard at him for a minute, my heart beating fast. This was horse-stealing. And horse-stealing was a hanging matter. But I had done so much already that I felt I might as well be hanged for a sheep as for a lamb. I was not sure that I had not incited to treason, and what was stealing a horse beside that? "I will do it!" I said desperately.

"Don't lose time, then," quoth my mentor.

I went out then and there, and found he had told the truth. Every soul in the place had gone to see the ducking, and the street was empty. Kicked aside in the roadway lay the bundle of letters, soiled but not torn, and in the gutter was the staff. I stooped and picked up one and the other--in for a lamb, in for a sheep! and they might be useful some day. Then I jumped into the saddle, and twitched the reins off the hook.

But before I could drive in the spurs, a hand fell on the bridle, and the monk's face appeared at my knee. "Well?" I said, glaring down at him--I was burning to be away.

"That is a good cloak you have got there," he muttered hurriedly. "There, strapped to the saddle, you fool. You do not want that, give it me. Do you hear? Quick, give it me," he cried, raising his voice and clutching at it fiercely, his face dark with greed and fear.

"I see," I replied, as I unstrapped it. "I am to steal the horse that you may get the cloak. And then you will lay the lot on my shoulders. Well, take it!" I cried, "and go your way as fast as you can."

Throwing it at him as hard as I could, I shook up the reins and went off down the road at a gallop. The wind whistled pleasantly past my ears. The sounds of the town grew faint and distant. Each bound of the good hack carried me farther and farther from present danger, farther and farther from the old life. In the exhilaration and excitement of the moment I forgot my condition; forgot that I had not a penny-piece in my pocket, and that I had left an unpaid bill behind me; forgot even that I rode a--well, a borrowed horse.

CHAPTER IV.

TWO SISTERS OF MERCY.

A younger generation has often posed me finely by asking, "What, Sir Francis! Did you not see *one* bishop burned? Did you not know *one* of the martyrs? Did you *never* come face to face with Queen Mary?" To all which questions I have one answer, No, and I watch small eyes grow large with astonishment. But the truth is, a man can only be at one place at a time. And though, in this very month of February, 1555, Prebendary Rogers--a good, kindly man, as I have heard, who had a wife and nine children--was burned in Smithfield in London for religion, and the Bishop of Gloucester suffered in his own city, and other inoffensive men were burned to death, and there was much talk of these things, and in thousands of breasts a smoldering fire was kindled which blazed high enough by and by--why, I was at Coton End, or on the London Road, at the time, and learned such things only dimly and by hearsay.

But the rill joins the river at last; and ofttimes suddenly and at a bound, as it were. On this very day, while I cantered easily southward with my face set toward St. Albans, Providence was at work shaping a niche for me in the lives of certain people who were at the time as unconscious of my existence as I was of theirs. In a great house in the Barbican in London there was much stealthy going and coming on this February afternoon and evening. Behind locked doors, and in fear and trembling, mails were being packed and bags strapped, and fingers almost too delicate for the task were busy with nails and hammers, securing this and closing that. The packers knew nothing of me, nor I of them. Yet but for me all that packing would have been of no avail; and but for them my fate might have been very different. Still, the sound of the hammer did not reach my ears, or, doing so, was covered by the steady tramp of the roadster; and no vision, so far as I ever heard, of a dusty youth riding Londonward came between the secret workers and their task.

I had made up my mind to sleep at St. Albans that night, and for this reason, and for others relating to the Sheriff of Buckinghamshire, in which county Stony Stratford lies, I pushed on briskly. I presently found time, however, to examine the packet of letters of which I had made spoil. On the outer wrapper I found there was no address, only an exhortation to be speedy. Off this came, therefore, without ceremony, and was left in the dirt. Inside I found two sealed epistles, each countersigned on the wrapper, "Stephen Winton."

"Ho! ho!" said I. "I did well to take them."

Over the signature on the first letter--it seemed to be written on parchment--were the words, "Haste! haste! haste!" This was the thicker and heavier of the two, and was addressed to Sir Maurice Berkeley, at St. Mary Overy's, Southwark, London. I turned it over and over in my hands, and peeped into it, hesitating. Twice I muttered, "All is fair in love and war!" And at last, with curiosity fully awake, and a glance behind me to make sure that the act was unobserved, I broke the seal. The document proved to be as short and pithy as it was startling. It was an order commanding Sir Maurice Berkeley forthwith in the Queen's name, and by the authority of the Council, and so on, and so on, to arrest Katherine Willoughby de Eresby, Duchess of Suffolk, and to deliver her into the custody of the Lieutenant of the Tower, "These presents to be his waranty for the detention of the said Duchess of Suffolk until her Grace's pleasure in the matter be known."

When it was too late I trembled to think what I had done. To meddle with matters of state might be more dangerous a hundred times than stealing horses, or even than ducking the Chancellor's messenger! Seeing at this moment a party of travelers approach, I crammed the letter into my pocket, and rode by them with a red face, and a tongue that stuttered so feebly that I could scarcely return their greetings. When they had gone by I pulled out the warrant again, having it in my mind to tear it up without a moment's delay--to tear it into the smallest morsels, and so get rid of a thing most dangerous. But the great red seal dangling at the foot of the parchment caught my eye, and I paused to think. It was so red, so large, so imposing, it seemed a pity to destroy it. It must surely be good for something. I folded up the warrant again, and put it away in my safest pocket. Yes, it might be good for something.

I took out the other letter. It was bound with green ribbon and sealed with extreme care, being directed simply to Mistress Clarence--there was no address. But over Gardiner's signature on the wrapper were the words, "These, on your peril, very privately."

I turned it over and over, and said the same thing about love and war, and even repeated to myself my old proverb about a sheep and a lamb. But somehow I could not do it. The letter was a woman's letter; the secret, her secret; and though my fingers itched as they hovered about the seals, my cheek tingled too. So at last, with a muttered, "What would Petronilla say?" I put it away unopened in the pocket where the warrant lay. The odds were immense that Mistress Clarence would never get it; but at least her secret should remain hers, my honor mine!

It was dark when I rode, thoroughly jaded, into St. Albans. I was splashed with mud up to the waist and wetted by a shower, and looked, I have no doubt, from the effect of my journeying on foot and horseback, as disreputable a fellow as might be. The consciousness too that I was without a penny, and the fear lest, careful as I had been to let no one outsrip me, the news of the riot at Stratford might have arrived, did not tend to give me assurance. I poked my head timidly into the great room, hoping that I might have it to myself. To my disgust it was full of people. Half-a-dozen travelers and as many townsfolk were sitting round the fire, talking briskly over their evening draught. Yet I had no choice. I was hungry, and the thing had to be done, and I swaggered in, something of the sneak, no doubt, peeping through my bravado. I remarked, as I took my seat by the fire and set to drying myself, that I was greeted by a momentary silence, and that two or three of the company began to eye me suspiciously.

There was one man, who sat on the settle in the warmest corner of the chimney, who seemed in particular to resent my damp neighborhood. His companions treated him with so much reverence, and he snubbed them so regularly, that I wondered who he was; and presently, listening to the conversation which went on round me, I had my curiosity satisfied. He was no less a personage than the Bailiff of St. Albans, and his manner befitted such a man; for it seemed to indicate that he thought himself heir to all the powers of the old Abbots under whose broad thumb his father and grandfather had groaned.

My conscience pricking me, I felt some misgiving when I saw him, after staring at me and whispering to two or three of his neighbors, beckon the landlord aside. His big round face and burly figure gave him a general likeness to bluff King Hal and he appeared to be aware of this himself, and to be inclined to ape the stout king's ways, which, I have heard my uncle say, were ever ways heavy for others' toes. For a while, however, seeing my supper come in, I forgot him. The bare-armed girl who brought it to me, and in whom my draggled condition seemed to provoke feelings of a different nature, lugged up a round table to the fire. On this she laid my meal, not scrupling to set aside some of the snug dry townsfolk. Then she set a chair for me well in the blaze, and folding her arms in her apron stood to watch me fall to. I did so with a will, and with each mouthful of beef and draught of ale, spirit and strength came back to me. The cits round me might sneer and shake their heads, and the travelers smile at my appetite. In five minutes I cared not a whit! I could give them back joke for joke, and laugh with the best of them.

Indeed, I had clean forgotten the Bailiff, when he stalked back to his place. But the moment our eyes met, I guessed there was trouble afoot. The landlord came with him and stood looking at me, sending off the wench with a flea in her ear; and I felt under his eye an uncomfortable consciousness that my purse was empty. Two or three late arrivals, to whom I suppose Master Bailiff had confided his suspicions, took their stand also in a half-circle and scanned me queerly. Altogether it struck me suddenly that I was in a tight place, and had need of my wits.

"Ahem!" said the Bailiff abruptly, taking skillful advantage of a lull in the talk. "Where from last, young man?" He spoke in a deep choky voice, and, if I was not mistaken, he winked one of his small eyes in the direction of his friends, as though to say, "Now see me pose him!"

But I only put another morsel in my mouth. For a moment indeed the temptation to reply "Towcester," seeing that such a journey over a middling road was something to brag of before the Highway Law came in, almost overcame me. But in time I bethought me of Stephen Gardiner's maxim, "Be slow to speak!" and I put another morsel in my mouth.

The Bailiff's face grew red, or rather, redder. "Come, young man, did you hear me speak?" he said pompously. "Where from last?"

"From the road, sir," I replied, turning to him as if I had not heard him before. "And a very wet road it was."

A man who sat next me chuckled, being apparently a stranger like myself. But the Bailiff puffed himself into a still more striking likeness to King Henry, and including him in his scowl shouted at me, "Sirrah! don't bandy words with me! Which way did you come along the road, I asked."

It was on the tip of my tongue to answer saucily, "The right way!" But I reflected that I might be stopped; and to be stopped might mean to be hanged at worst, and something very unpleasant at best. So I controlled myself, and answered--though the man's arrogance was provoking enough-- "I have come from Stratford, and I am going to London. Now you know as much as I do."

"Do I?" he said, with a sneer and a wink at the landlord.

"Yes, I think so," I answered patiently.

"Well, I don't!" he retorted, in vulgar triumph. "I don't. It is my opinion that you have come from London."

I went on with my supper.

"Do you hear?" he asked pompously, sticking his arms akimbo and looking round for sympathy. "You will have to give an account of yourself, young man. We will have no penniless rogues and sturdy vagabonds wandering about St. Albans."

"Penniless rogues do not go a-horseback," I answered. But it was wonderful how my spirits sank again under that word "penniless." It hit me hard.

"Wait a bit," he said, raising his finger to command attention for his next question. "What is your religion, young man?"

"Oh!" I replied, putting down my knife and looking open scorn at him, "you are an inquisitor, are you?" At which words of mine there was a kind of stir. "You would burn me as I hear they burned Master Sandars at Coventry last week, would you? They were talking about it down the road."

"You will come to a bad end, young man!" he retorted viciously, his outstretched finger shaking as if the palsy had seized him. For this time my taunt had gone home, and more than one of the listeners standing on the outer edge of the group, and so beyond his ken, had muttered "shame." More than one face had grown dark. "You will come to a bad end!" he repeated. "If it be not here, then somewhere else! It is my opinion that you have come from London, and that you have been in trouble. There is a hue-and-cry out for a young fellow just your age, and a cock of your hackle, I judge, who is wanted for heresy. A Londoner too. You do not leave here until you have given an account of yourself, Master Jack-a-Dandy!" The party had all risen round me, and some of the hindmost had got on benches to see me the better. Among these, between two bacon flitches, I caught a glimpse of the serving-maid's face as she peered at me, pale and scared, and a queer impulse led me to nod to her--a reassuring little nod. I found myself growing cool and confident, seeing myself so cornered.

"Easy! easy!" I said, "let a man finish his supper and get warmed in peace."

"Bishop Bonner will warm you!" cried the Bailiff.

"I dare say--as they warm people in Spain!" I sneered.

"He will be Bishop Burner to you!" shrieked the Bailiff, almost beside himself with rage at being so bearded by a lad.

"Take care!" I retorted. "Do not you speak evil of dignitaries, or you will be getting into trouble!"

He fairly writhed under this rejoinder.

"Landlord!" he spluttered. "I shall hold you responsible! If this person leaves your house, and is not forthcoming when wanted, you will suffer for it!"

The landlord scratched his head, being a good-natured fellow; but a bailiff is a bailiff, especially at St. Albans. And I was muddy and travel-stained, and quick of my tongue for one so young; which the middle-aged never like, though the old bear it better. He hesitated.

"Do not be a fool, Master Host!" I said. "I have something here----" and I touched my pocket, which happened to be near my sword-hilt--"that will make you rue it if you interfere with me!"

"Ho! ho!" cried the Bailiff, in haste and triumph. "So that is his tone! We have a tavern-brawler here, have we! A young swashbuckler! His tongue will not run so fast when he finds his feet in the stocks. Master landlord, call the watch! Call the watch at once, I command you!"

"You will do so at your peril!" I said sternly. Then, seeing that my manner had some effect upon all save the angry official, I gave way to the temptation to drive the matter home and secure my safety by the only means that seemed possible. It is an old story that one deception leads inevitably to another. I solemnly drew out the white staff I had taken from the apparitor. "Look here!" I continued, waving it. "Do you see this, you booby? I am traveling in the Queen's name, and on her service. By special commission, too, from the Chancellor! Is that plain speaking enough for you? And let me tell you, Master Bailiff," I added, fixing my eye upon him, "that my business is private, and that my Lord of Winchester will not be best pleased when he hears how I have had to declare myself. Do you think the Queen's servants go always in cloth of gold, you fool? The stocks indeed!"

I laughed out loudly and without effort, for there never was anything so absurd as the change in the Bailiff's visage. His color fled, his cheeks grew pendulous, his lip hung loose. He stared at me, gasping like a fish out of water, and seemed unable to move toe or finger. The rest enjoyed the scene, as people will enjoy a marvelous sudden stroke of fortune. It was as good as a stage pageant to them. They could not take their eyes from the pocket in which I had replaced my wand, and continued, long after I had returned to my meal, to gaze at me in respectful silence. The crestfallen Bailiff presently slipped out, and I was left cock of the walk, and for the rest of the evening enjoyed the fruits of victory.

They proved to be more substantial than I had expected, for, as I was on my way upstairs to bed, the landlord preceding me with a light, a man accosted me, and beckoned me aside mysteriously.

"The Bailiff is very much annoyed," he said, speaking in a muffled voice behind his hand, while his eyes peered into mine.

"Well, what is that to me?" I replied, looking sternly at him. I was tired and sleepy after my meal. "He should not make such a fool of himself."

"Tut, tut, tut, tut! You misunderstood me, young sir," the man answered, plucking my sleeve as I turned away. "He regrets the annoyance he has caused you. A mistake, he says, a pure mistake, and he hopes you will have forgotten it by morning." Then, with a skillful hand, which seemed not unused to the task, he slid two coins into my palm. I looked at them, for a moment not perceiving his drift. Then I found they were two gold angels, and I began to understand. "Ahem!" I said, fingering them uneasily. "Yes. Well, well, I will look over it, I will look over it! Tell him from me," I continued, gaining confidence as I proceeded with my new rôle, "that he shall hear no more about it. He is zealous--perhaps over zealous!"

"That is it!" muttered the envoy eagerly; "that is it, my dear sir! You see perfectly how it is. He is zealous. Zealous in the Queen's service!"

"To be sure; and so I will report him. Tell him that so I will report him. And here, my good friend, take one of these for yourself," I added, magnificently giving him back half my fortune--young donkey that I was. "Drink to the Queen's health; and so good-night to you."

He went away, bowing to the very ground, and, when the landlord likewise had left me, I was very merry over this, being in no mood for weighing words. The world seemed--to be sure, the ale was humming in my head, and I was in the landlord's best room--easy enough to conquer, provided one possessed a white staff. The fact that I had no right to mine only added--be it remembered I was young and foolish--to my enjoyment of its power. I went to bed in all comfort with it under my pillow, and slept soundly, untroubled by any dream of a mischance. But when did a lie ever help a man in the end?

When I awoke, which I seemed to do on a sudden, it was still dark. I wondered for a moment where I was, and what was the meaning of the shouting and knocking I heard. Then, discerning the faint outline of the window, I remembered the place in which I had gone to bed, and I sat up and listened. Some one--nay, several people--were drumming and kicking against the wooden doors of the inn-yard, and shouting besides, loud enough to raise the dead. In the next room to mine I caught the grumbling voices of persons disturbed, like myself, from sleep. And by and by a window was opened, and I heard the landlord ask what was the matter.

"In the Queen's name!" came the loud, impatient answer, given in a voice that rose above the ring of bridles and the stamping of iron hoofs, "open! and that quickly, Master Host. The watch are here, and we must search."

I waited to hear no more. I was out of bed, and huddling on my clothes, and thrusting my feet into my boots, like one possessed. My heart was beating as fast as if I had been running in a race, and my hands were shaking with the shock of the alarm. The impatient voice without was Master Pritchard's, and it rang with all the vengeful passion which I should have expected that gentleman, duped, ducked, and robbed, to be feeling. There would be little mercy to be had at his hands. Moreover, my ears, grown as keen for the moment as the hunted hare's, distinguished the tramping of at least half-a-dozen horses, so that it was clear that he had come with a force at his back. Resistance would be useless. My sole chance lay in flight--if flight should still be possible.

Even in my haste I did not forsake the talisman which had served me so well, but stayed an instant to thrust it into my pocket. The Cluddes have, I fancy, a knack of keeping cool in emergencies, getting, indeed, the cooler the greater the stress.

By this time the inn was thoroughly aroused. Doors were opening and shutting on all sides of me, and questions were being shouted in different tones from room to room. In the midst of the hubbub I heard the landlord come out muttering, and go downstairs to open the door. Instantly I unlatched mine, slipped through it stealthily, sneaked a step or two down the passage, and then came plump in the dark against some one who was moving as softly as myself. The surprise was complete, and I should have cried out at the unexpected collision, had not the unknown laid a cold hand on my mouth, and gently pushed me back into my room.

Here there was now a faint glimmer of dawn, and by this I saw that my companion was the serving-maid. "Hist!" she said, speaking under her breath, "Is it you they want?"

I nodded.

"I thought so," she muttered. "Then you must get out through your window. You cannot pass them. They are a dozen or more, and armed. Quick! knot this about the bars. It is no great depth to the bottom, and the ground is soft from the rain."

She tore, as she spoke, the coverlet from the bed, and, twisting it into a kind of rope, helped me to secure one corner of it about the window-bar. "When you are down," she whispered, "keep along the wall to the right until you come to a haystack. Turn to the left there--you will have to ford the water--and you will soon be clear of the town. Look about you then, and you will see a horse-track, which leads to Elstree, running in a line with the London Road, but a mile from it and through woods. At Elstree any path to the left will take you to Barnet, and not two miles lost."

"Heaven bless you!" I said, turning from the gloom, the dark sky, and driving scud without to peer gratefully at her. "Heaven bless you for a good woman!"

"And God keep you for a bonny boy," she whispered.

I kissed her, forcing into her hands--a thing the remembrance of which is very pleasant to me to this day--my last piece of gold.

A moment more, and I stood unhurt, but almost up to my knees in mud, in an alley bounded on both sides, as far as I could see, by blind walls. Stopping only to indicate by a low whistle that I was safe, I turned and sped away as fast as I could run in the direction which she had pointed out. There was no one abroad, and in a shorter time than I had expected I found myself outside the town, traveling over a kind of moorland tract bounded in the distance by woods.

Here I picked up the horse-track easily enough, and without stopping, save for a short breathing space, hurried along it, to gain the shelter of the trees. So far so good! I had reason to be thankful. But my case was still an indifferent one. More than once in getting out of the town I had slipped and fallen. I was wet through, and plastered with dirt owing to these mishaps; and my clothes were in a woeful plight. For a time excitement kept me up, however, and I made good way, warmed by the thought that I had again baffled the great Bishop. It was only when the day had come, and grown on to noon, and I saw no sign of any pursuers, that thought got the upper hand. Then I began to compare, with some bitterness of feeling, my present condition--wet, dirty, and homeless--with that which I had enjoyed only a week before; and it needed all my courage to support me. Skulking, half famished, between Barnet and Tottenham, often compelled to crouch in ditches or behind walls while travelers went by, and liable each instant to have to leave the highway and take to my heels, I had leisure to feel; and I did feel, more keenly, I think, that afternoon than at any later time, the bitterness of fortune. I cursed Stephen Gardiner a dozen times, and dared not let my thoughts wander to my father. I had said that I would build my house afresh. Well, truly I was building it from the foundation.

It added very much to my misery that it rained all day a cold, half-frozen rain. The whole afternoon I spent in hiding, shivering and shaking in a hole under a ledge near Tottenham; being afraid to go into London before nightfall, lest I should be waited for at the gate and be captured. Chilled and bedraggled as I was, and weak through want of food which I dared not go out to beg, the terrors of capture got hold of my mind and presented to me one by one every horrible form of humiliation, the stocks, the pillory, the cart-tail; so that even Master Pritchard, could he have seen me and known my mind, might have pitied me; so that I loathe to this day the hours I spent in that foul hiding-place. Between a man's best and worse, there is little but a platter of food.

The way this was put an end to, I well remember. An old woman came into the field where I lay hid, to drive home a cow. I had had my eyes on this cow for at least an hour, having made up my mind to milk it for my own benefit as soon as the dusk fell. In my disappointment at seeing it driven off, and also out of a desire to learn whether the old dame might not be going to milk it in a corner of the pasture, in which case I might still get an after taste, I crawled so far out of my hole that, turning suddenly, she caught sight of me. I expected to see her hurry off, but she did not. She took a long look, and then came back toward me, making, however, as it seemed to me, as if she did not see me. When she had come within a few feet of me, she looked down abruptly, and our eyes met. What she saw in mine I can only guess. In hers I read a divine pity. "Oh, poor lad!" she murmured; "oh, you poor, poor lad!" and there were tears in her voice.

I was so weak--it was almost twenty-four hours since I had tasted food, and I had come twenty-four miles in the time--that at that I broke down, and cried like a child.

I learned later that the old woman took me for just the same person for whom the Bailiff at St. Albans had mistaken me, a young apprentice named Hunter, who had got into trouble about religion, and was at this time hiding up and down the country; Bishop Bonner having clapped his father into jail until the son should come to hand. But her kind heart knew no distinction of creeds. She took me to her cottage as soon as night fell, and warmed, and dried, and fed me. She did not dare to keep me under her roof for longer than an hour or two, neither would I have stayed to endanger her. But she sent me out a new man, with a crust, moreover, in my pocket. A hundred times between Tottenham and Aldersgate I said "God bless her!" And I say so now.

So twice in one day, and that the gloomiest day of my life, I was succored by a woman. I have never forgotten it. I have tried to keep it always in mind; remembering too a saying of my uncle's, that "there is nothing on earth so merciful as a good woman, or so pitiless as a bad one!"

CHAPTER V.

MISTRESS BERTRAM.

"Ding! ding! ding! Aid ye the poor! Pray for the dead! Five o'clock and a murky morning."

The noise of the bell, and the cry which accompanied it, roused me from my first sleep in London, and that with a vengeance; the bell being rung and the words uttered within three feet of my head. Where did I sleep, then? Well, I had found a cozy resting-place behind some boards which stood propped against the wall of a baker's oven in a street near Moorgate. The wall was warm and smelt of new bread, and another besides myself had discovered its advantages. This was the watchman, who had slumbered away most of his vigil cheek by jowl with me, but, morning approaching, had roused himself, and before he was well out of his bed, certainly before he had left his bedroom, had begun--the ungrateful wretch--to prove his watchfulness by disturbing every one else.

I sat up and rubbed my eyes, grinding my shoulders well against the wall for warmth. I had no need to turn out yet, but I began to think, and the more I thought the harder I stared at the planks six inches before my nose. My thoughts turned upon a very knotty point; one that I had never seriously considered before. What was I going to do next? How was I going to live or to rear the new house of which I have made mention? Hitherto I had aimed simply at reaching London. London had paraded itself before my mind--though my mind should have known better--not as a town of cold streets and dreary alleys and shops open from seven to four with perhaps here and there a vacant place for an apprentice; but as a gilded city of adventure and romance, in which a young man of enterprise, whether he wanted to go abroad or to rise at home, might be sure of finding his sword weighed, priced, and bought up on the instant, and himself valued at his own standard.

But London reached, the hoarding in Moorgate reached, and five o'clock in the morning reached, somehow these visions faded rapidly. In the cold reality left to me I felt myself astray. If I would stay at home, who was going to employ me? To whom should I apply? What patron had I? Or if I would go abroad, how was I to set about it? how find a vessel, seeing that I might expect to be arrested the moment I showed my face in daylight?

Here all my experience failed me. I did not know what to do, though the time had come for action, and I must do or starve. It had been all very well when I was at Coton, to propose that I would go up to London, and get across the water--such had been my dim notion--to the Courtenays and Killigrews, who, with other refugees, Protestants for the most part, were lying on the French coast, waiting for better times. But now that I was in London, and as good as an outlaw myself, I saw no means of going to them. I seemed farther from my goal than I had been in Warwickshire.

Thinking very blankly over this I began to munch the piece of bread which I owed to the old dame at Tottenham; and had solemnly got through half of it, when the sound of rapid footsteps--the footsteps of women, I judged from the lightness of the tread--caused me to hold my hand and listen. Whoever they were--and I wondered, for it was still early, and I had heard no one pass since the watchman left me--they came to a stand in front of my shelter, and one of them spoke. Her words made me start; unmistakably the voice was a gentlewoman's, such as I had not heard for almost a week. And at this place and hour, on the raw borderland of day and night, a gentlewoman was the last person I expected to light upon. Yet if the speaker were not some one of station, Petronilla's lessons had been thrown away upon me.

The words were uttered in a low voice; but the planks in front of me were thin, and the speaker was actually leaning against them. I caught every accent of what seemed to be the answer to a question. "Yes, yes! It is all right!" she said, a covert ring of impatience in her tone. "Take breath a moment. I do not see him now."

"Thank Heaven!" muttered another voice. As I had fancied, there were two persons. The latter speaker's tone smacked equally of breeding with the former's, but was rounder and fuller, and more masterful; and she appeared to be out of breath. "Then perhaps we have thrown him off the trail," she continued, after a short pause, in which she seemed to have somewhat recovered herself. "I distrusted him from the first, Anne--from the first. Yet, do you know, I never feared him as I did Master Clarence; and as it was too much to hope that we should be rid of both at once--they took good care of that--why, the attempt had to be made while he was at home. But I always felt he was a spy."

"Who? Master Clarence?" asked she who had spoken first.

"Ay, he certainly. But I did not mean him, I meant Philip."

"Well, I--I said at first, you remember, that it was a foolhardy enterprise, mistress!"

"Tut, tut, girl!" quoth the other tartly--this time the impatience lay with her, and she took no pains to conceal it--"we are not beaten yet. Come, look about! Cannot you remember where we are, nor which way the river should be? If the dawn were come, we could tell."

"But with the dawn----"

"The streets would fill. True, and, Master Philip giving the alarm, we should be detected before we had gone far. The more need, girl, to lose no time. I have my breath again, and the child is asleep. Let us venture one way or the other, and Heaven grant it be the right one!"

"Let me see," the younger woman answered slowly, as if in doubt. "Did we come by the church? No; we came the other way. Let us try this turning, then."

"Why, child, we came that way," was the decided answer. "What are you thinking of? That would take us straight back into his arms, the wretch! Come, come! you loiter," continued this, the more masculine speaker, "and a minute may make all the difference between a prison and freedom. If we can reach the Lion Wharf by seven--it is like to be a dark morning and foggy--we may still escape before Master Philip brings the watch upon us."

They moved briskly away as she spoke, and her words were already growing indistinct from distance, while I remained still, idly seeking the clew to their talk and muttering over and over again the name Clarence, which seemed familiar to me, when a cry of alarm, in which I recognized one of their voices, cut short my reverie. I crawled with all speed from my shelter, and stood up, being still in a line with the boards, and not easily distinguishable. As she had said, it was a dark morning; but the roofs of the houses--now high, now low--could be plainly discerned against a gray, drifting sky wherein the first signs of dawn were visible; and the blank outlines of the streets, which met at this point, could be seen. Six or seven yards from me, in the middle of the roadway, stood three dusky figures, of whom I judged the nearer, from their attitudes, to be the two women. The farthest seemed to be a man.

I was astonished to see that he was standing cap in hand; nay, I was disgusted as well, for I had crept out hot-fisted, expecting to be called upon to defend the women. But, despite the cry I had heard, they were talking to him quietly enough, as far as I could hear. And in a minute or so I saw the taller woman give him something.

He took it with a low bow, and appeared almost to sweep the dirt with his bonnet. She waved her hand in dismissal, and he stood back still uncovered. And--hey, presto! the women tripped swiftly away.

By this time my curiosity was intensely excited, but for a moment I thought it was doomed to disappointment. I thought that it was all over. It was not, by any means. The man stood looking after them until they reached the corner, and the moment they had passed it, he followed. His stealthy manner of going, and his fashion of peering after them, was enough for me. I guessed at once that he was dogging them, following them unknown to them and against their will; and with considerable elation I started after him, using the same precautions. What was sauce for the geese was sauce for the gander! So we went, two--one--one, slipping after one another through half a dozen dark streets, tending generally southward.

Following him in this way I seldom caught a glimpse of the women. The man kept at a considerable distance behind them, and I had my attention fixed on him. But once or twice, when, turning a corner, I all but trod on his heels, I saw them; and presently an odd point about them struck me. There was a white kerchief or something attached apparently to the back of the one's cloak, which considerably assisted my stealthy friend to keep them in view. It puzzled me. Was it a signal to him? Was he really all the time acting in concert with them; and was I throwing away my pains? Or was the white object which so betrayed them merely the result of carelessness, and the lack of foresight of women grappling with a condition of things to which they were unaccustomed? Of course I could not decide this, the more as, at that distance, I failed to distinguish what the white something was, or even which of the two wore it.

Presently I got a clew to our position, for we crossed Cheapside close to Paul's Cross, which my childish memories of the town enabled me to recognize, even by that light. Here my friend looked up and down, and hung a minute on his heel before he followed the women, as if expecting or looking for some one. It might be that he was trying to make certain that the watch were not in sight. They were not, at any rate. Probably they had gone home to bed, for the morning was growing. And, after a momentary hesitation, he plunged into the narrow street down which the women had flitted.

He had only gone a few yards when I heard him cry out. The next instant, almost running against him myself, I saw what had happened. The women had craftily lain in wait for him in the little court into which the street ran and had caught him as neatly as could be. When I came upon them the taller woman was standing at bay with a passion that was almost fury in her pose and gesture. Her face, from which the hood of a coarse cloak had fallen back, was pale with anger; her gray eyes flashed, her teeth glimmered. Seeing her thus, and seeing the burden she carried under her cloak--which instinct told me was her child--I thought of a tigress brought to bay.

"You lying knave!" she hissed. "You Judas!"

The man recoiled a couple of paces, and in recoiling nearly touched me.

"What would you?" she continued. "What do you want? What would you do? You have been paid to go. Go, and leave us!"

"I dare not," he muttered, keeping away from her as if he dreaded a blow. She looked a woman who could deal a blow, a woman who could both love and hate fiercely and openly--as proud and frank and haughty a lady as I had ever seen in my life. "I dare not," he muttered sullenly; "I have my orders."

"Oh!" she cried, with scorn. "You have your orders, have you! The murder is out. But from whom, sirrah? Whose orders are to supersede mine? I would King Harry were alive, and I would have you whipped to Tyburn. Speak, rogue; who bade you follow me?"

He shook his head.

She looked about her wildly, passionately, and I saw that she was at her wits' end what to do, or how to escape him. But she was a woman. When she next spoke there was a marvelous change in her. Her face had grown soft, her voice low. "Philip," she said gently, "the purse was light. I will give you more. I will give you treble the amount within a few weeks, and I will thank you on my knees, and my husband shall be such a friend to you as you have never dreamed of, if you will only go home and be silent. Only that--or, better still, walk the streets an hour, and then report that you lost sight of us. Think, man, think!" she cried with energy--"the times may change. A little more, and Wyatt had been master of London last year. Now the people are fuller of discontent than ever, and these burnings and torturings, these Spaniards in the streets--England will not endure them long. The times will change. Let us go, and you will have a friend--when most you need one."

He shook his head sullenly. "I dare not do it," he said. And somehow I got the idea that he was telling the truth, and that it was not the man's stubborn nature only that withstood the bribe and the plea. He spoke as if he were repeating a lesson and the master were present.

When she saw that she could not move him, the anger, which I think came more naturally to her, broke out afresh. "You will not, you hound!" she cried. "Will neither threats nor promises move you?"

"Neither," he answered doggedly; "I have my orders."

So far, I had remained a quiet listener, standing in the mouth of the lane which opened upon the court where they were. The women had taken no notice of me; either because they did not see me, or because, seeing me, they thought that I was a hanger-on of the man before them. And he, having his back to me, and his eyes on them, could not see me. It was a surprise to him--a very great surprise, I think--when I took three steps forward, and gripped him by the scruff of his neck.

"You have your orders, have you?" I muttered in his ear, as I shook him to and fro, while the taller woman started back and the younger uttered a cry of alarm at my sudden appearance. "Well, you will not obey them. Do you hear? Your employer may go hang! You will do just what these ladies please to ask of you."

He struggled an instant; but he was an undersized man, and he could not loosen the hold which I had secured at my leisure. Then I noticed his hand going to his girdle in a suspicious way. "Stop that!" I said, flashing before his eyes a short, broad blade, which had cut many a deer's throat in Old Arden Forest. "You had better keep quiet, or it will be the worse for you! Now, mistress," I continued, "you can dispose of this little man as you please."

"Who are you?" she said, after a pause; during which she had stared at me in open astonishment. No doubt I was a wild-looking figure.

"A friend," I replied. "Or one who would be such. I saw this fellow follow you, and I followed him. For the last five minutes I have been listening to your talk. He was not amenable to reason then, but I think he will be now. What shall I do with him?"

She smiled faintly, but did not answer at once, the coolness and resolution with which she had faced him before failing her now, possibly in sheer astonishment, or because my appearance at her side, by removing the strain, sapped the strength. "I do not know," she said at length, in a vague, puzzled tone.

"Well," I answered, "you are going to the Lion Wharf, and----"

"Oh, you fool!" she screamed out loud. "Oh, you fool!" she repeated bitterly. "Now you have told him all."

I stood confounded. My cheeks burned with shame, and her look of contempt cut me like a knife. That the reproach was deserved I knew at once, for the man in my grasp gave a start, which proved that the information was not lost upon him. "Who told you?" the woman went on, clutching the child jealously to her breast, as though she saw herself menaced afresh. "Who told you about the Lion Wharf?"

"Never mind," I answered gloomily. "I have made a mistake, but it is easy to remedy it." And I took out my knife again. "Do you go on and leave us."

I hardly know whether I meant my threat or no. But my prisoner had no doubts. He shrieked out--a wild cry of fear which rang round the empty court--and by a rapid blow, despair giving him courage, he dashed the hunting-knife from my hand. This done he first flung himself on me, then tried by a sudden jerk to free himself. In a moment we were down on the stones, and tumbling over one another in the dirt, while he struggled to reach his knife, which was still in his girdle, and I strove to prevent him. The fight was sharp, but it lasted barely a minute. When the first effort of his despair was spent, I came uppermost, and he was but a child in my hands. Presently, with my knee on his chest, I looked up. The women were still there, the younger clinging to the other.

"Go! go!" I cried impatiently. Each second I expected the court to be invaded, for the man had screamed more than once.

But they hesitated. I had been forced to hurt him a little, and he was moaning piteously. "Who are you?" the elder woman asked--she who had spoken all through.

"Nay, never mind that!" I answered. "Do you go! Go, while you can. You know the way to the Wharf."

"Yes," she answered. "But I cannot go and leave him at your mercy. Remember he is a man, and has----"

"He is a treacherous scoundrel," I answered, giving his throat a squeeze. "But he shall have one more chance. Listen, sirrah!" I continued to the man, "and stop that noise or I will knock out your teeth with my dagger-hilt. Listen and be silent. I shall go with these ladies, and I promise you this: If they are stopped or hindered on their way, or if evil happen to them at that wharf, whose name you had better forget, it will be the worse for you. Do you hear? You will suffer for it, though there be a dozen guards about you! Mind you," I added, "I have nothing to lose myself, for I am desperate already."

He vowed--the poor craven--with his stuttering tongue, that he would be true, and vowed it again and again. But I saw that his eyes did not meet mine. They glanced instead at the knife-blade, and I knew, even while I pretended to trust him, that he would betray us. My real hope lay in his fears, and in this, that as the fugitives knew the way to the wharf, and it could not now be far distant, we might reach it, and go on board some vessel--I had gathered they were flying the country--before this wretch could recover himself and get together a force to stop us. That was my real hope, and in that hope only I left him.

We went as fast as the women could walk. I did not trouble them with questions; indeed, I had myself no more leisure than enabled me to notice their general appearance, which was that of comfortable tradesmen's womenfolk. Their cloaks and hoods were plainly fashioned, and of coarse stuff, their shoes were thick, and no jewel or scrap of lace, peeping out, betrayed them. Yet there was something in their carriage which could not be hidden, something which, to my eye, told tales; so that minute by minute I became more sure that this was really an adventure worth pursuing, and that London had kept a reward in store for me besides its cold stones and inhospitable streets.

The city was beginning to rouse itself. As we flitted through the lanes and alleys which lie between Cheapside and the river, we met many people, chiefly of the lower classes, on their way to work. Yet in spite of this, we had no need to fear observation, for, though the morning was fully come, with the light had arrived such a thick, choking, yellow fog as I, being for the most part country-bred, had never experienced. It was so dense and blinding that we had a difficulty in keeping together, and even hand in hand could scarcely see one another. In my wonder how my companions found their way, I presently failed to notice their condition, and only remarked the distress and exhaustion which one of them was suffering, when she began, notwithstanding all her efforts, to lag behind. Then I sprang forward, blaming myself much. "Forgive me," I said. "You are tired, and no wonder. Let me carry the child, mistress."

Exhausted as she was, she drew away from me jealously.

"No," she panted. "We are nearly there. I am better now." And she strained the child closer to her, as though she feared I might take it from her by force.

"Well, if you will not trust me," I answered, "let your friend carry it for a time. I can see you are tired out."

Through the mist she bent forward, and peered into my face, her eyes scarcely a foot from mine. The scrutiny seemed to satisfy her. She drew a long breath and held out her burden. "No," she said; "you shall take him. I will trust you."

I took the little wrapped-up thing as gently as I could. "You shall not repent it, if I can help it, Mistress----"

"Bertram," she said.

"Mistress Bertram," I repeated. "Now let us get on and lose no time."

A walk of a hundred yards or so brought us clear of the houses, and revealed before us, in place of all else, a yellow curtain of fog. Below this, at our feet, yet apparently a long way from us, was a strange, pale line of shimmering light, which they told me was the water. At first I could hardly believe this. But, pausing a moment while my companions whispered together, dull creakings and groanings and uncouth shouts and cries, and at last the regular beat of oars, came to my ears out of the bank of vapor, and convinced me that we really had the river before us.

Mistress Bertram turned to me abruptly. "Listen," she said, "and decide for yourself, my friend. We are close to the wharf now, and in a few minutes shall know our fate. It is possible that we may be intercepted at this point, and if that happen, it will be bad for me and worse for any one aiding me. You have done us gallant service, but you are young; and I am loath to drag you into perils which do not belong to you. Take my advice, then, and leave us now. I would I could reward you," she added hastily, "but that knave has my purse."

I put the child gently back into her arms. "Good-by," she said, with more feeling. "We thank you. Some day I may return to England, and have ample power----"

"Not so fast," I answered stiffly. "Did you think it possible, mistress, that I would desert you now? I gave you back the child only because it might hamper me, and will be safer with you. Come, let us on at once to the wharf."

"You mean it?" she said.

"Of a certainty!" I answered, settling my cap on my head with perhaps a boyish touch of the braggart.

At any rate, she did not take me at once at my word; and her thought for me touched me the more because I judged her--I know not exactly why--to be a woman not over prone to think of others. "Do not be reckless," she said slowly, her eyes intently fixed on mine. "I should be sorry to bring evil upon you. You are but a boy."

"And yet," I answered, smiling, "there is as good as a price upon my head already. I should be reckless if I stayed here. If you will take me with you, let us go. We have loitered too long already."

She turned then, asking no questions; but she looked at me from time to time in a puzzled way, as though she thought she ought to know me--as though I reminded her of some one. Paying little heed to this then, I hurried her and her companion down to the water, traversing a stretch of foreshore strewn with piles of wood and stacks of barrels and old rotting boats, between which the mud lay deep. Fortunately it was high tide, and so we had not far to go. In a minute or two I distinguished the hull of a ship looming large through the fog; and a few more steps placed us safely on a floating raft, on the far side of which the vessel lay moored.

There was only one man to be seen lounging on the raft, and the neighborhood was quiet. My spirits rose as I looked round. "Is this the *Whelp?*" the tall lady asked. I had not heard the other open her mouth since the encounter in the court.

"Yes, it is the *Whelp*, madam," the man answered, saluting her and speaking formally, and with a foreign accent. "You are the lady who is expected?"

"I am," she answered, with authority. "Will you tell the captain that I desire to sail immediately, without a moment's delay? Do you understand?"

"Well, the tide is going out," quoth the sailor, dubiously, looking steadily into the fog, which hid the river. "It has just turned, it is true. But as to sailing----"

She cut him short. "Go, go! man. Tell your captain what I say. And let down a ladder for us to get on board."

He caught a rope which hung over the side, and, swinging himself up, disappeared. We stood below, listening to the weird sounds which came off the water, the creaking and flapping of masts and canvas, the whir of wings and shrieks of unseen gulls, the distant hail of boatmen. A bell in the city solemnly tolled eight. The younger woman shivered. The elder's foot tapped impatiently on the planks. Shut in by the yellow walls of fog, I experienced a strange sense of solitude; it was as if we three were alone in the world--we three who had come together so strangely.

CHAPTER VI.

MASTER CLARENCE.

We had stood thus for a few moments when a harsh voice, hailing us from above, put an end to our several thoughts and forebodings. We looked up and I saw half a dozen night-capped heads thrust over the bulwarks. A rope ladder came hurtling down at our feet, and a man, nimbly descending, held it tight at the bottom. "Now, madame!" he said briskly. They all, I noticed, had the same foreign accent, yet all spoke English; a singularity I did not understand, until I learned later that the boat was the *Lions Whelp*, trading between London and Calais, and manned from the latter place.

Mistress Bertram ascended quickly and steadily, holding the baby in her arms. The other made some demur, lingering at the foot of the ladder and looking up as if afraid, until her companion chid her sharply. Then she too went up, but as she passed me--I was holding one side of the ladder steady--she shot at me from under her hood a look which disturbed me strangely.

It was the first time I had seen her face, and it was such a face as a man rarely forgets. Not because of its beauty; rather because it was a speaking face, a strange and expressive one, which the dark waving hair, swelling in thick clusters upon either temple, seemed to accentuate. The features were regular, but, the full red lips excepted, rather thin than shapely. The nose, too, was prominent. But the eyes! The eyes seemed to glorify the dark brilliant thinness of the face, and to print it upon the memory. They were dark flashing eyes, and their smile seemed to me perpetually to challenge, to allure and repulse, and even to goad. Sometimes they were gay, more rarely sad, sometimes soft, and again hard as steel. They changed in a moment as one or another approached her. But always at their gayest, there was a suspicion of weariness and fatigue in their depths. Or so I thought later.

Something of this flashed through my mind as I followed her up the side. But once on board I glanced round, forgetting her in the novelty of my position. The *Whelp* was decked fore and aft only, the blackness of the hold gaping amidships, spanned by a narrow gangway, which served to connect the two decks. We found ourselves in the forepart, amid coils of rope and windlasses and water-casks; surrounded by half a dozen wild-looking sailors wearing blue knitted frocks and carrying sheath-knives at their girdles.

The foremost and biggest of these seemed to be the captain, although, so far as outward appearances went, the only difference between him and his crew lay in a marlin-spike which he wore slung to a thong beside his knife. When I reached the deck he was telling a long story to Mistress Bertram, and telling it very slowly. But the drift of it I soon gathered. While the fog lasted he could not put to sea.

"Nonsense!" cried my masterful companion, chafing at his slowness of speech. "Why not? Would it be dangerous?"

"Well, madam, it would be dangerous," he answered, more slowly than ever. "Yes, it would be dangerous. And to put to sea in a fog? That is not seamanship. And your baggage has not arrived."

"Never mind my baggage!" she answered imperiously. "I have made other arrangements for it. Two or three things I know came on board last night. I want to start--to start at once, do you hear?"

The captain shook his head, and said sluggishly that it was impossible. Spitting on the deck he ground his heel leisurely round in a knothole. "Impossible," he repeated; "it would not be seamanship to start in a fog. When the fog lifts we will go. 'Twill be all the same to-morrow. We shall lie at Leigh to-night, whether we go now or go when the fog lifts."

"At Leigh?"

"That is it, madam."

"And when will you go from Leigh?" she cried indignantly.

"Daybreak to-morrow," he answered. "You leave it to me, mistress," he continued, in a tone of rough patronage, "and you will see your good man before you expect it."

"But, man!" she exclaimed, trembling with impotent rage. "Did not Master Bertram engage you to bring me across whenever I might be ready? Ay, and pay you handsomely for it? Did he not, sirrah?"

"To be sure, to be sure!" replied the giant unmoved. "Using seamanship, and not going to sea in a fog, if it please you."

"It does not please me!" she retorted. "And why stay at Leigh?"

He looked up at the rigging, then down at the deck. He set his heel in the knothole, and ground it round again. Then he looked at his questioner with a broad smile. "Well, mistress, for a very good reason. It is there your good man is waiting for you. Only," added this careful keeper of a secret, "he bade me not tell any one."

She uttered a low cry, which might have been an echo of her baby's cooing, and convulsively clasped the child more tightly to her. "He is at Leigh!" she murmured, flushing and trembling, another woman altogether. Even her voice was wonderfully changed. "He is really at Leigh, you say?"

"To be sure!" replied the captain, with a portentous wink and a mysterious roll of the head. "He is there safe enough! Safe enough, you may bet your handsome face to a rushlight. And we will be there to-night."

She started up with a wild gesture. For a moment she had sat down on a cask standing beside her, and forgotten our peril, and the probability that we might never see Leigh at all. Now, I have said, she started up. "No, no!" she cried, struggling for breath and utterance. "Oh, no! no! Let us go at once. We must start at once!" Her voice was hysterical in its sudden anxiety and terror, as the consciousness of our position rolled back upon her. "Captain! listen, listen!" she pleaded. "Let us start now, and my husband will give you double. I will promise you double whatever he said if you will chance the fog."

I think all who heard her were moved, save the captain only. He rubbed his head and grinned. Slow and heavy, he saw nothing in her prayer save the freak of a woman wild to get to her man. He did not weigh her promise at a groat; she was but a woman. And being a foreigner, he did not perceive a certain air of breeding which might have influenced a native. He was one of those men against whose stupidity Father Carey used to say the gods fight in vain. When he answered good-naturedly, "No, no, mistress, it is impossible. It would not be seamanship," I felt that we might as well try to stop the ebbing tide as move him from his position.

The feeling was a maddening one. The special peril which menaced my companions I did not know; but I knew they feared pursuit, and I had every reason to fear it for myself. Yet at any moment, out of the fog which encircled us so closely that we could barely see the raft below--and the shore not at all--might come the tramp of hurrying feet and the stern hail of the law. It was maddening to think of this, and to know that we had only to cast off a rope or two in order to escape; and to know also that we were absolutely helpless.

I expected that Mistress Bertram, brave as she had shown herself, would burst into a passion of rage or tears. But apparently she had one hope left. She looked at me.

I tried to think--to think hard. Alas, I seemed only able to listen. An hour had gone by since we parted from that rascal in the court, and we might expect him to appear at any moment, vengeful and exultant, with a posse at his back. Yet I tried hard to think; and the fog presently suggested a possible course. "Look here," I said suddenly, speaking for the first time, "if you do not start until the fog lifts, captain, we may as well breakfast ashore, and return presently."

"That is as you please," he answered indifferently.

"What do you think?" I said, turning to my companions with as much carelessness as I could command. "Had we not better do that?"

Mistress Bertram did not understand, but in her despair she obeyed the motion of my hand mechanically, and walked to the side. The younger woman followed more slowly, so that I had to speak to her with some curtness, bidding her make haste; for I was in a fever until we were clear of the *Whelp* and the Lion Wharf. It had struck me that, if the ship were not to leave at once, we were nowhere in so much danger as on board. At large in the fog we might escape detection for a time. Our pursuers might as well look for a needle in a haystack as seek us through it when once we were clear of the wharf. And this was not the end of my idea. But for the present it was enough. Therefore I took up Mistress Anne very short. "Come!" I said, "be quick! Let me help you."

She obeyed, and I was ashamed of my impatience when at the foot of the ladder she thanked me prettily. It was almost with good cheer in my voice and a rebound of spirits that I explained, as I hurried my companions across the raft, what my plan was.

The moment we were ashore I felt safer. The fog swallowed us up quick, as the Bible says. The very hull of the ship vanished from sight before we had gone half a dozen paces. I had never seen a London fog before, and to me it seemed portentous and providential; a marvel as great as the crimson hail which fell in the London gardens to mark her Majesty's accession.

Yet after all, without my happy thought, the fog would have availed us little. We had scarcely gone a score of yards before the cautious tread of several people hastening down the strand toward the wharf struck my ear. They were proceeding in silence, and we might not have noticed their approach if the foremost had not by chance tripped and fallen; whereupon one laughed and another swore. With a warning hand I grasped my companions' arms, and hurried them forward some paces until I felt sure that our figures could not be seen through the mist. Then I halted, and we stood listening, gazing into one another's strained eyes, while the steps came nearer and nearer, crossed our track and then with a noisy rush thundered on the wooden raft. My ear caught the jingle of harness and the clank of weapons.

"It is the watch," I muttered. "Come, and make no noise. What I want is a little this way. I fancy I saw it as we passed down to the wharf."

They turned with me, but we had not taken many steps before Mistress Anne, who was walking on my left side, stumbled over something. She tried to save herself, but failed and fell heavily, uttering as she did so a loud cry. I sprang to her assistance, and even before I raised her I laid my hand lightly on her mouth. "Hush!" I said softly, "for safety's sake, make no noise. What is the matter?"

"Oh!" she moaned, making no effort to rise, "my ankle! my ankle! I am sure I have broken it."

I muttered my dismay, while Mistress Bertram, stooping anxiously, examined the injured limb. "Can you stand?" she asked.

But it was no time for questioning, and I put her aside. The troop which had passed were within easy hearing, and if there should be one among them familiar with the girl's voice, we might be pounced upon, fog or no fog. I felt that it was no time for ceremony, and picked Mistress Anne up in my arms, whispering to the elder woman: "Go on ahead! I think I see the boat. It is straight before you."

Luckily I was right, it was the boat; and so far well. But at the moment I spoke I heard a sudden outcry behind us, and knew the hunt was up. I plunged forward with my burden, recklessly and blindly, through mud and over obstacles. The wherry for which I was making was moored in the water a few feet from the edge. I had remarked it idly and without purpose as we came down to the wharf, and had even noticed that the oars were lying in it. Now, if we could reach it and start down the river for Leigh, we might by possibility gain that place, and meet Mistress Bertram's husband.

At any late, nothing in the world seemed so desirable to me at the moment as the shelter of that boat. I plunged through the mud, and waded desperately through the water to it, Mistress Bertram scarce a whit behind me. I reached it, but reached it only as the foremost pursuer caught sight of us. I heard his shout of triumph, and somehow I bundled my burden into the boat--I remember that she clung about my neck in fear, and I had to loosen her hands roughly. But I did loosen them--in time. With one stroke of my hunting-knife, I severed the rope, and pushing off the boat with all my strength, sprang into it as it floated away--and was in time. But one second's delay would have undone us. Two men were already in the water up to their knees, and their very breath was hot on my face as we swung out into the stream.

Fortunately, I had had experience of boats on the Avon, at Bidford and Stratford, and could pull a good oar. For a moment indeed the wherry rolled and dipped as I snatched up the sculls; but I quickly got her in hand, and, bending to my work, sent her spinning through the mist, every stroke I pulled increasing the distance between us and our now unseen foes. Happily we were below London Bridge, and had not that dangerous passage to make. The river, too, was nearly clear of craft, and though once and again in the Pool a huge hulk loomed suddenly across our bows, and then faded behind us into the mist like some monstrous phantom, and so told of a danger narrowly escaped, I thought it best to run all risks, and go ahead as long as the tide should ebb.

It was strange how suddenly we had passed from storm into calm. Mistress Anne had bound her ankle with a handkerchief, and bravely made light of the hurt; and now the two women sat crouching in the stern watching me, their heads together, their faces pale. The mist had closed round us, and we were alone again, gliding over the bosom of the great river that runs down to the sea. I was oddly struck by the strange current of life which for a week had tossed me from one adventure to another, only to bring me into contact at length with these two, and sweep me into the unknown whirlpool of their fortunes.

Who were they? A merchant's wife and her sister flying from Bishop Bonner's inquisition? I thought it likely. Their cloaks and hoods indeed, and all that I could see of their clothes, fell below such a condition; but probably they were worn as a disguise. Their speech rose as much above it, but I knew that of late many merchant's wives had become scholars, and might pass in noblemen's houses; even as in those days when London waxed fat, and set up and threw down governments, every alderman had come to ride in mail.

No doubt the women, watching me in anxious silence, were as curious about me. I still bore the stains of country travel. I was unwashen, unkempt, my doublet was torn, the cloak I had cast at my feet was the very wreck of a cloak. Yet I read no distrust in their looks. The elder's brave eyes seemed ever thanking me. I never saw her lips move silently that they did not shape "Well done!" And though I caught Mistress Anne scanning me once or twice with an expression I could ill interpret, a smile took its place the moment her gaze met mine.

We had passed, but were still in sight of, Greenwich Palace--as they told me--when the mist rose suddenly like a curtain rolled away, and the cold, bright February sun, shining out, disclosed the sparkling river with the green hills rising on our right hand. Here and there on its surface a small boat such as our own moved to and fro, and in the distant Pool from which we had come rose a little forest of masts. I hung on the oars a moment, and my eyes were drawn to a two-masted vessel which, nearly half a mile below us, was drifting down, gently heeling over with the current as the crew got up the sails. "I wonder whither she is bound," I said thoughtfully, "and whether they would take us on board by any chance."

Mistress Bertram shook her head. "I have no money," she answered sadly. "I fear we must go on to Leigh, if it be any way possible. You are tired, and no wonder. But what is it?" with a sudden change of voice. "What is the matter?"

I had flashed out the oars with a single touch, and begun to pull as fast as I could down the stream. No doubt my face, too, proclaimed my discovery and awoke her fears. "Look behind!" I muttered between my set teeth.

She turned, and on the instant uttered a low cry. A wherry like our own, but even lighter--in my first glance up the river I had not noticed it-- had stolen nearer to us, and yet nearer, and now throwing aside disguise was in hot pursuit of us. There were three men on board, two rowing and one steering. When they saw that we had discovered them they hailed us in a loud voice, and I heard the steersman's feet rattle on the boards, as he cried to his men to give way, and stamped in very eagerness. My only reply was to take a longer stroke, and, pulling hard, to sweep away from them.

But presently my first strength died away, and the work began to tell upon me, and little by little they overhauled us. Not that I gave up at once for that. They were still some sixty yards behind, and for a few minutes at any rate I might put off capture. In that time something might happen. At the worst they were only three to one, and their boat looked light and cranky and easy to upset.

So I pulled on, savagely straining at the oars. But my chest heaved and my arms ached more and more with each stroke. The banks slid by us; we turned one bend, then another, though I saw nothing of them. I saw only the pursuing boat, on which my eyes were fixed, heard only the measured rattle of the oars in the rowlocks. A minute, two minutes, three minutes passed. They had not gained on us, but the water was beginning to waver before my eyes, their boat seemed floating in the air, there was a pulsation in my ears louder than that of the oars, I struggled and yet I flagged. My knees trembled. Their boat shot nearer now, nearer and nearer, so that I could read the smile of triumph on the steersman's dark face and hear his cry of exultation. Nearer! and then with a cry I dropped the oars.

"Quick!" I panted to my companions. "Change places with me! So!" Trembling and out of breath as I was, I crawled between the women and gained the stern sheets of the boat. As I passed Mistress Bertram she clutched my arm. Her eyes, as they met mine, flashed fire, her lips were white. "The man steering!" she hissed between her teeth. "Leave the others. He is Clarence, and I fear him!"

I nodded; but still, as the hostile boat bore swiftly down upon us, I cast a glance round to see if there were any help at hand. I saw no sign of any. I saw only the pale blue sky overhead, and the stream flowing swiftly under the boat. I drew my sword. The case was one rather for despair than courage. The women were in my charge, and if I did not acquit myself like a man now, when should I do so? Bah! it would soon be over.

There was an instant's confusion in the other boat, as the crew ceased rowing, and, seeing my attitude and not liking it, changed their seats. To my joy the man, who had hitherto been steering, flung a curse at the others and came forward to bear the brunt of the encounter. He was a tall, sinewy man, past middle age, with a clean-shaven face, a dark complexion, and cruel eyes. So he was Master Clarence! Well, he had the air of a swordsman and a soldier. I trembled for the women.

"Surrender, you fool!" he cried to me harshly. "In the Queen's name—do you hear? What do you in this company?"

I answered nothing, for I was out of breath. But softly, my eyes on his, I drew out with my left hand my hunting-knife. If I could beat aside his sword, I would spring upon him and drive the knife home with that hand. So, standing erect in bow and stern we faced one another, the man and the boy, the flush of rage and exertion on my cheek, a dark shade on his. And silently the boats drew together.

Thought is quick, quicker than anything else in the world I suppose, for in some drawn-out second before the boats came together I had time to wonder where I had seen his face before, and to rack my memory. I knew no Master Clarence, yet I had seen this man somewhere. Another second, and away with thought! He was crouching for a spring. I drew back a little, then lunged—lunged with heart and hand. Our swords crossed and whistled—just crossed—and even as I saw his eyes gleam behind his point, the shock of the two boats coming together flung us both backward and apart. A moment we reeled, staggering and throwing out wild hands. I strove hard to recover myself, nay, I almost did so; then I caught my foot in Mistress Anne's cloak, which she had left in her place, and fell heavily back into the boat.

I was up in a moment—on my knees at least—and unhurt. But another was before me. As I stooped half-risen, I saw one moment a dark shadow above me, and the next a sheet of flame shone before my eyes, and a tremendous shock swept all away. I fell senseless into the bottom of the boat, knowing nothing of what had happened to me.

CHAPTER VII.

ON BOARD THE "FRAMLINGHAM."

I am told by people who have been seasick that the sound of the waves beating against the hull comes in time to be an intolerable torment. But bad as this may be, it can be nothing in comparison with the pains I suffered from the same cause, as I recovered my senses. My brain seemed to be a cavern into which each moment, with a rhythmical regularity which added the pangs of anticipation to those of reality, the sea rushed, booming and thundering, jarring every nerve and straining the walls to bursting, and making each moment of consciousness a vivid agony. And this lasted long; how long I cannot say. But it had subsided somewhat when I first opened my eyes, and dully, not daring to move my head, looked up.

I was lying on my back. About a foot from my eyes were rough beams of wood disclosed by a smoky yellow light, which flickered on the knotholes and rude joists. The light swayed to and fro regularly; and this adding to my pain, I closed my eyes with a moan. Then some one came to me, and I heard voices which sounded a long way off, and promptly fell again into a deep sleep, troubled still, but less painfully, by the same rhythmical shocks, the same dull crashings in my brain.

When I awoke again I had sense to know what caused this, and where I was--in a berth on board ship. The noise which had so troubled me was that of the waves beating against her forefoot. The beams so close to my face formed the deck, the smoky light came from the ship's lantern swinging on a hook. I tried to turn. Some one came again, and with gentle hands arranged my pillow and presently began to feed me with a spoon. When I had swallowed a few mouthfuls I gained strength to turn.

Who was this feeding me? The light was at her back and dazzled me. For a short while I took her for Petronilla, my thoughts going back at one bound to Coton, and skipping all that had happened since I left home. But as I grew stronger I grew clearer, and recalling bit by bit what had happened in the boat, I recognized Mistress Anne. I tried to murmur thanks, but she laid a cool finger on my lips and shook her head, smiling on me. "You must not talk," she murmured, "you are getting well. Now go to sleep again."

I shut my eyes at once as a child might. Another interval of unconsciousness, painless this time, followed, and again I awoke. I was lying on my side now, and without moving could see the whole of the tiny cabin. The lantern still hung and smoked. But the light was steady now, and I heard no splashing without, nor the dull groaning and creaking of the timbers within. There reigned a quiet which seemed bliss to me; and I lay wrapped in it, my thoughts growing clearer and clearer each moment.

On a sea-chest at the farther end of the cabin were sitting two people engaged in talk. The one, a woman, I recognized immediately. The gray eyes full of command, the handsome features, the reddish-brown hair and gracious figure left me in no doubt, even for a moment, that I looked on Mistress Bertram. The sharer of her seat was a tall, thin man with a thoughtful face and dreamy, rather melancholy eyes. One of her hands rested on his knee, and her lips as she talked were close to his ear. A little aside, sitting on the lowest step of the ladder which led to the deck, her head leaning against the timbers, and a cloak about her, was Mistress Anne.

I tried to speak, and after more than one effort found my voice. "Where am I?" I whispered. My head ached sadly, and I fancied, though I was too languid to raise my hand to it, that it was bandaged. My mind was so far clear that I remembered Master Clarence and his pursuit and the fight in the boats, and knew that we ought to be on our way to prison. Who, then, was the mild, comely gentleman whose length of limb made the cabin seem smaller than it was? Not a jailer, surely? Yet who else?

I could compass no more than a whisper, but faint as my voice was they all heard me, and looked up. "Anne!" the elder lady cried sharply, seeming by her tone to direct the other to attend to me. Yet was she herself the first to rise, and come and lay her hand on my brow. "Ah! the fever is gone!" she said, speaking apparently to the gentleman, who kept his seat. "His head is quite cool. He will do well now, I am sure. Do you know me?" she continued, leaning over me.

I looked up into her eyes, and read only kindness. "Yes," I muttered. But the effort of looking was so painful that I closed my eyes again with a sigh. Nevertheless, my memory of the events which had gone before my illness grew clearer, and I fumbled feebly for something which should have been at my side. "Where is--where is my sword?" I made shift to whisper.

She laughed. "Show it to him, Anne," she said; "what a never-die it is! There, Master Knight Errant, we did not forget to bring it off the field, you see!"

"But how," I murmured, "how did you escape?" I saw that there was no question of a prison. Her laugh was gay, her voice full of content.

"That is a long story," she answered kindly. "Are you well enough to hear it? You think you are? Then take some of this first. You remember that knave Philip striking you on the head with an oar as you got up? No?

Well, it was a cowardly stroke, but it stood him in little stead, for we had drifted, in the excitement of the race, under the stern of the ship which you remember seeing a little before. There were English seamen on her; and when they saw three men in the act of boarding two defenseless women, they stepped in, and threatened to send Clarence and his crew to the bottom unless they sheered off."

"Ha!" I murmured. "Good!"

"And so we escaped. I prayed the captain to take us on board his ship, the *Framlingham*, and he did so. More, putting into Leigh on his way to the Nore, he took off my husband. There he stands, and when you are better he shall thank you."

"Nay, he will thank you now," said the tall man, rising and stepping to my berth with his head bent. He could not stand upright, so low was the deck. "But for you," he continued, his earnestness showing in his voice and eyes--the latter were almost too tender for a man's--"my wife would be now lying in prison, her life in jeopardy, and her property as good as gone. She has told me how bravely you rescued her from that cur in Cheapside, and how your presence of mind baffled the watch at the riverside. It is well, young gentleman. It is very well. But these things call for other returns than words. When it lies in her power my wife will make them; if not to-day, to-morrow, and if not to-morrow, the day after."

I was very weak, and his words brought the tears to my eyes. "She has saved my life already," I murmured.

"You foolish boy!" she cried, smiling down on me, her hand on her husband's shoulder. "You got your head broken in my defense. It was a great thing, was it not, that I did not leave you to die in the boat? There, make haste and get well. You have talked enough now. Go to sleep, or we shall have the fever back again."

"One thing first," I pleaded. "Tell me whither we are going."

"In a few hours we shall be at Dort in Holland," she answered. "But be content. We will take care of you, and send you back if you will, or you shall still come with us; as you please. Be content. Go to sleep now and get strong. Presently, perhaps, we shall have need of your help again."

They went and sat down then on their former seat and talked in whispers, while Mistress Anne shook up my pillows, and laid a fresh cool bandage on my head. I was too weak to speak my gratitude, but I tried to look it and so fell asleep again, her hand in mine, and the wondrous smile of those lustrous eyes the last impression of which I was conscious.

A long dreamless sleep followed. When I awoke once more the light still hung steady, but the peacefulness of night was gone. We lay in the midst of turmoil. The scampering of feet over the deck above me, the creaking of the windlass, the bumping and clattering of barrels hoisted in or hoisted out, the harsh sound of voices raised in a foreign tongue and in queer keys, sufficed as I grew wide-awake to tell me we were in port.

But the cabin was empty, and I lay for some time gazing at its dreary interior, and wondering what was to become of me. Presently an uneasy fear crept into my mind. What if my companions had deserted me? Alone, ill, and penniless in a foreign land, what should I do? This fear in my sick state was so terrible that I struggled to get up, and with reeling brain and nerveless hands did get out of my berth. But this feat accomplished I found that I could not stand. Everything swam before my eyes. I could not take a single step, but remained, clinging helplessly to the edge of my berth, despair at my heart. I tried to call out, but my voice rose little above a whisper, and the banging and shrieking, the babel without went on endlessly. Oh, it was cruel! cruel! They had left me!

I think my senses were leaving me too, when I felt an arm about my waist, and found Mistress Anne by my side guiding me to the chest. I sat down on it, the certainty of my helplessness and the sudden relief of her presence bringing the tears to my eyes. She fanned me, and gave me some restorative, chiding me the while for getting out of my berth.

"I thought that you had gone and left me," I muttered. I was as weak as a child.

She said cheerily: "Did you leave us when we were in trouble? Of course you did not. There, take some more of this. After all, it is well you are up, for in a short time we must move you to the other boat."

"The other boat?"

"Yes, we are at Dort, you know. And we are going by the Waal, a branch of the Rhine, to Arnheim. But the boat is here, close to this one, and, with help, I think you will be able to walk to it."

"I am sure I shall if you will give me your arm," I answered gratefully.

"But you will not think again," she replied, "that we have deserted you?"

"No," I said. "I will trust you always."

I wondered why a shadow crossed her face at that. But I had no time to do more than wonder, for Master Bertram, coming down, brought our sitting to an end. She bustled about to wrap me up, and somehow, partly walking, partly carried, I was got on deck. There I sat down on a bale to recover myself, and felt at once much the better for the fresh, keen air, the clear sky and wintry sunshine which welcomed me to a foreign land.

On the outer side of the vessel stretched a wide expanse of turbid water, five or six times as wide as the Thames at London, and foam-flecked here and there by the up-running tide. On the other side was a wide and spacious quay, paved neatly with round stones, and piled here and there with merchandise; but possessing, by virtue of the lines of leafless elms which bordered it, a quaint air of rusticity in the midst of bustle. The sober bearing of the sturdy landsmen, going quietly about their business, accorded well with the substantial comfort of the rows of tall, steep-roofed houses I saw beyond the quay, and seemed only made more homely by the occasional swagger and uncouth cry of some half-barbarous seaman, wandering aimlessly about. Above the town rose the heavy square tower of a church, a notable landmark where all around, land and water, lay so low, where the horizon seemed so far, and the sky so wide and breezy.

"So you have made up your mind to come with us," said Master Bertram, returning to my side--he had left me to make some arrangements. "You understand that if you would prefer to go home I can secure your tendance here by good, kindly people, and provide for your passage back when you feel strong enough to cross. You understand that? And that the choice is entirely your own? So which will you do?"

I changed color and felt I did. I shrunk, as being well and strong I should not have shrunk, from losing sight of those three faces which I had known for so short a time, yet which alone stood between myself and loneliness. "I would rather come with you," I stammered. "But I shall be a great burden to you now, I fear."

"It is not that," he replied, with hearty assurance in his voice. "A week's rest and quiet will restore you to strength, and then the burden will be on the other shoulder. It is for your own sake I give you the choice, because our future is for the time uncertain. Very uncertain," he repeated, his brow clouding over; "and to become our companion may expose you to fresh dangers. We are refugees from England; that you probably guess. Our plan was to go to France, where are many of our friends, and where we could live safely until better times. You know how that plan was frustrated. Here the Spaniards are masters--Prince Philip's people; and if we are recognized, we shall be arrested and sent back to England. Still, my wife and I must make the best of it. The hue and cry will not follow us for some days, and there is still a degree of independence in the cities of Holland which may, since I have friends here, protect us for a time. Now you know something of our position, my friend. You can make your choice with your eyes open. Either way we shall not forget you."

"I will go on with you, if you please," I answered at once. "I, too, cannot go home." And as I said this, Mistress Bertram also came up, and I took her hand in mine--which looked, by the way, so strangely thin I scarcely recognized it--and kissed it. "I will come with you, madam, if you will let me," I said.

"Good!" she replied, her eyes sparkling. "I said you would! I do not mind telling you now that I am glad of it. And if ever we return to England, as God grant we may and soon, you shall not regret your decision. Shall he, Richard?"

"If you say he shall not, my dear," he responded, smiling at her enthusiasm, "I think I may answer for it he will not."

I was struck then, as I had been before, by a certain air of deference which the husband assumed toward the wife. It did not surprise me, for her bearing and manner, as well as such of her actions as I had seen, stamped her as singularly self-reliant and independent for a woman; and to these qualities, as much as to the rather dreamy character of the husband, I was content to set down the peculiarity. I should add that a rare and pretty tenderness constantly displayed on her part toward him robbed it of any semblance of unseemliness.

They saw that the exertion of talking exhausted me, and so, with an encouraging nod, left me to myself. A few minutes later a couple of English sailors, belonging to the *Framlingham*, came up, and with gentle strength transported me, under Mistress Anne's directions, to a queer-looking wide-beamed boat which lay almost alongside. She was more like a huge Thames barge than anything else, for she drew little water, but had a great expanse of sail when all was set. There was a large deck-house, gay with paint and as clean as it could be; and in a compartment at one end of this--which seemed to be assigned to our party--I was soon comfortably settled.

Exhausted as I was by the excitement of sitting up and being moved, I knew little of what passed about me for the next two days, and remember less. I slept and ate, and sometimes awoke to wonder where I was. But the meals and the vague attempts at thought made scarcely more impression on my mind than the sleep. Yet all the while I was gaining strength rapidly, my youth and health standing me in good stead. The wound in my head, which had caused great loss of blood, healed all one way, as we say in Warwickshire; and about noon, on the second day after leaving Dort, I was well enough to reach the deck unassisted, and sit in the sunshine on a pile of rugs which Mistress Anne, my constant nurse, had laid for me in a corner sheltered from the wind.

* * * * *

Fortunately the weather was mild and warm, and the sunshine fell brightly on the wide river and the wider plain of pasture which stretched away on either side of the horizon, dotted, here and there only, by a windmill, a farmhouse, the steeple of a church, the brown sails of a barge, or at most broken by a low dike or a line of sand-dunes. All was open, free; all was largeness, space, and distance. I gazed astonished.

The husband and wife, who were pacing the deck forward, came to me. He noticed the wondering looks I cast round. "This is new to you?" he said smiling.

"Quite--quite new," I answered. "I never imagined anything so flat, and yet in its way so beautiful."

"You do not know Lincolnshire?"

"No."

"Ah, that is my native county," he answered. "It is much like this. But you are better, and you can talk again. Now I and my wife have been discussing whether we shall tell you more about ourselves. And since there is no time like the present I may say that we have decided to trust you."

"All in all or not at all," Mistress Bertram added brightly.

I murmured my thanks.

"Then, first to tell you who we are. For myself I am plain Richard Bertie of Lincolnshire, at your service. My wife is something more than appears from this, or"--with a smile--"from her present not too graceful dress. She is----"

"Stop, Richard! This is not sufficiently formal," my lady cried prettily. "I have the honor to present to you, young gentleman," she went on, laughing merrily and making a very grand courtesy before me, "Katherine, Duchess of Suffolk."

I made shift to get to my feet, and bowed respectfully, but she forced me to sit down again. "Enough of that," she said lightly, "until we go back to England. Here and for the future we are Master Bertram and his wife. And this young lady, my distant kinswoman, Anne Brandon, must pass as Mistress Anne. You wonder how we came to be straying in the streets alone and unattended when you found us?"

I did wonder, for the name of the gay and brilliant Duchess of Suffolk was well known even to me, a country lad. Her former husband, Charles Brandon, Duke of Suffolk, had been not only the one trusted and constant friend of King Henry the Eighth, but the king's brother-in-law, his first wife having been Mary, Princess of England and Queen Dowager of France. Late in his splendid and prosperous career the Duke had married Katherine, the heiress of Lord Willoughby de Eresby, and she it was who stood before me, still young and handsome. After her husband's death she had made England ring with her name, first by a love match with a Lincolnshire squire, and secondly by her fearless and outspoken defense of the reformers. I did wonder indeed how she had come to be wandering in the streets at daybreak, an object of a chance passer's chivalry and pity.

"It is simple enough," she said dryly; "I am rich, I am a Protestant, and I have an enemy. When I do not like a person I speak out. Do I not, Richard?"

"You do indeed, my dear," he answered smiling.

"And once I spoke out to Bishop Gardiner. What! Do you know Stephen Gardiner?"

For I had started at the name, after which I could scarcely have concealed my knowledge if I would. So I answered simply, "Yes, I have seen him." I was thinking how wonderful this was. These people had been utter strangers to me until a day or two before, yet now we were all looking out together from the deck of a Dutch boat on the low Dutch landscape, united by one tie, the enmity of the same man.

"He is a man to be dreaded," the Duchess continued, her eyes resting on her baby, which lay asleep on my bundle of rugs--and I guessed what fear it was had tamed her pride to flight. "His power in England is absolute. We learned that it was his purpose to arrest me, and determined to leave England. But our very household was full of spies, and though we chose a time when Clarence, our steward, whom we had long suspected of being Gardiner's chief tool, was away, Philip, his deputy, gained a clew to our design, and watched us. We gave him the slip with difficulty, leaving our luggage, but he dogged and overtook us, and the rest you know."

I bowed. As I gazed at her, my admiration, I know, shone in my eyes. She looked, as she stood on the deck, an exile and fugitive, so gay, so bright, so indomitable, that in herself she was at once a warranty and an omen of better times. The breeze had heightened her color and loosened here and there a tress of her auburn hair. No wonder Master Bertie looked proudly on his Duchess.

Suddenly a thing I had clean forgotten flashed into my mind, and I thrust my hand into my pocket. The action was so abrupt that it attracted their attention, and when I pulled out a packet--two packets--there were three pairs of eyes upon me. The seal dangled from one missive. "What have you there?" the Duchess asked briskly, for she was a woman, and curious. "Do you carry the deeds of your property about with you?"

"No," I said, not unwilling to make a small sensation. "This touches your Grace."

"Hush!" she cried, raising one imperious finger. "Transgressing already? From this time forth I am Mistress Bertram, remember. But come," she went on, eying the packet with the seal inquisitively, "how does it touch me?"

I put it silently into her hands, and she opened it and read a few lines, her husband peeping over her shoulder. As she read her brow darkened, her eyes grew hard. Master Bertie's face changed with hers, and they both peeped suddenly at me over the edge of the parchment, suspicion and hostility in their glances. "How came you by this, young sir?" he said slowly, after a long pause. "Have we escaped Peter to fall into the hands of Paul?"

"No, no!" I cried hurriedly. I saw that I had made a greater sensation than I had bargained for. I hastened to tell them how I had met with Gardiner's servant at Stony Stratford, and how I had become possessed of his credentials. They laughed of course--indeed they laughed so loudly that the placid Dutchmen, standing aft with their hands in their breeches-pockets, stared open-mouthed at us, and the kindred cattle on the bank looked mildly up from the knee-deep grass.

"And what was the other packet?" the Duchess asked presently. "Is that it in your hand?"

"Yes," I answered, holding it up with some reluctance. "It seems to be a letter addressed to Mistress Clarence."

"Clarence!" she cried. "Clarence!" arresting the hand she was extending. "What! Here is our friend again then. What is in it? You have opened it?"

"No."

"You have not? Then quick, open it!" she exclaimed. "This too touches us, I will bet a penny. Let us see at once what it contains. Clarence indeed! Perhaps we may have him on the hip yet, the arch-traitor!"

But I held the pocket-book back, though my cheeks reddened and I knew I must seem foolish. They made certain that this letter was a communication to some spy, probably to Clarence himself under cover of a feminine address. Perhaps it was, but it bore a woman's name and it was sealed; and foolish though I might be, I would not betray the woman's secret.

"No, madam," I said confused, awkward, stammering, yet withholding it with a secret obstinacy; "pardon me if I do not obey you--if I do not let this be opened. It may be what you say," I added with an effort; "but it may also contain an honest secret, and that a woman's."

"What do you say?" cried the Duchess; "here are scruples!" At that her husband smiled, and I looked in despair from him to Mistress Anne. Would she sympathize with my feelings? I found that she had turned her back on us, and was gazing over the side. "Do you really mean," continued the Duchess, tapping her foot sharply on the deck, "that you are not going to open that, you foolish boy?"

"I do--with your Grace's leave," I answered.

"Or without my Grace's leave! That is what you mean," she retorted pettishly, a red spot in each cheek. "When people will not do what I ask, it is always, Grace! Grace! Grace! But I know them now."

I dared not smile; and I would not look up, lest my heart should fail me and I should give her her way.

"You foolish boy!" she again said, and sniffed. Then with a toss of her head she went away, her husband following her obediently.

I feared that she was grievously offended, and I got up restlessly and went across the deck to the rail on which Mistress Anne was leaning, meaning to say something which should gain for me her sympathy, perhaps her advice. But the words died on my lips, for as I approached she turned her face abruptly toward me, and it was so white, so haggard, so drawn, that I uttered a cry of alarm. "You are ill!" I exclaimed. "Let me call the Duchess!"

She gripped my sleeve almost fiercely, "Hush!" she muttered. "Do nothing of the kind. I am not well. It is the water. But it will pass off, if you do not notice it. I hate to be noticed," she added, with an angry shrug.

I was full of pity for her and reproached myself sorely. "What a selfish brute I have been!" I said. "You have watched by me night after night, and nursed me day after day, and I have scarcely thanked you. And now you are ill yourself. It is my fault!"

She looked at me, a wan smile on her face. "A little, perhaps," she answered faintly. "But it is chiefly the water. I shall be better presently. About that letter--did you not come to speak to me about it?"

"Never mind it now," I said anxiously. "Will you not lie down on the rugs awhile? Let me give you my place," I pleaded.

"No, no!" she cried impatiently; and seeing I vexed her by my importunity, I desisted. "The letter," she went on; "you will open it by and by?"

"No," I said slowly, considering, to tell the truth, the strength of my resolution, "I think I shall not."

"You will! you will!" she repeated, with a kind of scorn. "The Duchess will ask you again, and you will give it to her. Of course you will!"

Her tone was strangely querulous, and her eyes continually flashed keen, biting glances at me. But I thought only that she was ill and excited, and I fancied it was best to humor her. "Well, perhaps I shall," I said soothingly. "Possibly. It is hard to refuse her anything. And yet I hope I may not. The girl--it may be a girl's secret."

"Well?" she asked, interrupting me abruptly, her voice harsh and unmusical. "What of her?" She laid her hand on her bosom as though to still some secret pain. I looked at her, anxious and wondering, but she had again averted her face. "What of her?" she repeated.

"Only that--I would not willingly hurt her!" I blurted out.

She did not answer. She stood a moment, then to my surprise she turned away without a word, and merely commanding me by a gesture of the hand not to follow, walked slowly away. I watched her cross the deck and pass through the doorway into the deck-house. She did not once turn her face, and my only fear was that she was ill; more seriously ill, perhaps, than she had acknowledged.

CHAPTER VIII.

A HOUSE OF PEACE.

As the day went on, therefore, I looked eagerly for Mistress Anne's return, but she appeared no more, though I maintained a close watch on the cabin-door. All the afternoon, too, the Duchess kept away from me, and I feared that I had seriously offended her; so that it was with no very pleasant anticipations that, going into that part of the deck-house which served us for a common room, to see if the evening meal was set, I found only the Duchess and Master Bertie prepared to sit down to it. I suppose that something of my feeling was expressed in my face, for while I was yet half-way between door and table, my lady gave way to a peal of merriment.

"Come, sit down, and do not be afraid!" she cried pleasantly, her gray eyes still full of laughter. "I vow the lad thinks I shall eat him. Nay, when all is said and done, I like you the better, Sir Knight Errant, for your scruples. I see that you are determined to act up to your name. But that reminds me," she added in a more serious vein. "We have been frank with you. You must be equally frank with us. What are we to call you, pray?"

I looked down at my plate and felt my face grow scarlet. The wound which the discovery of my father's treachery had dealt me had begun to heal. In the action, the movement, the adventure of the last fortnight, I had well-nigh lost sight of the blot on my escutcheon, of the shame which had driven me from home. But the question, "What are we to call you?" revived the smart, and revived it with an added pang. It had been very well, in theory, to proudly discard my old name. It was painful, in practice, to be unable to answer the Duchess, "I am a Cludde of Coton, nephew to Sir Anthony, formerly esquire of the body to King Henry. I am no unworthy follower and associate even for you," and to have instead to reply, "I have no name. I am nobody. I have all to make and win." Yet this was my ill-fortune.

Her woman's eye saw my trouble as I hesitated, confused and doubting what I should reply. "Come!" she said good-naturedly, trying to reassure me. "You are of gentle birth. Of that we feel sure."

I shook my head. "Nay, I am of no birth, madam," I answered hurriedly. "I have no name, or at any rate no name that I can be proud of. Call me--call me, if it please you, Francis Carey."

"It is a good name," quoth Master Bertie, pausing with his knife suspended in the air. "A right good Protestant name!"

"But I have no claim to it," I rejoined, mere and more hurt. "I have all to make. I am a new man. Yet do not fear!" I added quickly, as I saw what I took to be a cloud of doubt cross my lady's face. "I will follow you no less faithfully for that!"

"Well," said the Duchess, a smile again transforming her open features, "I will answer for that, Master Carey. Deeds are better than names, and as for being a new man, what with Pagets and Cavendishes and Spencers, we have nought but new men nowadays. So, cheer up!" she continued kindly. "And we will poke no questions at you, though I doubt whether you do not possess more birth and breeding than you would have us think. And if, when we return to England, as I trust we may before we are old men and women, we can advance your cause, then let us have your secret. No one can say that Katherine Willoughby ever forgot her friend."

"Or forgave her enemy over quickly," quoth her husband naïvely.

She rapped his knuckles with the back of her knife for that; and under cover of this small diversion I had time to regain my composure. But the matter left me sore at heart, and more than a little homesick. And I sought leave to retire early.

"You are right!" said the Duchess, rising graciously. "To-night, after being out in the air, you will sleep soundly, and to-morrow you will be a new man," with a faint smile. "Believe me, I am not ungrateful, Master Francis, and I will diligently seek occasion to repay both your gallant defense of the other day and your future service." She gave me her hand to kiss, and I bent over it. "Now," she continued, "do homage to my baby, and then I shall consider that you are really one of us, and pledged to our cause."

I kissed the tiny fist held out to me, a soft pink thing looking like some dainty sea-shell. Master Bertie cordially grasped my hand. And so under the oil-lamp in the neat cabin of that old Dutch boat, somewhere on the Waal between Gorcum and Nimuegen, we plighted our troth to one another, and in a sense I became one of them.

I went to my berth cheered and encouraged by their kindness. But the interview, satisfactory as it was, had set up no little excitement in my brain, and it was long before I slept. When I did I had a strange dream. I dreamed that I was sitting in the hall at Coton, and that Petronilla was standing on the dais looking fixedly at me with gentle, sorrowful eyes. I wanted to go to her, but I could not move; every dreamer knows the sensation. I tried to call to her, to ask her what was the matter, and why she so looked at me.

But I could utter no sound. And still she continued to fix me with the same sad, reproachful eyes, in which I read a warning, yet could not ask its meaning.

I struggled so hard that at last the spell was in a degree broken. Following the direction of her eyes I looked down at myself, and saw fastened to the breast of my doublet the knot of blue velvet which she had made for my sword-hilt, and which I had ever since carried in my bosom. More, I saw, with a singular feeling of anger and sorrow, that a hand which came over my shoulder was tugging hard at the ribbon in the attempt to remove it.

This gave me horrible concern, yet at the moment I could not move nor do anything to prevent it. At last, making a stupendous effort, I awoke, my last experience, dreaming, being of the strange hand working at my breast. My first waking idea was the same, so that I threw out my arms, and cried aloud, and sat up. "Ugh!" I exclaimed, trembling in the intensity of my relief, as I looked about and welcomed the now familiar surroundings. "It was only a dream. It was----"

I stopped abruptly, my eyes falling on a form lurking in the doorway. I could see it only dimly by the light of a hanging lamp, which smoked and burned redly overhead. Yet I could see it. It was real, substantial--a waking figure; nevertheless, a faint touch of superstitious terror still clung to me. "Speak, please!" I asked. "Who is it?"

"It is only I," answered a soft voice, well known to me--Mistress Anne's. "I came in to see how you were," she continued, advancing a little, "and whether you were sleeping. I am afraid I awoke you. But you seemed," she added, "to be having such painful dreams that perhaps it was as well I did."

I was fumbling in my breast while she spoke; and certainly, whether in my sleep I had undone the fastenings or had loosened them intentionally before I lay down (though I could not remember doing so), my doublet and shirt were open at the breast. The velvet knot was safe, however, in that tiny inner pocket beside the letter, and I breathed again. "I am very glad you did awake me!" I replied, looking gratefully at her. "I was having a horrible dream. But how good it was of you to think of me--and when you are not well yourself, too."

"Oh, I am better," she murmured, her eyes, which glistened in the light, fixed steadily on me. "Much better. Now go to sleep again, and happier dreams to you. After to-night," she added pleasantly, "I shall no longer consider you as an invalid, nor intrude upon you."

And she was gone before I could reiterate my thanks. The door fell to, and I was alone, full of kindly feelings toward her, and of thankfulness that my horrible vision had no foundation. "Thank Heaven!" I murmured more than once, as I lay down; "it was only a dream."

Next day we reached Nimuegen, where we stayed a short time. Leaving that place in the afternoon, twenty-four hours' journeying, partly by river, partly, if I remember rightly, by canal, brought us to the neighborhood of Arnheim on the Rhine. It was the 1st of March, but the opening month belied its reputation. There was a brightness, a softness in the air, and a consequent feeling as of spring which would better have befitted the middle of April. All day we remained on deck enjoying the kindliness of nature, which was especially grateful to me, in whom the sap of health was beginning to spring again; and we were still there when one of those gorgeous sunsets which are peculiar to that country began to fling its hues across our path. We turned a jutting promontory, the boat began to fall off, and the captain came up, his errand to tell us that our journey was done.

We went eagerly forward at the news, and saw in a kind of bay, formed by a lake-like expansion of the river, a little island green and low, its banks trimly set with a single row of poplars. It was perhaps a quarter of a mile every way, and a channel one-fourth as wide separated it from the nearer shore of the river; to which, however, a long narrow bridge of planks laid on trestles gave access. On the outer side of the island, facing the river's course, stood a low white house, before which a sloping green terrace, also bordered with poplars, led down to a tiny pier. Behind and around the house were meadows as trim and neat as a child's toys, over which the eye roved with pleasure until it reached the landward side of the island, and there detected, nestling among gardens, a tiny village of half a dozen cottages. It was a scene of enchanting peace and quietude. As we slowly plowed our way up to the landing-place, I saw the rabbits stand to gaze at us, and then with a flick of their heels dart off to their holes. I marked the cattle moving homeward in a string, and heard the wild fowl rise in creek and pool with a whir of wings. I turned with a full heart to my neighbor. "Is it not lovely?" I cried with enthusiasm. "Is it not a peaceful place--a very Garden of Eden?"

I looked to see her fall into raptures such as women are commonly more prone to than men. But all women are not the same. Mistress Anne was looking, indeed, when I turned and surprised her, at the scene which had so moved me, but the expression of her face was sad and bitter and utterly melancholy. The weariness and fatigue I had often seen lurking in her eyes had invaded all her features. She looked five years older; no longer a girl, but a gray-faced, hopeless woman whom the sight of this peaceful haven rather smote to the heart than filled with anticipations of safety and repose.

It was but for a moment I saw her so. Then she dashed her hand across her eyes--though I saw no tears in them--and with a pettish exclamation turned away. "Poor girl!" I thought. "She, too, is homesick. No doubt this reminds her of some place at home, or of some person." I thought this the more likely, as Master Bertie came from Lincolnshire, which he said had many of the features of this strange land. And it was conceivable enough that she should know Lincolnshire too, being related to his wife.

I soon forgot the matter in the excitement of landing. A few minutes of bustle and it was over. The boat put out again; and we four were left face to face with two strangers, an elderly man and a girl, who had come down to the pier to meet us. The former, stout, bluff, and red-faced, with a thick gray beard and a gold chain about his neck, had the air of a man of position. He greeted us warmly. His companion, who hung behind him, somewhat shyly, was as pretty a girl as one could find in a month. A second look assured me of something more--that she formed an excellent foil to the piquant brightness and keen vivacity, the dark hair and nervous features of Mistress Anne. For the Dutch girl was fair and plump and of perfect complexion. Her hair was very light, almost flaxen indeed, and her eyes were softly and limpidly blue; grave, innocent, wondering eyes they were, I remember. I guessed rightly that she was the elderly man's daughter. Later I learned that she was his only child, and that her name was Dymphna.

He was a Master Lindstrom, a merchant of standing in Arnheim. He had visited England and spoke English fairly, and being under some obligations, it appeared, to the Duchess Katherine, was to be our host.

We all walked up the little avenue together. Master Lindstrom talking as he went to husband or wife, while his daughter and Mistress Anne came next, gazing each at each in silence, as women when they first meet will gaze, taking stock, I suppose, of a rival's weapons. I walked last, wondering why they had nothing to say to one another.

As we entered the house the mystery was explained. "She speaks no English," said Mistress Anne, with a touch of scorn.

"And we no Dutch," I answered, smiling. "Here in Holland I am afraid that she will have somewhat the best of us. Try her with Spanish."

"Spanish! I know none."

"Well, I do, a little."

"What, you know Spanish?" Mistress Anne's tone of surprise amounted almost to incredulity, and it flattered me, boy that I was. I dare say it would have flattered many an older head than mine. "You know Spanish? Where did you learn it?" she continued sharply.

"At home."

"At home! Where is that?" And she eyed me still more closely. "Where is your home, Master Carey? You have never told me."

But I had said already more than I intended, and I shook my head. "I mean," I explained awkwardly, "that I learned it in a home I once had. Now my home is here. At any rate I have no other."

The Dutch girl, standing patiently beside us, had looked first at one face and then at the other as we talked. We were all by this time in a long, low parlor, warmed by a pretty closed fireplace covered with glazed tiles. On the shelves of a great armoire, or dresser, at one end of the room appeared a fine show of silver plate. At the other end stood a tall linen-press of walnut-wood, handsomely carved; and even the gratings of the windows and the handles of the doors were of hammered iron-work. There were no rushes on the floor, which was made of small pieces of wood delicately joined and set together and brightly polished. But everything in sight was clean and trim to a degree which would have shamed our great house at Coton, where the rushes sometimes lay for a week unchanged. With each glance round I felt a livelier satisfaction. I turned to Mistress Dymphna.

"Señorita!" I said, mustering my noblest accent. "Beso los pies de usted! Habla usted Castillano?"

Mistress Anne stared, while the effect on the girl whom I addressed was greater than I had looked for, but certainly of a different kind. She started and drew back, an expression of offended dignity and of something like anger ruffling her placid face. Did she not understand? Yes, for after a moment's hesitation, and with a heightened color, she answered, "Si, Señor."

Her constrained manner was not promising, but I was going on to open a conversation if I could--for it looked little grateful of us to stand there speechless and staring--when Mistress Anne interposed. "What did you say to her? What was it?" she asked eagerly.

"I asked her if she spoke Spanish. That was all," I replied, my eyes on Dymphna's face, which still betrayed trouble of some kind, "except that I paid her the usual formal compliment. But what is she saying to her father?"

It was like the Christmas game of cross-questions. The girl and I had spoken in Spanish. I translated what we had said into English for Mistress Anne, and Mistress Dymphna turned it into Dutch for her father; an anxious look on her face which needed no translation.

"What is it?" asked Master Bertie, observing that something was wrong.

"It is nothing--nothing!" replied the merchant apologetically, though, as he spoke, his eyes dwelt on me curiously. "It is only that I did not know that you had a Spaniard in your company."

"A Spaniard?" Master Bertie answered. "We have none. This," pointing to me, "is our very good friend and faithful follower, Master Carey--an Englishman."

"To whom," added the Duchess, smiling gravely, "I am greatly indebted."

I hurriedly explained the mistake, and brought at once a smile of relief to the Mynheer's face. "Ah! pardon me, I beseech you," he said. "My daughter was in error." And he added something in Dutch which caused Mistress Dymphna to blush. "You know," he continued--"I may speak freely to you, since our enemies are in the main the same--you know that our Spanish rulers are not very popular with us, and grow less popular every day, especially with those who are of the reformed faith. We have learned some of us to speak their language, but we love them none the better for that."

"I can sympathize with you, indeed," cried the Duchess impulsively. "God grant that our country may never be in the same plight: though it looks as if this Spanish marriage were like to put us in it. It is Spain! Spain! Spain! and nothing else nowadays!"

"Nevertheless, the Emperor is a great and puissant monarch," rejoined the Arnheimer thoughtfully; "and could he rule us himself, we might do well. But his dominions are so large, he knows little of us. And worse, he is dying, or as good as dying. He can scarcely sit his horse, and rumor says that before the year is out he will resign the throne. Then we hear little good of his successor, your queen's husband, and look to hear less. I fear that there is a dark time before us, and God only knows the issue."

"And alone will rule it," Master Bertie rejoined piously.

This saying was in a way the keynote to the life we found our host living on his island estate. Peace, but peace with constant fear for an assailant, and religion for a supporter. Several times a week Master Lindstrom would go to Arnheim to superintend his business, and always after his return he would shake his head, and speak gravely, and Dymphna would lose her color for an hour or two. Things were going badly. The reformers were being more and more hardly dealt with. The Spaniards were growing more despotic. That was his constant report. And then I would see him, as he walked with us in orchard or garden, or sat beside the stove, cast wistful glances at the comfort and plenty round him. I knew that he was asking himself how long they would last. If they escaped the clutches of a tyrannical government, would they be safe in the times that were coming from the violence of an ill-paid soldiery? The answer was doubtful, or rather it was too certain.

I sometimes wondered how he could patiently foresee such possibilities, and take no steps, whatever the risk, to prevent them. At first I thought his patience sprang from the Dutch character. Later I traced its deeper roots to a simplicity of faith and a deep religious feeling, which either did not at that time exist in England, or existed only among people with whom I had never come into contact. Here they seemed common enough and real enough. These folks' faith sustained them. It was a part of their lives; a bulwark against the fear that otherwise would have overwhelmed them. And to an extent, too, which then surprised me, I found, as time went on, that the Duchess and Master Bertie shared this enthusiasm, although with them it took a less obtrusive form.

I was led at the time to think a good deal about this; and just a word I may say of myself, and of those days spent on the Rhine inland--that whereas before I had taken but a lukewarm interest in religious questions, and, while clinging instinctively to the teaching of my childhood, had conformed with a light heart rather than annoy my uncle, I came to think somewhat differently now; differently and more seriously. And so I have continued to think since, though I have never become a bigot; a fact I owe, perhaps, to Mistress Dymphna, in whose tender heart there was room for charity as well as faith. For she was my teacher.

Of necessity, since no other of our party could communicate with her, I became more or less the Dutch girl's companion. I would often, of an evening, join her on a wooden bench which stood under an elm on a little spit of grass looking toward the city, and at some distance from the house. Here, when the weather was warm, she would watch for her father's return; and here one day, while talking with her, I had the opportunity of witnessing a sight unknown in England, but which year by year was to become more common in the Netherlands, more heavily fraught with menace in Netherland eyes.

We happened to be so deeply engaged in watching the upper end of the reach at the time in question, where we expected each moment to see Master Lindstrom's boat round the point, that we saw nothing of a boat coming the other way, until the flapping of its sails, as it tacked, drew our eyes toward it. Even then in the boat itself I saw nothing strange, but in its passengers I did. They were swarthy, mustachioed men, who in the hundred poses they assumed, as they lounged on deck or leaned over the side, never lost a peculiar air of bravado. As they drew nearer to us the sound of their loud voices, their oaths and laughter reached us plainly, and seemed to jar on the evening stillness. Their bold, fierce eyes, raking the banks unceasingly, reached us at last. The girl by my side uttered a cry of alarm, and rose as if to retreat. But she sat down again, for behind us was an open stretch of turf, and to escape unseen was impossible. Already a score of eyes had marked her beauty, and as the boat drew abreast of us, I had to listen to the ribald jests and laughter of those on board. My ears tingled and my cheeks burned. But I could do nothing. I could only glare at them, and grind my teeth.

"Who are they?" I muttered. "The cowardly knaves!"

"Oh, hush! hush!" the girl pleaded. She had retreated behind me. And indeed I need not have put my question, for though I had never seen the Spanish soldiery, I had heard enough about them to recognize them now. In the year 1555 their reputation was at its height. Their fathers had overcome the Moors after a contest of centuries, and they themselves had overrun Italy and lowered the pride of France. As a result they had many military virtues and all the military vices. Proud, bloodthirsty, and licentious everywhere, it may be imagined that in the subject Netherlands, with their pay always in arrear, they were, indeed, people to be feared. It was seldom that even their commanders dared to check their excesses.

Yet, when the first flush of my anger had subsided, I looked after them, odd as it may seem, with mingled feelings. With all their faults they were few against many, a conquering race in a foreign land. They could boast of blood and descent. They were proud to call themselves the soldiers and gentlemen of Europe. I was against them, yet I admired them with a boy's admiration for the strong and reckless.

Of course I said nothing of this to my companion. Indeed, when she spoke to me I did not hear her. My thoughts had flown far from the burgher's daughter sitting by me, and were with my grandmother's people. I saw, in imagination, the uplands of Old Castile, as I had often heard them described, hot in summer and bleak in winter. I pictured the dark, frowning walls of Toledo, with its hundred Moorish trophies, the castles that crowned the hills around, the gray olive groves, and the box-clad slopes. I saw Palencia, where my grandmother, Petronilla de Vargas, was born; Palencia, dry and brown and sun-baked, lying squat and low on its plain, the eaves of its cathedral a man's height from the ground. All this I saw. I suppose the Spanish blood in me awoke and asserted itself at sight of those other Spaniards. And then--then I forgot it all as I heard behind me an alien voice, and I turned and found Dymphna had stolen from me and was talking to a stranger.

CHAPTER IX.

PLAYING WITH FIRE.

He was a young man, and a Dutchman, but not a Dutchman of the stout, burly type which I had most commonly seen in the country. He had, it is true, the usual fair hair and blue eyes, and he was rather short than tall; but his figure was thin and meager, and he had a pointed nose and chin, and a scanty fair beard. I took him to be nearsighted: at a second glance I saw that he was angry. He was talking fast to Dymphna--of course in Dutch--and my first impulse, in face of his excited gestures and queer appearance, was to laugh. But I had a notion what his relationship to the girl was, and I smothered this, and instead asked, as soon as I could get a word in, whether I should leave them.

"Oh, no!" Dymphna answered, blushing slightly, and turning to me with a troubled glance. I believe she had clean forgotten my presence. "This is Master Jan Van Tree, a good friend of ours. And this," she continued, still in Spanish, but speaking to him, "is Master Carey, one of my father's guests."

We bowed, he formally, for he had not recovered his temper, and I--I dare say I still had my Spanish ancestors in my head--with condescension. We disliked one another at sight, I think. I dubbed him a mean little fellow, a trader, a peddler; and, however he classed me, it was not favorably. So it was no particular desire to please him which led me to say with outward solicitude, "I fear you are annoyed at something, Master Van Tree?"

"I am!" he said bluntly, meeting me half-way.

"And am I to know the cause?" I asked, "or is it a secret?"

"It is no secret!" he retorted. "Mistress Lindstrom should have been more careful. She should not have exposed herself to the chance of being seen by those miserable foreigners."

"The foreigners--in the boat?" I said dryly.

"Yes, of course--in the boat," he answered. He was obliged to say that, but he glared at me across her as he spoke. We had turned and were walking back to the house, the poplars casting long shadows across our path.

"They were rude," I observed carelessly, my chin very high. "But there is no particular harm done that I can see, Master Van Tree."

"Perhaps not, as far as you can see," he retorted in great excitement. "But perhaps also you are not very far-sighted. You may not see it now, yet harm will follow."

"Possibly," I said, and I was going to follow up this seemingly candid admission by something very boorish, when Mistress Dymphna struck in nervously.

"My father is anxious," she explained, speaking to me, "that I should have as little to do with our Spanish governors as possible, Master Carey. It always vexes him to hear that I have fallen in their way, and that is why my friend feels annoyed. It was not, of course, your fault, since you did not know of this. It was I," she continued hurriedly, "who should not have ventured to the elm tree without seeing that the coast was clear."

I knew that she was timidly trying, her color coming and going, to catch my eye; to appease me as the greater stranger, and to keep the peace between her ill-matched companions, who, indeed, stalked along eying one another much as a wolf-hound and a badger-dog might regard each other across a choice bone. But the young Dutchman's sudden appearance had put me out. I was not in love with her, yet I liked to talk to her, and I grudged her to him, he seemed so mean a fellow. And so--churl that I was-- in answer to her speech I let drop some sneer about the great fear of the Spaniards which seemed to prevail in these parts.

"*You* are not afraid of them, then?" Van Tree said, with a smile.

"No, I am not," I answered, my lip curling also.

"Ah!" with much meaning. "Perhaps you do not know them very well."

"Perhaps not," I replied. "Still, my grandmother was a Spaniard."

"So I should have thought," he retorted swiftly.

So swiftly that I felt the words as I should have felt a blow. "What do you mean?" I blurted out, halting before him, with my cheek crimson. In vain were all Dymphna's appealing glances, all her signs of distress. "I will have you explain, Master Van Tree, what you mean by that?" I repeated fiercely.

"I mean what I said," he answered, confronting me stubbornly, and shaking off Dymphna's hand. His blue eyes twinkled with rage, his thin beard bristled; he was the color of a turkey-cock's comb. At home we should have thought him a comical little figure; but he did not seem so absurd here. For one thing, he looked spiteful enough for anything; and for another, though I topped him by a head and shoulders, I could not flatter myself that he was afraid of me. On the contrary, I felt that in the presence of his mistress, small and short-sighted as he was, he would have faced a lion without winking.

His courage was not to be put to the proof. I was still glaring at him, seeking some retort which should provoke him beyond endurance, when a hand was laid on my shoulder, and I turned to find that Master Bertie and the Duchess had joined us.

"So here are the truants," the former said pleasantly, speaking in English, and showing no consciousness whatever of the crisis in the middle of which he had come up, though he must have discerned in our defiant attitudes, and in Dymphna's troubled face, that something was wrong. "You know who this is, Master Francis," he continued heartily. "Or have you not been introduced to Master Van Tree, the betrothed of our host's daughter?"

"Mistress Dymphna has done me that honor," I said stiffly, recovering myself in appearance, while at heart sore and angry with everybody. "But I fear the Dutch gentleman has not thanked her for the introduction, since he learned that my grandmother was Spanish."

"*Your* grandmother, do you mean?" cried the Duchess, much astonished.

"Yes, madam."

"Well, to be sure!" she exclaimed, lifting up her hands and appealing whimsically to the others. "This boy is full of starts and surprises. You never know what he will produce next. The other day it was a warrant! To-day it is a grandmother, and a temper!"

I could not be angry with her; and perhaps I was not sorry now that my quarrel with the young Dutchman had stopped where it had. I affected, as well as I could, to join in the laugh at my expense, and took advantage of the arrival of our host--who at this moment came up the slope from the landing-place, his hands outstretched and a smile of greeting on his kindly face--to slip away unnoticed, and make amends to my humor by switching off the heads of the withes by the river.

But naturally the scene left a degree of ill-feeling behind it; and for the first time, during the two months we had spent under Master Lindstrom's roof, the party who sat down to supper were under some constraint. I felt that the young Dutchman had had the best of the bout in the garden; and I talked loudly and foolishly in the boyish attempt to assert myself, and to set myself right at least in my own estimation. Master Van Tree meanwhile sat silent, eying me from time to time in no friendly fashion. Dymphna seemed nervous and frightened, and the Duchess and her husband exchanged troubled glances. Only our host and Mistress Anne, who was in particularly good spirits, were unaffected by the prevailing chill.

Mistress Anne, indeed, in her ignorance, made matters worse. She had begun to pick up some Dutch, and was fond of airing her knowledge and practicing fresh sentences at meal-times. By some ill-luck she contrived this evening--particularly after, finding no one to contradict me, I had fallen into comparative silence--to frame her sentences so as to cause as much embarrassment as possible to all of us. "Where did you walk with Dymphna this morning?" was the question put to me. "You are fond of the water; Englishmen are fond of the water," she said to Dymphna. "Dymphna is tall; Master Francis is tall. I sit by you to-night; the Dutch lady sat by you last night," and soon, and so on, with prattle which seemed to amuse our host exceedingly--he was never tired of correcting her mistakes--but which put the rest of us out of countenance, bringing the tears to poor Dymphna's eyes--she did not know where to look--and making her lover glower at me as though he would eat me.

It was in vain that the Duchess made spasmodic rushes into conversation, and in the intervals nodded and frowned at the delinquent. Mistress Anne in her innocence saw nothing. She went on until Van Tree could stand it no longer, and with a half-smothered threat, which was perfectly intelligible to me, rose roughly from the table, and went to the door as if to look out at the night.

"What is the matter?" Mistress Anne said, wonderingly, in English. Her eyes seemed at length to be opened to the fact that something was amiss with us.

Before I could answer, the Duchess, who had risen, came behind her. "You little fool!" she whispered fiercely, "if fool you are. You deserve to be whipped!"

"Why, what have I done?" murmured the girl, really frightened now, and appealing to me.

"Done!" whispered the Duchess; and I think she pinched her, for my neighbor winced. "More harm than you guess, you minx! And for you, Master Francis, a word with you. Come with me to my room, please."

I went with her, half-minded to be angry, and half-inclined to feel ashamed of myself. She did not give me time, however, to consider which attitude I should take up, for the moment the door of her room was closed behind us, she turned upon me, the color high in her cheeks. "Now, young man," she said in a tone of ringing contempt, "do you really think that that girl is in love with you?"

"What girl?" I asked sheepishly. The unexpected question and her tone put me out of countenance.

"What girl? What girl?" she replied impatiently. "Don't play with me, boy! You know whom I mean. Dymphna Lindstrom!"

"Oh, I thought you meant Mistress Anne," I said, somewhat impertinently.

Her face fell in an extraordinary fashion, as if the suggestion were not pleasant to her. But she answered on the instant: "Well! The vanity of the lad! Do you think all the girls are in love with you? Because you have been sitting with a pretty face on each side of you, do you think you have only to throw the handkerchief, this way or that? If you do, open your eyes, and you will find it is not so. My kinswoman can take care of herself, so we will leave her out of the discussion, please. And for this pink and white Dutch girl," my lady continued viciously, "let me tell you that she thinks more of Van Tree's little finger than of your whole body."

I shrugged my shoulders, but still I was mortified. A young man may not be in love with a girl, yet it displeases him to hear that she is indifferent to him.

The Duchess noticed the movement. "Don't do that," she cried in impatient scorn. "You do not see much in Master Van Tree, perhaps? I thought not. Therefore you think a girl must be of the same mind as yourself. Well," with a fierce little nod, "you will learn some day that it is not so, that women are not quite what men think them; and particularly, Master Francis, that six feet of manhood, and a pretty face on top of it, do not always have their way. But there, I did not bring you here to tell you that. I want to know whether you are aware what you are doing?"

I muttered something to the effect that I did not know I was doing any harm.

"You do not call it harm, then," the Duchess retorted with energy, "to endanger the safety of every one of us? Cannot you see that if you insult and offend this young man--which you are doing out of pure wanton mischief, for you are not in love with the girl--he may ruin us?"

"Ruin us?" I repeated incredulously.

"Yes, ruin us!" she cried. "Here we are, living more or less in hiding through the kindness of Master Lindstrom--living in peace and quietness. But do you suppose that inquiries are not being made for us? Why, I would bet a dozen gold angels that Master Clarence is in the Netherlands, at this moment, tracking us."

I was startled by this idea, and she saw I was. "We can trust Master Lindstrom, were it only for his own sake," she continued more quietly, satisfied perhaps with the effect she had produced. "And this young man, who is the son of one of the principal men of Arnheim, is also disposed to look kindly on us, as I fancy it is his nature to look. But if you make mischief between Dymphna and him----"

"I have not," I said.

"Then do not," she replied sharply. "Look to it for the future. And more, do not let him fancy it possible. Jealousy is as easily awakened as it is hardly put to sleep. A word from this young man to the Spanish authorities, and we should be hauled back to England in a trice, if worse did not befall us here. Now, you will be careful?"

"I will," I said, conscience-stricken and a little cowed.

"That is better," she replied smiling. "I think you will. Now go."

I went down again with some food for thought--with some good intentions, too. But I was to find--the discovery is made by many--that good resolutions commonly come too late. When I went downstairs I found my host and Master Bertie alone in the parlor. The girls had disappeared, so had Van Tree, and I saw at once that something had happened. Master Bertie was standing gazing at the stove very thoughtfully, and the Dutchman was walking up and down the room with an almost comical expression of annoyance and trouble on his pleasant face.

"Where are the young ladies?" I asked.

"Upstairs," said Master Bertie, not looking at me.

"And--and Van Tree?" I asked mechanically. Somehow I anticipated the answer.

"Gone!" said the Englishman curtly.

"Ay, gone, the foolish lad!" the Dutchman struck in, tugging at his beard. "What has come to him? He is not wont to show temper. I have never known him and Dymphna have a cross word before. What has come to the lad, I say, to go off in a passion at this time of night? And no one knows whither he has gone, or when he will come back again!"

He seemed as he spoke hardly conscious of my presence; but Master Bertie turned and looked at me, and I hung my head, and very shortly afterward, I slunk out. The thought of what I might have brought upon us all by my petulance and vanity made me feel sick. I crept up to bed nervous and fearful of the morrow, listening to every noise without, and praying inwardly that my alarm might not be justified.

When the morrow came I went downstairs as anxious to see Van Tree in the flesh as I had been yesterday disappointed by his appearance. But no Van Tree was there to be seen. Nothing had been heard of him. Dymphna moved restlessly about, her cheeks pale, her eyes downcast, and if I had ever flattered myself that I was anything to the girl, I was undeceived now. The Duchess shot angry glances at me from time to time. Master Bertie kept looking anxiously at the door. Every one seemed to fear and to expect something. But none of them feared and expected it as I did.

"He must have gone home; he must have gone to Arnheim," said our host, trying to hide his vexation. "He will be back in a day or two. Young men will be young men."

But I found that the Duchess did not share the belief that Van Tree had gone home; for in the course of the morning she took occasion, when we were alone, to charge me to be careful not to come into collision with him.

"How can I, now he has gone?" I said meekly, feeling I was in disgrace.

"He has not gone far," replied the Duchess meaningly. "Depend upon it, he will not go far out of sight unless there is more harm done than I think, or he is very different from English lovers. But if you come across him, I pray you to keep clear of him, Master Francis."

I nodded assent.

But of what weight are resolutions, with fate in the other scale! It was some hours after this, toward two o'clock indeed, when Mistress Anne came to me, looking flurried and vexed. "Have you seen Dymphna?" she asked abruptly.

"No," I answered. "Why?"

"Because she is not in the house," the girl answered, speaking quickly, "nor in the garden; and the last time I saw her she was crossing the island toward the footbridge. I think she has gone that way to be on the lookout-- you can guess for whom [with a smile]. But I am fearful lest she shall meet some one else, Master Francis; she is wearing her gold chain, and one of the maids says that she saw two of the Spanish garrison on the road near the end of the footbridge this morning. That is the way by land to Arnheim, you know."

"That is bad," I said. "What is to be done?"

"You must go and look for her," Anne suggested. "She should not be alone."

"Let her father go, or Master Bertie," I answered.

"Her father has gone down the river--to Arnheim, I expect; and Master Bertie is fishing in a boat somewhere. It will take time to find him. Why cannot you go? If she has crossed the footbridge she will not be far away."

She seemed so anxious as she spoke for the Dutch girl's safety, that she infected me with her fears, and I let myself be persuaded. After all there might be danger, and I did not see what else was to be done. Indeed, Mistress Anne did not leave me until she had seen me clear of the orchard and half across the meadows toward the footbridge. "Mind you bring her back," she cried after me. "Do not let her come alone!" And those were her last words.

After we had separated I did think for a moment that it was a pity I had not asked her to come with me. But the thought occurred too late, and I strode on toward the head of the bridge, resolving that, as soon as I had sighted Dymphna, I would keep away from her and content myself with watching over her from a distance. As I passed by the little cluster of cottages on the landward side of the island, I glanced sharply about me, for I thought it not unlikely that Master Van Tree might be lurking in the neighborhood. But I saw nothing either of her or him. All was quiet, the air full of spring sunshine and warmth and hope and the blossoms of fruit trees; and with an indefinable pleasure, a feeling of escape from control and restraint, I crossed the long footbridge, and set foot, almost for the first time since our arrival--for at Master Lindstrom's desire we had kept very close--on the river bank.

To the right a fair road or causeway along the waterside led to Arnheim. At the point where I stood, this road on its way from the city took a turn at right angles, running straight away from the river to avoid a wide track of swamp and mere which lay on my left--a quaking marsh many miles round, overgrown with tall rushes and sedges, which formed the head of the bay in which our island lay. I looked up the long, straight road to Arnheim, and saw only a group of travelers moving slowly along it, their backs toward me. The road before me was bare of passengers. Where, then, was Dymphna, if she had crossed the bridge? In the last resort I scanned the green expanse of rushes and willows, which stretched, with intervals of open water, as far as the eye could reach on my left. It was all rustling and shimmering in the light breeze, but my eye picked out one or two raised dykes which penetrated it here and there, and served at once as pathways to islets in the mere and as breastworks against further encroachments of the river. Presently, on one of these, of which the course was fairly defined by a line of willows, I made out the flutter of a woman's hood. And I remembered that the day before I had heard Dymphna express a wish to go to the marsh for some herb which grew there.

"Right!" I said, seating myself with much satisfaction on the last post of the bridge. "She is safe enough there! And I will go no nearer. It is only on the road she is likely to be in danger from our Spanish gallants!"

My eyes, released from duty, wandered idly over the landscape for a while, but presently returned to the dyke across the mere. I could not now see Dymphna. The willows hid her, and I waited for her to reappear. She did not, but some one else did; for by and by, on the same path and crossing an interval between the willows, there came into sight a man's form.

"Ho! ho!" I said, following it with my eyes. "So I may go home! Master Van Tree is on the track. And now I hope they will make it up!" I added pettishly.

Another second and I started up with a low cry. The sunlight had caught a part of the man's dress, a shining something which flashed back a point of intense light. The something I guessed at once was a corselet, and it needed scarce another thought to apprise me that Dymphna's follower was not Van Tree at all, but a Spanish soldier!

I lost no time; yet it took me a minute--a minute of trembling haste and anxiety--to discover the path from the causeway on to the dyke. When once I had stumbled on to the latter I found I had lost sight of both figures; but I ran along at the top of my speed, calculating that the two, who could not be far apart, the man being the nearer to me, were about a quarter of a mile or rather more from the road. I had gone one-half of this distance perhaps when a shrill scream in front caused me to redouble my efforts. I expected to find the ruffian in the act of robbing the girl, and clutched my cudgel--for, alas! I had left my sword at home--more tightly in my grasp, so that it was an immense relief to me when, on turning an angle in the dyke, I saw her running toward me. Her face, still white with fear, however, and her hair streaming loosely behind her, told how narrow had been her escape--if escape it could be called. For about ten feet behind her, the hood he had plucked off still in his grasp, came Master Spaniard, hot-foot and panting, but gaining on her now with every stride.

I STOOD OVER HIM WATCHING HIM

He was a tall fellow, gayly dressed, swarthy, mustachioed, and fierce-eyed. His corselet and sword-belt shone and jingled as he ran and swore; but he had dropped his feathered bonnet in the slight struggle which had evidently taken place when she got by him; and it lay a black spot in the middle of the grassy avenue behind him. The sun--it was about three hours after noon--was at my back, and shining directly into his eyes, and I marked this as I raised my cudgel and jumped aside to let the girl pass; for she in her blind fear would have run against me.

It was almost the same with him. He did not see me until I was within a few paces of him, and even then I think he noticed my presence merely as that of an unwelcome spectator. He fancied I should step aside; and he cursed me, calling me a Dutch dog for getting in his way.

The next moment--he had not drawn his sword nor made any attempt to draw it--we came together violently, and I had my hand on his throat. We swayed as we whirled round one another in the first shock of the collision. A cry of astonishment escaped him--astonishment at my hardihood. He tried, his eyes glaring into mine, and his hot breath on my cheek, to get at his dagger. But it was too late. I brought down my staff, with all the strength of an arm nerved at the moment by rage and despair, upon his bare head.

He went down like a stone, and the blood bubbled from his lips. I stood over him watching him. He stretched himself out and turned with a convulsive movement on his face. His hands clawed the grass. His leg moved once, twice, a third time faintly. Then he lay still.

There was a lark singing just over my head, and its clear notes seemed, during the long, long minute while I stood bending over him in an awful fascination, to be the only sounds in nature. I looked so long at him in that dreadful stillness and absorption, I dared not at last look up lest I should see I knew not what. Yet when a touch fell on my arm I did not start.

"You have killed him!" the girl whispered, shuddering.

"Yes, I have killed him," I answered mechanically.

I could not take my eyes off him. It was not as if I had done this thing after a long conflict, or in a *mêlée* with others fighting round me, or on the battle-field. I should have felt no horror then such as I felt now, standing over him in the sunshine with the lark's song in my ears. It had happened so quickly, and the waste about us was so still; and I had never killed a man before, nor seen a man die.

"Oh, come away!" Dymphna wailed suddenly. "Come away!"

I turned then, and the sight of the girl's wan face and strained eyes recalled me in some degree to myself. I saw she was ill; and hastily I gave her my arm, and partly carried, partly supported, her back to the road. The way seemed long and I looked behind me often. But we reached the causeway at last, and there in the open I felt some relief. Yet even then, stopping to cast a backward glance at the marsh, I shuddered anew, espying a bright white spark gleaming amid the green of the rushes. It was the dead man's corselet. But if it had been his eye I could scarcely have shrunk from it in greater dread.

It will be imagined that we were not long in crossing the island. Naturally I was full of what had happened, and never gave a thought to Van Tree's jealousy, or the incidents of his short visit. I had indeed forgotten his existence until we reached the porch. There entering rapidly, with Dymphna clinging to my arm, I was so oblivious of other matters that when the young Dutchman rose suddenly from the seat on one side of the door, and at the same moment the Duchess rose from the bench on the other, I did not understand in the first instant of surprise what was the matter, though I let Dymphna's hand fall from my arm. The dark scowling face of the one, however, and the anger and chagrin written on the features of the other, as they both glared at us, brought all back to me in a flash. But it was too late. Before I could utter a word the girl's lover pushed by me with a fierce gesture and fiercer cry, and disappeared round a corner of the house.

"Was ever such folly!" cried the Duchess, stamping her foot, and standing before us, her face crimson. "Or such fools! You idiot! You----"

"Hush, madam," I said sternly--had I really grown older in doing the deed? "something has happened."

And Dymphna, with a low cry of "The Spaniard! The Spaniard!" tottered up to her and fainted in her arms.

CHAPTER X.

THE FACE IN THE PORCH.

"This is a serious matter," said Master Bertie thoughtfully, as we sat in conclave an hour later round the table in the parlor. Mistress Anne was attending to Dymphna upstairs, and Van Tree had not returned again; so that we had been unable to tell him of the morning's adventure. But the rest of us were there. "It considerably adds to the danger of our position," Bertie continued.

"Of course it does," his wife said promptly. "But Master Lindstrom here can best judge of that, and of what course it will be safest to take."

"It depends," our host answered slowly, "upon whether the dead man be discovered before night. You see if the body be not found----"

"Well?" said my lady impatiently, as he paused.

"Then we must some of us go after dark and bury him," he decided. "And perhaps, though he will be missed at the next roll-call in the city, his death may not be proved, or traced to this neighborhood. In that case the storm will blow over, and things be no worse than before."

"I fear there is no likelihood of that," I said; "for I am told he had a companion. One of the maids noticed them lurking about the end of the bridge more than once this morning."

Our host's face fell.

"That is bad," he said, looking at me in evident consternation. "Who told you?"

"Mistress Anne. And one of the maids told her. It was that which led me to follow your daughter."

The old man got up for about the fortieth time, and shook my hand, while the tears stood in his eyes and his lip trembled. "Heaven bless you, Master Carey!" he said. "But for you, my girl might not have escaped."

He could not finish. His emotion choked him, and he sat down again. The event of the morning--his daughter's danger, and my share in averting it--had touched him as nothing else could have touched him. I met the Duchess's eyes and they too were soft and shining, wearing an expression very different from that which had greeted me on my return with Dymphna.

"Ah, well! she is safe," Master Lindstrom resumed, when he had regained his composure. "Thanks to Heaven and your friend, madam! Small matter now if house and lands go!"

"Still, let us hope they will not," Master Bertie said. "Do you think these miscreants were watching the island on our account? That some information had been given as to our presence, and they were sent to learn what they could?"

"No, no!" the Dutchman answered confidently. "It was the sight of the girl and her gewgaws yesterday brought them--the villains! There is nothing safe from them and nothing sacred to them. They saw her as they passed up in the boat, you remember."

"But then, supposing the worst to come to the worst?"

"We must escape across the frontier to Wesel, in the Duchy of Cleves," replied Lindstrom in a matter-of-fact tone, as if he had long considered and settled the point. "The distance is not great, and in Wesel we may find shelter, at any rate for a time. Even there, if pressure be brought to bear upon the Government to give us up, I would not trust it. Yet for a time it may do."

"And you would leave all this?" the Duchess said in wonder, her eyes traveling round the room, so clean and warm and comfortable, and settling at length upon the great armoire of plate, which happened to be opposite to her. "You would leave all this at a moment's notice?"

"Yes, madam, all we could not carry with us," he answered simply. "Honor and life, these come first. And I thank Heaven that I live here within reach of a foreign soil, and not in the interior, where escape would be hopeless."

"But if the true facts were known," the Duchess urged, "would you still be in danger? Would not the magistrates protect you? The Schout and Schepen as you call them? They are Dutchmen."

"Against a Spanish governor and a Spanish garrison?" he replied with emphasis. "Ay, they would protect me--as one sheep protects another against the wolves. No! I dare not risk it. Were I in prison, what would become of Dymphna?"

"Master Van Tree?"

"He has the will to shelter her, no doubt. And his father has influence; but such as mine--a broken reed to trust to. Then Dymphna is not all. Once in prison, whatever the charge, there would be questioning about religion; perhaps," with a faint smile, "questioning about my guests."

"I suppose you know best," said the Duchess, with a sigh. "But I hope the worst will not come to the worst."

"Amen to that!" he answered quite cheerfully.

Indeed, it was strange that we seemed to feel more sorrow at the prospect of leaving this haven of a few weeks, than our host of quitting the home of a lifetime. But the necessity had come upon us suddenly, while he had contemplated it for years. So much fear and humiliation had mingled with his enjoyment of his choicest possessions that this long-expected moment brought with it a feeling akin to relief.

For myself I had a present trouble that outweighed any calamity of to-morrow. Perforce, since I alone knew the spot where the man lay, I must be one of the burying party. My nerves had not recovered from the blow which the sight of the Spaniard lying dead at my feet had dealt them so short a time before, and I shrank with a natural repulsion from the task before me. Yet there was no escaping it, no chance of escaping it, I saw.

None the less, throughout the silent meal to which we four sat down together, neither the girls nor Van Tree appearing, were my thoughts taken up with the business which was to follow. I heard our host, who was to go with me, explaining that there was a waterway right up to the dyke, and that we would go by boat; and heard him with apathy. What matter how we went, if such were the object of our journey? I wondered how the man's face would look when we came to turn him over, and pictured it in all ghastliest shapes. I wondered whether I should ever forget the strange spasmodic twitching of his leg, the gurgle--half oath, half cry--which had come with the blood from his throat. When Lindstrom said the moon was up and bade me come with him to the boat, I went mechanically. No one seemed to suspect me of fear. I suppose they thought that, as I had not feared to kill him, I should not fear him dead. And in the general silence and moodiness I escaped notice.

"It is a good night for the purpose," the Dutchman said, looking about when we were outside. "It is light enough for us, yet not so light that we run much risk of being seen."

I assented, shivering. The moon was almost at the full, and the weather was dry, but scud after scud of thin clouds, sweeping across the breezy sky, obscured the light from time to time, and left nothing certain. We loosed the smallest boat in silence, and getting in, pulled gently round the lower end of the island, making for the fringe of rushes which marked the line of division between river and fen. We could hear the frogs croaking in the marsh, and the water lapping the banks, and gurgling among the tree-roots, and making a hundred strange noises to which daylight ears are deaf. Yet as long as I was in the open water I felt bold enough. I kept my tremors for the moment when we should brush through the rustling belt of reeds, and the willows should whisper about our heads, and the rank vegetation, the mysterious darkness of the mere should shut us in.

For a time I was to be spared this. Master Lindstrom suddenly stopped rowing. "We have forgotten to bring a stone, lad," he said in a low voice.

"A stone?" I answered, turning. I was pulling the stroke oar, and my back was toward him. "Do we want a stone?"

"To sink the body," he replied. "We cannot bury it in the marsh, and if we could it were trouble thrown away. We must have a stone."

"What is to be done?" I asked, leaning on my oar and shivering, as much in impatience as nervousness. "Must we go back?"

"No, we are not far from the causeway now," he answered, with Dutch coolness. "There are some big stones, I fancy, by the end of the bridge. If not, there are some lying among the cottages just across the bridge. Your eyes are younger than mine, so you had better go. I will pull on, and land you."

I assented, and the boat's course being changed a point or two, three minutes' rowing laid her bows on the mud, some fifty yards from the landward bend of the bridge, and just in the shadow of the causeway. I sprang ashore and clambered up. "Hist!" he cried, warning me as I was about to start on my errand. "Go about it quietly, Master Francis. The people will probably be in bed. But be secret."

I nodded and moved off, as warily as he could desire. I spent a minute or two peering about the causeway, but I found nothing that would serve our purpose. There was no course left then but to cross the planks, and seek what I wanted in the hamlet. Remembering how the timbers had creaked and clattered when I went over them in the daylight, I stole across on tiptoe. I fancied I had seen a pile of stones near one of the posts at that end, but I could not find them now, and after groping about a while--for this part was at the moment in darkness--I crept cautiously past the first hovel, peering to right and left as I went. I did not like to confess to myself that I was afraid to be alone in the dark, but that was nearly the truth. I was feverishly anxious to find what I wanted and return to my companion.

Suddenly I paused and held my breath. A slight sound had fallen on my ears, nervously ready to catch the slightest. I paused and listened. Yes, there it was again; a whispering of cautious voices close by me, within a few feet of me. I could see no one. But a moment's thought told me that the speakers were hidden by the farther corner of the cottage abreast of which

I stood. The sound of human voices, the assurance of living companionship, steadied my nerves, and to some extent rid me of my folly. I took a step to one side, so as to be more completely in the shadow cast by the reed-thatched eaves, and then softly advanced until I commanded a view of the whisperers.

They were two, a man and a woman. And the woman was of all people Dymphna! She had her back to me, but she stood in the moonlight, and I knew her hood in a moment. The man--surely the man was Van Tree then, if the woman was Dymphna? I stared. I felt sure it must be Van Tree. It was wonderful enough that Dymphna should so far have regained nerve and composure as to rise and come out to meet him. But in that case her conduct, though strange, was explicable. If not, however, if the man were not Van Tree----

Well, he certainly was not. Stare as I might, rub my eyes as I might, I could not alter the man's figure, which was of the tallest, whereas I have said that the young Dutchman was short. This man's face, too, though it was obscured as he bent over the girl by his cloak, which was pulled high up about his throat, was swarthy; swarthy and beardless, I made out. More, his cap had a feather, and even as he stood still I thought I read the soldier in his attitude. The soldier and the Spaniard!

What did it mean? On what strange combination had I lit? Dymphna and a Spaniard! Impossible. Yet a thousand doubts and thoughts ran riot in my brain, a thousand conjectures jostled one another to get uppermost. What was I to do? What ought I to do? Go nearer to them, as near as possible, and listen and learn the truth? Or steal back the way I had come, and fetch Master Lindstrom? But first, was it certain that the girl was there of her own free will? Yes, the question was answered as soon as put. The man laid his hand gently on her shoulder. She did not draw back.

Confident of this, and consequently of Dymphna's bodily safety, I hesitated, and was beginning to consider whether the best course might not be to withdraw and say nothing, leaving the question of future proceedings to be decided after I had spoken to her on the morrow, when a movement diverted my thoughts. The man at last raised his head. The moonlight fell cold and bright on his face, displaying every feature as clearly as if it had been day. And though I had only once seen his face before, I knew it again.

And knew him! In a second I was back in England, looking on a far different scene. I saw the Thames, its ebb tide rippling in the sunshine as it ripples past Greenwich, and a small boat gliding over it, and a man in the bow of the boat, a man with a grim lip and a sinister eye. Yes, the tall soldier talking to Dymphna in the moonlight, his cap the cap of a Spanish guard, was Master Clarence! the Duchess's chief enemy!

* * * * *

I stayed my foot. With a strange settling into resolve of all my doubts I felt if my sword, which happily I had brought with me, was loose in its sheath, and leaned forward scanning him. So he had tracked us! He was here! With wonderful vividness I pictured all the dangers which menaced the Duchess, Master Bertie, the Lindstroms, myself, through his discovery of us, all the evils which would befall us if the villain went away with his tale. Forgetting Dymphna's presence, I set my teeth hard together. He should not escape me this time.

But man can only propose. As I took a step forward, I trod on a round piece of wood which turned under my foot, and I stumbled. My eye left the pair for a second. When it returned to them they had taken the alarm. Dymphna had started away, and I saw her figure retreating swiftly in the direction of the house. The man poised himself a moment irresolute opposite to me; then dashed aside and disappeared behind the cottage.

I was after him on the instant, my sword out, and caught sight of his cloak as he whisked round a corner. He dodged me twice round the next cottage, the one nearer the river. Then he broke away and made for the bridge, his object evidently to get off the island. But he seemed at last to see that I was too quick for him--as I certainly was--and should catch him half way across the narrow planking; and changing his mind again he doubled nimbly back and rushed into the open porch of a cottage, and I heard his sword ring out. I had him at bay.

At bay indeed! But ready as I was, and resolute to capture or kill him, I paused. I hesitated to run in on him. The darkness of the porch hid him, while I must attack with the moonlight shining on me. I peered in cautiously. "Come out!" I cried. "Come out, you coward!" Then I heard him move, and for a moment I thought he was coming, and I stood a-tiptoe waiting for his rush. But he only laughed a derisive laugh of triumph. He had the odds, and I saw he would keep them.

I took another cautious step toward him, and shading my eyes with my left hand, tried to make him out. As I did so, gradually his face took dim form and shape, confronting mine in the darkness. I stared yet more intently. The face became more clear. Nay, with a sudden leap into vividness, as it were, it grew white against the dark background--white and whiter. It seemed to be thrust out nearer and nearer, until it almost touched mine. It--his face? No, it was not his face! For one awful moment a terror, which seemed to still my heart, glued me to the ground where I stood, as it flashed upon my brain that it was another face that grinned at me so close to mine, that it was another face I was looking on; the livid, bloodstained face and stony eyes of the man I had killed!

With a wild scream I turned and fled. By instinct, for terror had deprived me of reason, I hied to the bridge, and keeping, I knew not how, my footing upon the loose clattering planks, made one desperate rush across it. The shimmering water below, in which I saw that face a thousand times reflected, the breeze, which seemed the dead man's hand clutching me, lent wings to my flight. I sprang at a bound from the bridge to the bank, from the bank to the boat, and overturning, yet never seeing, my startled companion, shoved off from the shore with all my might--and fell a-crying.

A very learned man, physician to the Queen's Majesty has since told me, when I related this strange story to him, that probably that burst of tears saved my reason. It so far restored me at any rate that I presently knew where I was--cowering in the bottom of the boat, with my eyes covered; and understood that Master Lindstrom was leaning over me in a terrible state of mind, imploring me in mingled Dutch and English to tell him what had happened. "I have seen him!" was all I could say at first, and I scarcely dared remove my hands from my eyes. "I have seen him!" I begged my host to row away from the shore, and after a time was able to tell him what the matter was, he sitting the while with his arm round my shoulder.

"You are sure that it was the Spaniard?" he said kindly, after he had thought a minute.

"Quite sure," I answered shuddering, yet with less violence. "How could I be mistaken? If you had seen him----"

"And you are sure--did you feel his heart this morning? Whether it was beating?"

"His heart?" Something in his voice gave me courage to look up, though I still shunned the water, lest that dreadful visage should rise from the depths. "No, I did not touch him."

"And you tell me that he fell on his face. Did you turn him over?"

"No." I saw his drift now. I was sitting erect. My brain began to work again. "No," I admitted; "I did not."

"Then how----" asked the Dutchman roughly--"how do you know that he was dead, young sir? Tell me that."

When I explained, "Bah!" he cried. "There is nothing in that! You jumped to a conclusion. I thought a Spaniard's head was harder to break. As for the blood coming from his mouth, perhaps he bit his tongue, or did any one of a hundred things--except die, Master Francis. That you may be sure is just what he did not do."

"You think so?" I said gratefully. I began to look about me, yet still with a tremor in my limbs, and an inclination to start at shadows.

"Think?" he rejoined, with a heartiness which brought conviction home tome; "I am sure of it. You may depend upon it that Master Clarence, or the man you take for Master Clarence--who no doubt was the other soldier seen with the scoundrel this morning--found him hurt late in the evening. Then, seeing him in that state, he put him in the porch for shelter, either because he could not get him to Arnheim at once, or because he did not wish to give the alarm before he had made his arrangements for netting your party."

"That is possible!" I allowed, with a sigh of relief. "But what of Master Clarence?"

"Well," the old man said; "let us get home first. We will talk of him afterward."

I felt he had more in his mind than appeared, and I obeyed; growing ashamed now of my panic, and looking forward with no very pleasant feelings to hearing the story narrated. But when we reached the house, and found Master Bertie and the Duchess in the parlor waiting for us--they rose startled at sight of my face--he bade me leave that out, but tell the rest of the story.

I complied, describing how I had seen Dymphna meet Clarence, and what I had observed to pass between them. The astonishment of my hearers may be imagined. "The point is very simple," said our host coolly, when I had, in the face of many exclamations and some incredulity, completed the tale; "it is just this! The woman certainly was not Dymphna. In the first place, she would not be out at night. In the second place, what could she know of your Clarence, an Englishman and a stranger? In the third place, I will warrant she has been in her room all the evening. Then if Master Francis was mistaken in the woman, may he not have been mistaken in the man? That is the point."

"No," I said boldly. "I only saw her back. I saw his face."

"Certainly, that is something," Master Lindstrom admitted reluctantly.

"But how many times had you seen him before?" put in my lady very pertinently. "Only once."

In answer to that I could do no more than give further assurance of my certainty on the point. "It was the man I saw in the boat at Greenwich," I declared positively. "Why should I imagine it?"

"All the same, I trust you have," she rejoined. "For, if it was indeed that arch scoundrel, we are undone."

"Imagination plays us queer tricks sometimes," Master Lindstrom said, with a smile of much meaning. "But come, lad, I will ask Dymphna, though I think it useless to do so. For whether you are right or wrong as to your friend, I will answer for it you are wrong as to my daughter."

He was rising to go from them for the purpose, when Mistress Anne opened the door and came in. She looked somewhat startled at finding us all in conclave. "I thought I heard your voices," she explained timidly, standing between us and the door. "I could not sleep."

She looked indeed as if that were so. Her eyes were very bright, and there was a bright spot of crimson in each cheek. "What is it?" she went on abruptly, looking hard at me and shutting her lips tightly. There was so much to explain that no one had taken it in hand to begin.

"It is just this," the Duchess said, opening her mouth with a snap. "Have you been with Dymphna all the time?"

"Yes, of course," was the prompt answer.

"What is she doing?"

"Doing?" Mistress Anne repeated in surprise. "She is asleep."

"Has she been out since nightfall?" the Duchess continued. "Out of her room? Or out of the house?"

"Out? Certainly not. Before she fell asleep she was in no state to go out, as you know, though I hope she will be all right when she awakes. Who says she has been out?" Anne added sharply. She looked at me with a challenge in her eyes, as much as to say, "Is it you?"

"I am satisfied," I said, "that I was mistaken as to Mistress Dymphna. But I am just as sure as before that I saw Clarence."

"Clarence?" Mistress Anne repeated, starting violently, and the color for an instant fleeing from her cheeks. She sat down on the nearest seat.

"You need not be afraid, Anne," my lady said smiling. She had a wonderfully high courage herself. "I think Master Francis was mistaken, though he is so certain about it."

"But where--where did he see him?" the girl asked. She still trembled.

Once more I had to tell the tale; Mistress Anne, as was natural, listening to it with the liveliest emotions. And this time so much of the ghost story had to be introduced--for she pressed me closely as to where I had left Clarence, and why I had let him go--that my assurances got less credence than ever.

"I think I see how it is," she said, with a saucy scorn that hurt me not a little. "Master Carey's nerves are in much the same state to-night as Dymphna's. He thought he saw a ghost, and he did not. He thought he saw Dymphna, and he did not. And he thought he saw Master Clarence, and he did not."

"Not so fast, child!" cried the Duchess sharply, seeing me wince. "Your tongue runs too freely. No one has had better proofs of Master Carey's courage--for which I will answer myself--than we have!"

"Then he should not say things about Dymphna!" the young lady retorted, her foot tapping the floor, and the red spots back in her cheeks. "Such rubbish I never heard!"

CHAPTER XI.

A FOUL BLOW.

They none of them believed me, it seemed; and smarting under Mistress Anne's ridicule, hurt by even the Duchess's kindly incredulity, what could I do? Only assert what I had asserted already, that it was undoubtedly Clarence, and that before twenty-four hours elapsed they would have proof of my words.

At mention of this possibility Master Bertie looked up. He had left the main part in the discussion to others, but now he intervened. "One moment!" he said. "Take it that the lad is right, Master Lindstrom. Is there any precaution we can adopt, any back door, so to speak, we can keep open, in case of an attempt to arrest us being made? What would be the line of our retreat to Wesel?"

"The river," replied the Dutchman promptly.

"And the boats are all at the landing-stage?"

"They are, and for that reason they are useless in an emergency," our host answered thoughtfully. "Knowing the place, any one sent to surprise and arrest us would secure them first, and the bridge. Then they would have us in a trap. It might be well to take a boat round, and moor it in the little creek in the farther orchard," he added, rising. "It is a good idea, at any rate. I will go and do it."

He went out, leaving us four--the Duchess, her husband, Anne, and myself--sitting round the lamp.

"If Master Carey is so certain that it was Clarence," my lady began, "I think he ought to----"

"Yes, Kate?" her husband said. She had paused and seemed to be listening.

"Ought to open that letter he has!" she continued impetuously. "I have no doubt it is a letter to Clarence. Now the rogue has come on the scene again, the lad's scruples ought not to stand in the way. They are all nonsense. The letter may throw some light on the Bishop's schemes and Clarence's presence here; and it should be read. That is what I think."

"What do you say, Carey?" her husband asked, as I kept silence. "Is not that reasonable?"

Sitting with my elbows on the table, I twisted and untwisted the fingers of my clasped hands, gazing at them the while as though inspiration might come of them. What was I to do? I knew that the three pairs of eyes were upon me, and the knowledge distracted me, and prevented me really thinking, though I seemed to be thinking so hard. "Well," I burst out at last, "the circumstances are certainly altered. I see no reason why I should not----"

Crash!

I stopped, uttering an exclamation, and we all sprang to our feet. "Oh, what a pity!" the Duchess cried, clasping her hands. "You clumsy, clumsy girl! What have you done?"

Mistress Anne's sleeve as she turned had swept from the table a Florentine jug, one of Master Lindstrom's greatest treasures, and it lay in a dozen fragments on the floor. We stood and looked at it, the Duchess in anger, Master Bertie and I in comic dismay. The girl's lip trembled, and she turned quite white as she contemplated the ruin she had caused.

"Well, you have done it now!" the Duchess said pitilessly. What woman could ever overlook clumsiness in another woman! "It only remains to pick up the pieces, miss. If a man had done it--but there, pick up the pieces. You will have to make your tale good to Master Lindstrom afterward."

I went down on my knees and helped Anne, the annoyance her incredulity had caused me forgotten. She was so shaken that I heard the bits of ware in her hand clatter together. When we had picked up all, even to the smallest piece, I rose, and the Duchess returned to the former subject. "You will open this letter, then?" she said; "I see you will. Then the sooner the better. Have you got it about you?"

"No, it is in my bedroom," I answered. "I hid it away there, and I must fetch it. But do you think," I continued, pausing as I opened the door for Mistress Anne to go out with her double handful of fragments, "it is absolutely necessary to read it, my lady?"

"Most certainly," she answered, gravely nodding with each syllable, "I think so. I will be responsible." And Master Bertie nodded also.

"So be it," I said reluctantly. And I was about to leave the room to fetch the letter--my bedroom being in a different part of the house, only connected with the main building by a covered passage--when our host returned. He told us that he had removed a boat, and I stayed a while to hear if he had anything more to report, and then, finding he had not, went out to go to my room, shutting the door behind me.

- 102 -

The passage I have mentioned, which was merely formed of rough planks, was very dark. At the nearer end was the foot of the staircase leading to the upper rooms. Farther along was a door in the side opening into the garden. Going straight out of the lighted room, I had almost to grope my way, feeling the walls with my hands. When I had about reached the middle I paused. It struck me that the door into the garden must be open, for I felt a cold draught of air strike my brow, and saw, or fancied I saw, a slice of night sky and the branch of a tree waving against it. I took a step forward, slightly shivering in the night air as I did so, and had stretched out my hand with the intention of closing the door, when a dark form rose suddenly close to me, I saw a knife gleam in the starlight, and the next moment I reeled back into the darknesss of the passage, a sharp pain in my breast.

I knew at once what had happened to me, and leaned a moment against the planking with a sick, faint feeling, saying to myself, "I have it this time!" The attack had been so sudden and unexpected, I had been taken so completely off my guard, that I had made no attempt either to strike or to clutch my assailant, and I suppose only the darkness of the passage saved me from another blow. But was one needed? The hand which I had raised instinctively to shield my throat was wet with the warm blood trickling fast down my breast. I staggered back to the door of the parlor, groped blindly for the latch, seemed to be an age finding it, found it at last, and walked in.

The Duchess sprang up at sight of me. "What," she cried, backing from me, "what has happened?"

"I have been stabbed," I said, and I sat down.

It amused me afterward to recall what they all did. The Dutchman stared, my lady screamed loudly, Master Bertie whipped out his sword; he could make up his mind quickly enough at times.

"I think he has gone," I said faintly.

The words brought the Duchess to her knees by my chair. She tore open my doublet, through which the blood was oozing fast. I made no doubt that I was a dead man, for I had never been wounded in this way before, and the blood scared me. I remember my prevailing idea was a kind of stunned pity for myself. Perhaps later--I hope so--I should have come to think of Petronilla and my uncle and other people. But before this stage was readied, the Duchess reassured me. "Courage, lad!" she cried heartily. "It is all right, Dick. The villain struck him on the breastbone an inch too low, and has just ripped up a scrap of skin. It has blooded him for the spring, that is all. A bit of plaster----"

"And a drink of strong waters," suggested the Dutchman soberly--his thoughts were always to the point when they came.

"Yes, that too," quoth my lady, "and he will be all right."

I thought so myself when I had emptied the cup they offered me. I had been a good deal shaken by the events of the day. The sight of blood had further upset me. I really think it possible I might have died of this slight hurt and my imagination, if I had been left to myself. But the Duchess's assurance and the draught of schnapps, which seemed to send new blood through my veins, made me feel ashamed of myself. If the Duchess would have let me, I would at once have gone to search the premises; as it was, she made me sit still while she ran to and fro for hot water and plaster, and the men searched the lower rooms and secured the door afresh.

"And so you could see nothing of him?" our host asked, when he and Master Bertie returned, weapons in hand. "Nothing of his figure or face?"

"Nothing, save that he was short," I answered; "shorter than I am, at any rate, and I fancy a good deal."

"A good deal shorter than you are?" my lady said uneasily; "that is no clew. In this country nine people out of ten are that. Clarence, now, is not."

"No," I said; "he is about the same height. It was not Clarence."

"Then who could it be?" she muttered, rising, and then with a quick shudder sitting down again. "Heaven help us, we seem to be in the midst of foes! What could be the motive? And why should the villain have selected you? Why pick you out?"

Thereupon a strange thing happened. Three pairs of English eyes met, and signaled a common message eye to eye. No word passed, but the message was "Van Tree!" When we had glanced at one another we looked all of us at our host--looked somewhat guiltily. He was deep in thought, his eyes on the stove; but he seemed to feel our gaze upon him, and he looked up abruptly. "Master Van Tree----" he said, and stopped.

"You know him well?" the Duchess said, appealing to him softly. We felt a kind of sorrow for him, and some delicacy, too, about accusing one of his countrymen of a thing so cowardly. "Do you think it is possible," she continued with an effort--"possible that he can have done this, Master Lindstrom?"

"I have known him from a boy," the merchant said, looking up, a hand on either knee, and speaking with a simplicity almost majestic, "and never knew him do a mean thing, madam. I know no more than that." And he looked round on us.

"That is a good deal; still, he went off in a fit of jealousy when Master Carey brought Dymphna home. We must remember that."

"Yes, I would he knew the rights of that matter," said the Dutchman heartily.

"And he has been hanging about the place all day," my lady persisted.

"Yes," Master Lindstrom rejoined patiently; "yet I do not think he did this."

"Then who did?" she said, somewhat nettled.

That was the question. I had my opinion, as I saw Master Bertie and the Duchess had. I did not doubt it was Van Tree. Yet a thought struck me. "It might be well," I suggested, "that some one should ask Mistress Anne whether the door was open when she left the room. She passed out just in front of me."

"But she does not go by the door," my lady objected.

"No, she would turn at once and go upstairs," I agreed. "But she could see the door from the foot of the stairs--if she looked that way, I mean."

The Duchess assented, and went out of the room to put the question. We three, left together, sat staring at the dull flame of the lamp, and were for the most part silent, Master Bertie only remarking that it was after midnight. The suspicion he and I entertained of Van Tree's guilt seemed to raise a barrier between us and our host. My wound, slight as it was, smarted and burned, and my head ached. After midnight, was it? What a day it had been!

When the Duchess came back, as she did in a few minutes, both Anne and Dymphna came with her. The girls had risen hastily, and were shivering with cold and alarm. Their eyes were bright, their manner was excited. They were full of sympathy and horror and wonder, as was natural; of nervous fear for themselves, too. But my lady cut short their exclamations. "Anne says she did not notice the door," she said.

"No," the girl answered, trembling visibly as she spoke. "I went up straight to bed. But who could it be? Did you see nothing of him as he struck you? Not a feature? Not an outline?"

"No," I murmured.

"Did he not say a word?" she continued, with strange insistence. "Was he tall or short?" Her dark eyes dwelling on mine seemed to probe my thoughts, as though they challenged me to keep anything back from her. "Was it the man you hurt this morning?" she suggested.

"No," I answered reluctantly. "This man was short."

"Short, was he? Was it Master Van Tree, then?"

We, who felt also certain that it was Van Tree, started, nevertheless, at hearing the charge put into words before Dymphna. I wondered, and I think the others did, too, at Mistress Anne's harshness. Even my lady, so blunt and outspoken by nature, had shrunk from trying to question the Dutch girl about her lover. We looked at Dymphna, wondering how she would take it.

We had forgotten that she could not understand English. But this did not serve her; for without a pause Mistress Anne turned to her, and unfalteringly said something in her scanty Dutch which came to the same thing. A word or two of questioning and explanation followed. Then the meaning of the accusation dawned at last on Dymphna's mind. I looked for an outburst of tears or protestations. Instead, with a glance of wonder and great scorn, with a single indignant widening of her beautiful eyes, she replied by a curt Dutch sentence.

"What does she say?" my lady exclaimed eagerly.

"She says," replied Master Lindstrom, who was looking on gravely, "that it is a base lie, madam."

On that we became spectators. It seemed to me, and I think to all of us, that the two girls stood apart from us in a circle of light by themselves; confronting one another with sharp glances as though a curtain had been raised from between them, and they saw one another in their true colors and recognized some natural antagonism, or, it might be, some rivalry each in the other. I think I was not peculiar in feeling this, for we all kept silence for a space as though expecting something to follow. In the middle of this silence there came a low rapping at the door.

One uttered a faint shriek; another stood as if turned to stone. The Duchess cried for her child. The rest of us looked at one another. Midnight was past. Who could be abroad, who could want us at this hour? As a rule we should have been in bed and asleep long ago. We had no neighbors save the cotters on the far side of the island. We knew of no one likely to arrive at this time with any good intent.

"I will open," said Master Lindstrom. But he looked doubtfully at the women-folk as he said it.

"One minute," whispered the Duchess. "That table is solid and heavy. Could you not----"

"Put it across the door?" concluded her husband. "Yes, we will." And it was done at once, the two men--my lady would not let me help--so arranging it that it prevented the door being opened to its full width.

"That will stop a rush," said Master Bertie with satisfaction.

It did strengthen the position, yet it was a nervous moment when our host prepared to lower the bar. "Who is there?" he cried loudly.

We waited, listening and looking at one another, the fear of arrest and the horrors of the Inquisition looming large in the minds of some of us at least. The answer, when it came, did not reassure us. It was uttered in a voice so low and muffled that we gained no information, and rather augured treachery the more. I remember noticing how each took the crisis; how Mistress Anne's face was set hard, and her breath came in jerks; how Dymphna, pale and trembling, seemed yet to have eyes only for her father; how the Duchess faced the entrance like a queen at bay. All this I took in at a glance. Then my gaze returned to Master Lindstrom, as he dropped the bar with a jerk. The door was pushed open at once as far as it would go. A draught of cold air came in, and with it Van Tree. He shut the door behind him.

Never were six people so taken aback as we were. But the newcomer, whose face was flushed with haste and excitement, observed nothing. Apparently he saw nothing unexpected even in our presence downstairs at that hour, nothing hostile or questioning in the half circle of astonished faces turned toward him. On the contrary, he seemed pleased. "Ah!" he exclaimed gutturally. "It is well! You are up! You have taken the alarm!"

It was to me he spoke, and I was so surprised by that, and by his sudden appearance, so dumfounded by his easy address and the absence of all self-consciousness on his part, so struck by a change in him, that I stared in silence. I could not believe that this was the same half-shy, half-fierce young man who had flung away a few hours before in a passion of jealousy. My theory that he was the assassin seemed on a sudden extravagant, though here he was on the spot. When Master Lindstrom asked, "Alarm! What alarm?" I listened for his answer as I should have listened for the answer of a friend and ally, without hesitation, without distrust. For in truth the man was transfigured; changed by the rise of something to the surface which ordinarily lay hid in him. Before, he had seemed churlish, awkward, a boor. But in this hour of our need and of his opportunity he showed himself as he was. Action and purpose lifted him above his outward seeming. I caught the generous sparkle in his eye, and trusted him.

"What!" he said, keeping his voice low. "You do not know? They are coming to arrest you. Their plan is to surround the house before daybreak. Already there is a boat lying in the river watching the landing-stage."

"Whom are they coming to arrest?" I asked. The others were silent, looking at this strange messenger with mingled feelings.

"All, I fear," he replied. "You, too, Master Lindstrom. Some one has traced your English friends hither and informed against you. I know not on what ground you are included, but I fear the worst. There is not a moment to be lost if you would escape by the bridge, before the troop who are on the way to guard it arrives."

"The landing-stage, you say, is already watched?" our host asked, his phlegmatic coolness showing at its best. His eyes roved round the room, and he tugged, as was his habit when deep in thought, at his beard. I felt sure that he was calculating which of his possessions he could remove.

"Yes," Van Tree answered. "My father got wind of the plan in Arnheim. An English envoy arrived there yesterday on his way to Cleves or some part of Germany. It is rumored that he has come out of his road to inquire after certain English fugitives whom his Government are anxious to seize. But come, we have no time to lose! Let us go!"

"Do you come too?" Master Lindstrom said, pausing in the act of turning away. He spoke in Dutch, but by some inspiration born of sympathy I understood both his question and the answer.

"Yes, I come. Where Dymphna goes I go, and where she stops I stop, though it be at Madrid itself," the young man answered gallantly. His eyes kindled, and he seemed to grow taller and to gain majesty. The barrier of race, which had hindered me from viewing him fairly before, fell in a trice. I felt now only a kindly sorrow that he had done this noble thing, and not I. I went to him and grasped his hand; and though I said nothing, he seemed, after a single start of surprise, to understand me fully. He understood me even better, if that were possible, an hour later, when Dymphna had told him of her adventure with the Spaniard, and he came to me to thank me.

Ordered myself to be idle, I found all busy round me, busy with a stealthy diligence. Master Lindstrom was packing his plate. Dymphna, pale, but with soft, happy eyes--for had she not cause to be proud?--was preparing food and thick clothing. The Duchess had fetched her child and was dressing it for the journey. Master Bertie was collecting small matters, and looking to our arms. In one or other of these occupations--I can guess in which--Van Tree was giving his aid. And so, since the Duchess would not let me do anything, it chanced that presently I found myself left alone for a few minutes with Anne.

I was not watching her. I was gnawing my nails in a fit of despondency, reflecting that I was nothing but a hindrance and a drawback to my friends, since whenever a move had to be made I was sure to be invalided, when I became aware, through some mysterious sense, that my companion, who was kneeling on the floor behind me, packing, had desisted from her work and was gazing fixedly at me. I turned. Yes, she was looking at me; her eyes, in which a smoldering fire seemed to burn, contrasting vividly with her pale face and contracted brows. When she saw that I had turned--of which at first she did not seem aware--she rose and came to me, and laid a hand on my shoulder and leaned over me. A feeling that was very like fright fell upon me, her manner was so strange. "What is it?" I stammered, as she still pored on me in silence, still maintained her attitude. "What is the matter, Anne?"

"Are you *quite* a fool?" she whispered, her voice almost a hiss, her hot breath on my cheek. "Have you no sense left, that you trust that man?"

For a moment I failed to understand her. "What man?" I said. "Oh, Van Tree!"

"Ay, Van Tree! Who else? Will you go straight into the trap he has laid for you?" She moistened her lips with her tongue, as though they were parched. "You are all mad! Mad, I think! Don't you see," she continued, stooping over me again and whispering hurriedly, her wild eyes close to mine, "that he is jealous of you?"

"He was," I said uneasily. "That is all right now."

"He was? He is!" she retorted. "He went away wild with you. He comes back smiling and holding out his hand. Do you trust him? Don't you see--don't you see," she cried, rocking me to and fro with her hand in her excitement, "that he is fooling you? He is leading us all into a trap that has been laid carefully enough. What is this tale of an English envoy on his way to Germany? Rubbish! Rubbish, I tell you."

"But Clarence----"

"Bah! It was all your fancy!" she cried fiercely, her eyes for the moment flitting to the door, then returning to my face. "How should he find us here? Or what has Clarence to do with an English envoy?"

"I do not know," I said. She had not in the least persuaded me. In a rare moment I had seen into Van Tree's soul and trusted him implicitly. "Please take care," I added, wincing under her hand. "You hurt me!"

She sprang back with a sudden change of countenance as if I had struck her, and for a moment cowered away from me, her former passion still apparent fighting for the mastery in her face. I set down her condition to terror at the plight we were all in, or to vexation that no one would take her view. The next moment I went farther. I thought her mad, when she turned abruptly from me and, flying to the door by which Van Tree had entered, began with trembling fingers to release the pin which confined the bar.

"Stop! stop! you will ruin all!" I cried in horror. "They can see that door from the river, and if they see the light, they will know we are up and have taken the alarm; and they may make a dash to secure us. Stop, Anne! Stop!" I cried. But the girl was deaf. She tugged desperately at the pin, and had already loosened the bar when I caught her by the arms, and, pushing her away, set my back against the door. "Don't be foolish!" I said gently. "You have lost your head. You must let us men settle these things, Anne."

She was indeed beside herself, for she faced me during a second or two as though she would spring upon me and tear me from the door. Her hands worked, her eyes gleamed, her strong white teeth showed themselves. I shuddered. I had never pictured her looking like that. Then, as steps sounded on the stairs and cheerful voices--cheerful they seemed to me as they broke in on that strange scene--drew nearer, she turned, and walking deliberately to a seat, fell to weeping hysterically.

"What are you doing to that door?" cried the Duchess sharply, as she entered with the others. I was securing the bar again.

"Nothing," I said stolidly. "I am seeing that it is fast."

"And hoity toity, miss!" she continued, turning to Anne. "What has come over you, I would like to know? Stop crying, girl; what is the matter with you? Will you shame us all before this Dutch maid? Here, carry these things to the back door."

Anne somehow stifled her sobs and rose. Seeming by a great effort to recover composure, she went out, keeping her face to the last averted from me.

We all followed, variously laden, Master Lindstrom and Van Tree, who carried between them the plate-chest, being the last to leave. There was not one of us--even of us who had only known the house a few weeks--who did not heave a sigh as we passed out of the warm lamp-lit parlor, which, littered as it was with the debris of packing, looked still pleasant and comfortable in comparison with the darkness outside and the uncertain future before us. What, then, must have been the pain of parting to those who had never known any other home? Yet they took it bravely. To Dymphna, Van Tree's return had brought great happiness. To Master Lindstrom, any ending to a long series of anxieties and humiliations was welcome. To Van Tree--well, he had Dymphna with him, and his side of the plate-chest was heavy, and gave him ample employment.

We passed out silently through the back door, leaving the young Dutchman to lock it behind us, and flitted, a line of gliding shadows, through the orchard. It was two o'clock, the sky was overcast, a slight drizzle was falling. Once an alarm was given that we were being followed; and we huddled together, and stood breathless, a clump of dark figures gazing affrightedly at the tree trunks which surrounded us, and which seemed--at least to the women's eyes--to be moving, and to be men closing in on us. But the alarm was groundless, and with no greater mishap than a few stumbles when we came to the slippery edge of the creek, we reached the boat, and one by one, admirably ordered by our host, got in and took our seats. Van Tree and Master Lindstrom pushed us off; then they swung themselves in and paddled warily along, close under the bank, where the shadows of the poplars fell across us, and our figures blended darkly with the line of rushes on the shore.

CHAPTER XII.

ANNE'S PETITION.

We coasted along in this silent fashion, nearly as far as the hamlet and bridge, following, but farther inshore, the course which Master Lindstrom and I had taken when on our way to bury the Spaniard. A certain point gained, at a signal from our host we struck out into the open, and rowed swiftly toward the edge of the marsh. This was the critical moment; but, so far as we could learn, our passage was unnoticed. We reached the fringe of rushes; with a prolonged hissing sound the boat pushed through them; a flight of water-fowl rose, whirring and clapping about us, and we floated out into a dim misty lake, whose shores and surface stretched away on every side, alike dark, shifting, and uncertain.

Across this the Dutchman steered us, bringing us presently to a narrow opening, through which we glided into a second and smaller mere. At the farther end of this one the way seemed barred by a black, impenetrable wall of rushes, which rose far above our heads. But the tall stems bent slowly with many a whispered protest before our silent onset, and we slid into a deep water-lane, here narrow, there widening into a pool, in one place dark, in another reflecting the gray night sky. Down this we sped swiftly, the sullen plash of the oars and the walls of rushes always with us. For ourselves, we crouched still and silent, shivering and listening for sounds of pursuit; now starting at the splash of a frog, again shuddering at the cry of a night-bird. The Duchess, her child, and I were in the bows, Master Lindstrom, his daughter, and Mistress Anne in the stern. They had made me comfortable with the baggage and some warm coverings, and would insist on treating me as helpless. Even when the others began to talk in whispers, the Duchess enjoined silence on me, and bade me sleep. Presently I did so, my last impression one of unending water-ways and shoreless, shadowy lakes.

When I awoke the sun was high and the scene was changed indeed. We lay on the bosom of a broad river, our boat seeming now to stand still as the sail flapped idly, now to heel over and shoot forward as the light breeze struck us. The shores abreast of us were still low and reedy, but ahead the slopes of green wooded hills rose gently from the stream. Master Bertie was steering, and, seeing me lift my head, greeted me with a smile. The girls in the stern were covered up and asleep. Amidships, too, Master Lindstrom and Van Tree had curled themselves up between the thwarts, and were slumbering peacefully. I turned to look for the Duchess, and found her sitting wide awake at my elbow, her eyes on her husband.

"Well," she said smiling, "do you feel better now? You have had a good sleep."

"How long have I been asleep, please?" I asked, bewildered by the sunshine, by the shining river and the green hills, by the fresh morning air, by the change in everything; and answering in a question, as people freshly aroused do nine times out of ten. "Where are we?"

"You have been asleep nearly six hours, and we are on the Rhine, near Emmerich," she answered, smiling. She was pale, and the long hours of watching had drawn dark circles round her eyes. But the old undaunted courage shone in them still, and her smile was as sweet as ever.

"Have we passed the frontier?" I asked eagerly.

"Well, nearly," she answered. "But how does your wound feel?"

"Rather stiff and sore," I said ruefully, after making an experiment by moving my body to and fro. "And I am very thirsty, but I could steer."

"So you shall," she said. "Only first eat something. We broke our fast before the others lay down. There is bread and meat behind you, and some hollands and water in the bottle."

I seized the latter and drank greedily. Then, finding myself hungry now I came to think about it, I fell upon the eatables.

"You will do now, I think," she said, when she had watched me for some time.

I laughed for answer, pleased that the long dark night, its gloom and treachery were past. But its memories remained and presently I said, "If Van Tree did not try to kill me--and I am perfectly sure he did not----"

"So am I," she said. "We were all wrong."

"Then," I continued, looking at her gravely, "who did? that is the question. And why?"

"You are sure that it was not the Spaniard whom you hurt in defense of Dymphna?" my lady asked.

"Quite sure."

"And sure that it was not Clarence?" she persisted.

"Quite sure. It was a short man," I explained again, "and dressed in a cloak. That is all I can tell about him."

"It might be some one employed by Clarence," she suggested, her face gloomy, her brows knit.

"True, I had not thought of that," I answered. "And it reminds me. I have heard so much of Clarence----"

"And seen some little--even that little more than was good for you."

"Yes, he has had the better of me, on both occasions," I allowed. "But I was going to ask you," I continued, "to tell me something about him. He was your steward, I know. But how did he come to you? How was it you trusted him?"

"We are all fools at times," she answered grimly. "We wanted to have persons of our own faith about us, and he was highly commended to us by Protestants abroad, as having seen service in the cause. He applied to us just at the right moment, too. And at the first we felt a great liking for him. He was so clever in arranging things, he kept such excellent order among the servants; he was so ready, so willing, so plausible! Oh!" she added bitterly, "he had ways that enabled him to twist nine women out of ten round his fingers! Richard was fond of him; I liked him; we had talked more than once of how we might advance his interests. And then, like a thunderbolt on a clear day, the knowledge of his double-dealing fell upon us. We learned that he had been seen talking with a known agent of Gardiner, and this at a time when the Bishop was planning our ruin. We had him watched, and just when the net had all but closed round us we discovered that he had been throughout in Gardiner's pay."

"Ah!" I said viciously. "The oddest thing to me is the way he has twice escaped me when I had him at the sword's point!"

"The third time may bring other fortune, Master Francis," she answered smiling. "Yet be wary with him. He is a good swordsman, as my husband, who sometimes fenced with him, will tell you."

"He can be no common man," I said.

"He is not. He is well-bred, and has seen service. He is at once bold and cunning. He has a tongue would win most women, and a hardihood that would chain them to him. Women love bold men," my lady added naïvely. And she smiled on me--yet humorously--so that I blushed.

There was silence for a moment. The sail flapped, then filled again. How delicious this morning after that night, this bright expanse after the dark, sluggish channels! Far away in front a great barge, high-laden with a mighty stack of rushes, crept along beside the bank, the horse that drew it covered by a kind of knitted rug. When my lady spoke next, it was abruptly. "Is it Anne?" she asked.

I knew quite well what she meant, and blushed again. I shook my head.

"I think it was going to be," she said sagely, "only Mistress Dymphna came upon the scene. You have heard the story of the donkey halting between two bundles of hay, Master Francis? And in the multitude of sweethearts there is safety."

"I do not think that was my case," I said. Instinctively my hand went to my breast, in which Petronilla's velvet sword-knot lay safe and warm. The Duchess saw the gesture and instantly bent forward and mimicked it. "Ha! ha!" she cried, leaning back with her hands clasped about her knees, and her eyes shining with fun and amusement. "Now I understand. You have left her at home; now, do not deny it, or I will tell the others. Be frank and I will keep your secret, on my honor."

"She is my cousin," I said, my cheeks hot.

"And her name?"

"Petronilla."

"Petronilla?" my lady repeated shrewdly. "That was the name of your Spanish grandmother, then?"

"Yes, madam."

"Petronilla? Petronilla?" she repeated, stroking her cheek with her hand. "She would be before my time, would she not? Yet there used to be several Petronillas about the court in Queen Catherine of Aragon's days, I remember. There was Petronilla de Vargas for one. But there, I guess at random. Why do you not tell me more about yourself, Master Francis? Do you not know me well enough now?"

"There is nothing to tell, madam," I said in a low voice.

"Your family? You come, I am sure, of a good house."

"I did, but it is nothing to me now. I am cut off from it. I am building my house afresh. And," I added bitterly, "I have not made much way with it yet."

She broke, greatly to my surprise, into a long peal of laughter. "Oh, you vain boy!" she cried. "You valiant castle-builder! How long have you been about the work? Three months? Do you think a house is to be built in a day? Three months, indeed? Quite a lifetime!"

Was it three months? It seemed to me to be fully three years. I seemed to have grown more than three years older since that February morning when I had crossed Arden Forest with the first light, and looked down on

Wootton Wawen sleeping in its vale, and roused the herons fishing in the bottoms.

"Come, tell me all about it!" she said abruptly. "What did you do to be cut off?"

"I cannot tell you," I answered.

A shade of annoyance clouded her countenance. But it passed away almost on the instant. "Very well," she said, with a little nod of disdain and a pretty grimace. "So be it. Have your own way. But I prophesy you will come to me with your tale some day."

I went then and took Master Bertie's place at the tiller; and, he lying down, I had the boat to myself until noon, and drew no little pleasure from the placid picture which the moving banks and the wide river presented. About noon there was a general uprising; and, coming immediately afterward to a little island lying close to one bank, we all landed to stretch our legs and refresh ourselves after the confinement on board.

"We are over the border now and close to Emmerich," said Master Lindstrom, "though the mere line of frontier will avail us little if the Spanish soldiers can by hook or crook lay hands on us! Therefore, we must lose no time in getting within the walls of some town. We should be fairly secure for a few days either in Wesel or Santon."

"I thought Wesel was the point we were making for," Master Bertie said in some surprise.

"It was Wesel I mentioned the other day," the Dutchman admitted frankly. "And it is the bigger town and the stronger. But I have more friends in Santon. To Wesel the road from Emmerich runs along the right bank. To Santon we go by a cross-country road, starting from the left bank opposite Emmerich, a road longer and more tedious. But we are much less likely to be followed that way than along the Wesel road, and on second thoughts I incline to Santon."

"But why adopt either road? Why not go on by river?" I asked.

"Because we should be overtaken. The wind is falling, and the boat," our late host explained, more truly than politely, "with the women in it is heavy."

"I understand," I said. "And you feel sure we shall be pursued?"

For answer he pointed with a smile to his plate-chest. "Quite sure," he added. "With that before them they will think nothing of the frontier. I fancy that for you, if the English Government be in earnest, there will be no absolutely safe place short of the free city of Frankfort. Unless indeed you have interest with the Duke of Cleves."

"Ah!" said the Duchess. And she looked at her husband.

"Ah!" said Master Bertie, and he looked very blankly at his wife. So that I did not derive much comfort from that suggestion.

"Then it is Santon, is it?" said my lady.

"That first, at any rate. Then, if they follow us along the Wesel road, we shall still give them the slip."

So it was settled, neither Van Tree nor the girls having taken any part in the discussion. The former and Dymphna were talking aside, and Mistress Anne was sitting low down on the bank, with her feet almost in the water, immersed to all appearance in her own thoughts. There was a little bustle as we rose to get into the boat, which we had drawn up on the landward side of the island so as to be invisible from the main channel; and in the middle of this I was standing with one foot in the boat and one on shore, taking from Anne various articles which we had landed for rearrangement, when she whispered to me that she wanted to speak to me alone.

"I want to tell you something," she said, raising her eyes to my face, and then averting them. "Follow me this way."

She strolled, as if accidentally, twenty or thirty paces along the bank; and in a minute I joined her. I found her gazing down the river in the direction from which we had come. "What is it?" I said anxiously. "You do not see anything, do you?" For there had been a hint of bad news in her voice.

She dropped the hand with which she had been shading her eyes and turned to me. "Master Francis, you will not think me very foolish?" she said. Then I perceived that her lip was quivering and that there were tears in her eyes. They were very beautiful eyes when, as now, they grew soft, and appeal took the place of challenge.

"What is it?" I replied, speaking cheerfully to reassure her. She had scarcely got over her terror of last night. She trembled as she stood.

"It is about Santon," she answered with a miserable little catch in her voice. "I am so afraid of going there! Master Lindstrom says it is a rough, long road, and when we are there we are not a bit farther from those wretches than at Wesel, and--and----"

"There, there!" I said. She was on the point of bursting into tears, and was clearly much overwrought. "You are making the worst of it. If it were not for Master Lindstrom I should be inclined to choose Wesel myself. But he ought to know best."

"But that is not all," she said, clasping her hands and looking up at me with her face grown full of solemn awe; "I have had a dream."

"Well, but dreams----" I objected.

"You do not believe in dreams?" she said, dropping her head sorrowfully.

"No, no; I do not say that," I admitted, naturally startled. "But what was your dream?"

"I thought we took the road to Santon. And mind," she added earnestly, "this was before Master Lindstrom had uttered a word about going that way, or any other way save to Wesel. I dreamt that we followed the road through such a dreadful flat country, a country all woods and desolate moorland, under a gray sky, and in torrents of rain, to----"

"Well, well?" I said, with a passing shiver at the picture. She described it with a rapt, absent air, which made me creep--as if even now she were seeing something uncanny.

"And then I thought that in the middle of these woods, about half-way to Santon, they overtook us, and there was a great fight."

"There would be sure to be that!" I muttered, with shut teeth.

"And I thought you were killed, and we women were dragged back! There, I cannot tell you the rest!" she added wildly. "But try, try to get them to go the old way. If not, I know evil will come of it. Promise me to try?"

"I will tell them your dream," I said.

"No, no!" she exclaimed still more vehemently. "They would only laugh. Madam does not believe in dreams. But they will listen to you if you say you think the other way better. Promise me you will! Promise me!" she pleaded, her hands clasping my arm, and her tearful eyes looking up to mine.

"Well," I agreed reluctantly, "I will try. After all, the shortest way may be the best. But if I do," I said kindly, "you must promise me in return not to be alarmed any longer, Anne."

"I will try," she said gratefully; "I will indeed, Francis."

We were summoned at that minute, for the boat was waiting for us. The Duchess scanned us rather curiously as we ran up--we were the last. But Anne kept her word, and concealed her fears so bravely that, as she jumped in from the bank, her air of gayety almost deceived me, and would have misled the sharpest-sighted person who had not been present at our interview, so admirably was it assumed.

We calculated that our pursuers would not follow us down the river for some hours. They would first have to search the island, and the watch which they had set on the landing-stage would lead them to suspect rather that we had fled by land. We hoped, therefore, to reach Emmerich unmolested. There Master Lindstrom said we could get horses, and he thought we might be safe in Santon by the following evening.

"If you really think we had better go to Santon," I said. This was an hour or two after leaving the island, and when we looked to sight Emmerich very soon, the hills which we had seen in front all day, and which were grateful to eyes sated with the monotony of Holland, being now pretty close to us.

"I thought that we had settled that," replied the Dutchman promptly.

I felt they were all looking at me. "I look at it this way," I said, reddening. "Wesel is not far from Emmerich by the road. Should we not have an excellent chance of reaching it before our pursuers come up?"

"You might reach it," Master Lindstrom said gravely. "Though, again, you might not."

"And, Wesel once reached," I persisted, "there is less fear of violence being attempted there than in Santon. It is a larger town."

"True," he admitted. "But it is just this. Will you be able to reach Wesel? It is the getting there--that is the difficulty; the getting there before you are caught."

"If we have a good start, why should we not?" I urged; and urged it the more persistently, the more I found them opposed to it. Naturally there ensued a warm discussion. At first they all sided against me, save of course Anne, and she sat silent, though she was visibly agitated, as from minute to minute I or they seemed likely to prevail. But presently when I grew warmer, and urged again and again the strength of Wesel, my own party veered round, yet still with doubt and misgiving. The Dutchman shrugged his shoulders to the end and remained unpersuaded. But finally it was decided that I should have my own way. We would go to Wesel.

Every one knows how a man feels when he comes victorious out of such a battle. He begins on the instant to regret his victory, and to see the possible evils which may result from it; to repent the hot words he has used in the strife and the declarations he has flung broadcast. That dreadful phrase, "I told you so!" rises like an avenging fury before his fancy, and he quails.

I felt all this the moment the thing was settled. But I was too young to back out and withdraw my words. I hoped for the best, and resolved inwardly to get the party mounted the moment we reached Emmerich.

I soon had the opportunity of proving this resolution to be more easily made than carried out. About three o'clock we reached the little town dominated, as we saw from afar, by an ancient minster, and, preferring not to enter it, landed at the steps of an inn a quarter of a mile short of the gates, and marking a point where we might take the road to Wesel, or, crossing the river, the road to Santon. Master Lindstrom seemed well known, but there were difficulties about the horses. The German landlord listened to his story with apparent sympathy--but no horses! We could not understand the tongue in which the two talked, but the Dutchman's questions, quick and animated for once, and the landlord's slow replies, reminded me of the foggy morning when in a similar plight we had urged the master of the *Lion's Whelp* to put to sea. And I feared a similar result.

"He says he cannot get so many horses to-night," said Master Lindstrom with a long face.

"Offer him more money!" quoth the Duchess.

"If we cannot have horses until the morning, we may as well go on in the boat," I urged.

"He says, too, that the water is out on the road," continued the Dutchman.

"Nonsense! Double the price!" cried my lady impatiently.

I suppose that this turned the scale. The landlord finally promised that in an hour four saddle-horses for Master Bertie and the Duchess, Anne and myself, should be ready, with a couple of pack-horses and a guide. Master Lindstrom, his daughter, and Van Tree would start a little later for Cleves, five miles on the road to Santon, if conveyance could be got. "And if not," our late host added, as we said something about our unwillingness to leave him in danger, "I shall be safe enough in the town, but I hope to sleep in Cleves."

It was all settled very hastily. We felt--and I in particular, since my plan had been adopted--an unreasonable impatience to be off. As we stood on the bank by the inn-door, we had a straight reach of river a mile long in full view below us; and now we were no longer moving ourselves, but standing still, expected each minute to see the Spanish boat, with its crew of desperadoes, sweep round the corner before our eyes. Master Lindstrom assured us that if we were once out of sight our pursuers would get no information as to the road we had taken, either from the inn-keeper or his neighbors. "There is no love lost between them and the Spaniards," he said shrewdly. "And I know the people here, and they know me. The burghers may not be very keen to come to blows with the Spaniards or to resent their foray. But the latter, on their part, will be careful not to go too far or to make themselves obnoxious."

We took the opportunity of supping then, not knowing when we might get food again. I happened to finish first, and, hearing the horses' hoofs, went out and watched the lads who were to be our guides fastening the baggage on the sumpter beasts. I gave them a hand--not without a wince or two, for the wound in my chest was painful--and while doing so had a flash of remembrance. I went to the unglazed window of the kitchen in which the others sat, and leaned my elbows on the sill. "I say!" I said, full of my discovery, "there is something we have forgotten!"

"What?" asked the Duchess, rising and coming toward me, while the others paused in their meal to listen.

"The letter to Mistress Clarence," I answered. "I was going to get it when I was stabbed, you remember, and afterward we forgot all about it. Now it is too late. It has been left behind."

She did not answer then, but came out to me, and turned with me to look at the horses. "This comes of your foolish scruples, Master Francis!" she said severely. "Where was it?"

"I slipped it between the leathers of the old haversack you gave me," I answered, "which I used to have for a pillow. Van Tree brought my things down, but overlooked the haversack, I suppose. At any rate, it is not here."

"Well, it is no good crying over spilt milk," she said.

She called the others out then, and there was no mistaking Mistress Anne's pleasure at escaping the Santon road. She was radiant, and vouchsafed me a very pretty glance of thanks, in which her relief as well as her gratitude shone clearly. By half-past four we had got, wearied as we were, to horse, and with three hours of daylight before us hoped to reach Wesel without mishap. But for most of us the start was saddened by the parting--though we hoped it would be only for a time--from our Dutch friends. We remembered how good and stanch they had been to us. We feared--though Master Lindstrom would not hear of it--that we had brought misfortune upon them, and neither the Duchess's brave eyes nor Dymphna's blue ones were free from tears as they embraced.

I wrung Van Tree's hand as if I had known him for months instead of days, for a common danger is a wondrous knitter of hearts; and he only smiled--though Dymphna blushed--when I kissed her cheek. A few broken words, a last cry of farewell, and we four, with our two guides behind us, moved down the Wesel road, the last I heard of our good friends being Master Lindstrom's charge, shouted after us, "to beware of the water if it was out!"

CHAPTER XIII.

A WILLFUL MAN'S WAY.

Only to feel that we were moving was a relief, though our march was very slow. Master Bertie carried the child slung in a cloak before him, and, thus burdened, could not well go beyond a smooth amble, while the guides, who were on foot, and the pack-horses, found this pace as much as they could manage. A little while and the exhilaration of the start died away. The fine morning was followed by a wet evening, and before we had left Emmerich three miles behind us Master Bertie and I had come to look at one another meaningly. We were moving in a dreary, silent procession through heavy rain, with the prospect of the night closing in early. The road, too, grew more heavy with each furlong, and presently began to be covered with pools of water. We tried to avoid this inconvenience by resorting to the hill slopes on our left, but found the attempt a waste of time, as a deep stream or backwater, bordered by marshes, intervened. The narrow road, raised but little above the level of the swiftly flowing river on our right, turned out to be our only possible path; and when Master Bertie discerned this his face grew more and more grave.

We soon found, indeed, as we plodded along, that a sheet of water, which palely reflected the evening light, was taking the place of the road; and through this we had to plash and plash at a snail's pace, one of the guides on a pack-horse leading the way, and Master Bertie in charge of his wife coming next; then, at some distance, for her horse did not take kindly to the water, the younger woman followed in my care. The other guide brought up the rear. In this way, stopped constantly by the fears of the horses, which were scared by the expanse of flood before them, we crept wearily on until the moon rose. It brought, alas, an access of light, but no comfort! The water seemed continually to grow deeper, the current on our right swifter; and each moment I dreaded the announcement that farther advance was impossible.

It seemed to have come to that at last, for I saw the Duchess and her husband stop and stand waiting for me, their dark shadows projected far over the moonlit surface.

"What is to be done?" Master Bertie called out, as we moved up to them. "The guide tells me that there is a broken piece of road in front which will be impassable with this depth of water."

I had expected to hear this; yet I was so dumfounded--for, this being true, we were lost indeed--that for a time I could not answer. No one had uttered a word of reproach, but I knew what they must be thinking. I had brought them to this. It was my foolish insistence had done it. The poor beast under me shivered. I struck him with my heels. "We must go forward!" I said desperately. "Or what? What do you think? Go back?"

"Steady! steady, Master Knight Errant!" the Duchess cried in her calm, brave voice. "I never knew you so bad a counselor before!"

"It is my fault that you are here," I said, looking dismally around.

"Perhaps the other road is as bad," Master Bertie replied. "At any rate, that is past and gone. The question is, what are we to do now? To remain here is to die of cold and misery. To go back may be to run into the enemy's arms. To go forward----"

"Will be to be drowned!" Mistress Anne cried with a pitiful sob.

I could not blame her. A more gloomy outlook than ours, as we sat on our jaded horses in the middle of this waste of waters, which appeared in the moonlight to be boundless, could scarcely be imagined. The night was cold for the time of year, and the keen wind pierced our garments and benumbed our limbs. At any moment the rain might begin afresh, and the moon be overcast. Of ourselves, we could not take a step without danger, and our guides had manifestly lost their heads and longed only to return.

"Yet, I am for going forward," the Duchess urged. "If there be but this one bad place we may pass it with care."

"We may," her husband assented dubiously. "But suppose when we have passed it we can go no farther. Suppose the----"

"It is no good supposing!" she retorted with some sharpness. "Let us cross this place first, Richard, and we will deal with the other when we come to it."

He nodded assent, and we moved slowly forward, compelling the guides to go first. In this order we waded some hundred yards through water, which grew deeper with each step, until it rose nearly to our girths. Then the lads stopped.

"Are we over?" said the Duchess eagerly.

For answer one of them pointed to the flood before him, and peering forward I made out a current sweeping silently and swiftly across our path--a current with an ominous rush and swirl.

"Over?" grunted Master Bertie. "No, this is the place. See, the road has given way, and the stream is pouring through from the river. I expect it is getting worse every minute as the banks crumble."

We all craned forward, looking at it. It was impossible to say how deep the water was, or how far the deep part might extend. And we had with us a child and two women.

"We must go back!" said Master Bertie resolutely. "There is no doubt about it. The flood is rising. If we do not take care, we shall be cut off, and be able to go neither backward nor forward. I cannot see a foot of dry land, as it is, before or behind us."

He was right. Far and wide, wherever our eyes could reach, the moonlight was reflected in a sheet of water. We were nearly up to our girths in water. On one side was the hurrying river, on the other were the treacherous depths of the backwater. I asked the guide as well as I could whether the road was good beyond. He answered that he did not know. He and his companion were so terrified that we only kept them beside us by threats.

"I fear we must go back," I said, assenting sorrowfully.

Even the Duchess agreed, and we were in the act of turning to retrace our steps with what spirit we might, when a distant sound brought us all to a standstill again. The wind was blowing from the quarter whence we had come--from Emmerich; and it brought to us the sound of voices. We all stopped to listen. Yes, they were voices we heard--loud, strident tones, mingled now with the sullen plash of horses tramping through the water. I looked at the Duchess. Her face was pale, but her courage did not fail her. She understood in a trice that the danger we had so much dreaded was upon us--that we were followed, and the followers were at our heels; and she turned her horse round again. Without a word she spurred it back toward the deep part. I seized Anne's rein and followed, notwithstanding that the poor girl in her terror would have resisted. Letting the guides go as they pleased, we four in a moment found ourselves abreast again, our horses craning over the stream, while we, with whip and spur, urged them on.

In cold blood we should scarcely have done it. Indeed, for a minute, as our steeds stumbled, and recovered themselves, and slid forward, only to draw back trembling--as the water rose above our boots or was flung by our fellows in our eyes, and all was flogging and scrambling and splashing, it seemed as if we were to be caught in a trap despite our resolve. But at last Master Bertie's horse took the plunge. His wife's followed; and both, partly floundering and partly swimming, set forward snorting the while in fear. To my joy I saw them emerge safely not ten yards away, and, shaking themselves, stand comparatively high out of the water.

"Come!" cried my lady imperatively, as she turned in her saddle with a gesture of defiance. "Come! It is all right."

Come, indeed! I wanted nothing better, for I was beside myself with passion. But, flog as I might, I could not get Anne's brute to take the plunge. The girl herself could give me no aid; clinging to her saddle, pale and half-fainting, she could only beg me to leave her, crying out again and again in a terrified voice that she would be drowned. With her cry there suddenly mingled another, the hail of our pursuers as they sighted us. I could hear them drawing nearer, and I grew desperate. Luckily they could not make any speed in water so deep, and time was given me for one last furious effort. It succeeded. My horse literally fell into the stream; it dragged Anne's after it. How we kept our seats, how they their footing, I never understood; but, somehow, splashing and stumbling and blinded by the water dashed in our faces, we came out on the other side, where the Duchess and her husband, too faithful to us to save themselves, had watched the struggle in an agony of suspense. I did but fling the girl's rein to Master Bertie; and then I wheeled my horse to the stream again. I had made up my mind what I must do. "Go on," I cried, waving my hand with a gesture of farewell. "Go on! I can keep them here for a while."

"Nonsense!" I heard the Duchess cry, her voice high and shrill. "It is----"

"Go on!" I cried. "Go on! Do not lose a moment, or it will be useless."

Master Bertie hesitated. But he too saw that this was the only chance. The Spaniards were on the brink of the stream now, and must, if they passed it, overtake us easily. He hesitated, I have said, for a moment. Then he seized his wife's rein and drew her on, and I heard the three horses go splashing away through the flood. I threw a glance at them over my shoulder, bethinking me that I had not told the Duchess my story, and that Sir Anthony and Petronilla would never--but, pish! What was I thinking of? That was a thought for a woman. I had only to harden my heart now, and set my teeth together. My task was very simple indeed. I had just to keep these men--there were four--here as long as I could, and if possible to stop Clarence's pursuit altogether.

For I had made no mistake. The first man to come up was Clarence-- Clarence himself. He let fall a savage word as his horse stopped suddenly with its fore feet spread out on the edge of the stream, and his dark face grew darker as he saw the swirling eddies, and me standing fronting him in the moonlight with my sword out. He discerned at once, I think, the strength of my position. Where I stood the water was scarcely over my horse's fetlocks. Where he stood it was over his horse's knees. And between us it flowed nearly four feet deep.

He held a hasty parley with his companions. And then he hailed me. "Will you surrender?" he cried in English. "We will give you quarter."

"Surrender? To whom?" I said. "And why--why should I surrender? Are you robbers and cutpurses?"

"Surrender in the name of the Emperor, you fool!" he answered sternly and roughly.

"I know nothing about the Emperor!" I retorted. "What Emperor?"

"In the Queen's name, then!"

"The Duke of Cleves is queen here!" I cried. "And as the flood is rising," I added scornfully, "I would advise you to go home again."

"You would advise, would you? Who *are* you?" he replied, in a kind of wrathful curiosity.

I gave him no answer. I have often since reflected, with a fuller knowledge of certain facts, that no stranger interview ever took place than this short colloquy between us, that no stranger fight ever was fought than that which we contemplated as we stood there bathed in the May moonlight, with the water all round us, and the cold sky above. A strange fight indeed it would have been between him and me, had it ever come to the sword's point!

But this was what happened. His last words had scarcely rung out when my horse began to quiver under me and sway backward and forward. I had just time to take the alarm, when the poor beast sank down and rolled gently over, leaving me bestriding its body, my feet in the water. Whatever the cause of this, I had to disentangle myself, and that quickly, for the four men opposite me, seeing me dismounted, plunged with a cry of triumph into the water, and began to flounder across. Without more ado I stepped forward to keep the ford.

The foremost and nearest to me was Clarence, whose horse began, half-way across, to swim. It was still scrambling to regain its footing when it came within my reach, and I slashed it cruelly across the nostrils. It turned in an instant on its side. I saw the rider's face gleam white in the water; his stirrup shone a moment as the horse rolled over, then in a second the two were gone down the stream. It was done so easily, so quickly, it amazed me. One gone! hurrah! I turned quickly to the others, who were about landing. My blood was fired, and my yell of victory, as I dashed at them, scared back two of the horses. Despite their riders' urging, they turned and scrambled out on the side from which they had entered. Only one was left, the farthest from me. He got across indeed. Yet he was the most unlucky of all, for his horse stumbled on landing, came down heavily on its head, and flung him at my very feet.

I LUNGED TWICE AT THE RIDER

It was no time for quarter--I had to think of my friends--and while with one hand I seized the flying rein as the horse scrambled trembling to its feet, with the other I lunged twice at the rider as he half tried to rise, half tried to grasp at me. The second time I ran him through, and he screamed shrilly. In those days I was young and hotheaded, and I answered only by a shout of defiance, as I flung myself into the saddle and dashed away through the water after my friends.

Væ victis! I had done enough to check the pursuit, and had yet escaped myself. If I could join the others again, what a triumph it would be! I had no guide, but neither had those in front of me; and luckily at this point a row of pollard willows defined the line between the road and the river. Keeping this on my right, I made good way. The horse seemed strong under me, the water was shallow, and appeared to be growing more so, and presently across the waste of flood I discerned before me a dark, solitary tower, the tower seemingly of a church, for it was topped by a stumpy spire, which daylight would probably have shown to be of wood.

There was a little dry ground round the church, a mere patch in a sea of water, but my horse rang its hoofs on it with every sign of joy, and arched its neck as it trotted up to the neighborhood of the church, whinnying with pleasure. From the back of the building, I was not surprised, came an answering neigh. As I pulled up, a man, his weapon in his hand, came from the porch, and a woman followed him. I called to them gayly. "I fancied you would be here the moment I saw the church!" I said, sliding to the ground.

"Thank Heaven you are safe!" the Duchess answered, and to my astonishment she flung her arms round my neck and kissed me. "What has happened?" she asked, looking in my eyes, her own full of tears.

"I think I have stopped them," I answered, turning suddenly shy, though, boylike, I had been longing a few minutes before to talk of my victory. "They tried to cross, and----"

I had not sheathed my sword. Master Bertie caught my wrist, and, lifting the blade, looked at it. "So, so!" he said nodding. "Are you hurt?"

"Not touched!" I answered. Before more was said he compelled his wife to go back into the porch. The wind blew keenly across the open ground, and we were all wet and shivering. When we had fastened up the horse we followed her. The door of the church was locked, it seemed, and the porch afforded the best shelter to be had. Its upper part was of open woodwork, and freely admitted the wind; but wide eaves projected over these openings, and over the door, so that at least it was dry within. By huddling together on the floor against the windward side we got some protection. I hastily told what had happened.

"So Clarence is gone!" My lady's voice as she said the words trembled, but not in sorrow or pity as I judged. Rather in relief. Her dread and hatred of the man were strange and terrible, and so seemed to me then. Afterward, I learned that something had passed between them which made almost natural such feelings on her part, and made natural also a bitter resentment on his. But of that no more. "You are quite sure," she said--pressing me anxiously for confirmation--"that it was he!"

"Yes. But I am not sure that he is dead," I explained.

"You seem to bear a charmed life yourself," she said.

"Hush!" cried her husband quickly. "Do not say that to the lad. It is unlucky. But do you think," he continued--the porch was in darkness, and we could scarcely make out one another's faces--"that there is any further chance of pursuit?"

"Not by that party to-night," I said grimly. "Nor I think to-morrow."

"Good!" he answered. "For I can see nothing but water ahead, and it would be madness to go on by night without a guide. We must stay here until morning, whatever the risk."

He spoke gloomily--and with reason. Our position was a miserable, almost a desperate one, even on the supposition that pursuit had ceased. We had lost all our baggage, food, wraps. We had no guides, and we were in the midst of a flooded country, with two tender women and a baby, our only shelter the porch of God's house. Mistress Anne, who was crouching in the darkest corner next the church, seemed to have collapsed entirely. I remembered afterward that I did not once hear her speak that night. The Duchess tried to maintain our spirits and her own; but in the face of cold, damp, and hunger, she could do little. Master Bertie and I took it by turns to keep a kind of watch, but by morning--it was a long night and a bitter one--we were worn out, and slept despite our misery. We should have been surprised and captured without a blow if the enemy had come upon us then.

I awoke with a start to find the gray light of a raw misty morning falling upon and showing up our wretched group. The Duchess's head was hidden in her cloak; her husband's had sunk on his breast; but Mistress Anne--I looked at her and shuddered. Had she sat so all night? Sat staring with that stony face of pain, and those tearless eyes on the moonlight, on the darkness which had been before the dawn, on the cold first rays of morning? Stared on all alike, and seen none? I shuddered and peered at her, alarmed, doubtful, wondering, asking myself what this was that had happened to her. Had fear and cold killed her, or turned her brain? "Anne!" I said timidly. "Anne!"

She did not answer nor turn; nor did the fixed gaze of her eyes waver. I thought she did not hear. "Anne!" I cried again, so loudly that the Duchess stirred, and muttered something in her sleep. But the girl showed no sign of consciousness. I put out my hand and touched her.

She turned sharply and saw me, and in an instant drew her skirt away with a gesture of such dread, loathing repulsion as froze me; while a violent shudder convulsed her whole frame. Afterward she seemed unable to withdraw her eyes from me, but sat in the same attitude, gazing at me with a fixed look of horror, as one might gaze at a serpent, while tremor after tremor shook her.

I was frightened and puzzled, and was still staring at her, wondering what I had done, when a footstep fell on the road outside and called away my attention. I turned from her to see a man's figure looming dark in the doorway. He looked at us--I suppose he had found the horses outside--gazing in surprise at the queer group. I bade him good-morning in Dutch, and he answered as well as his astonishment would let him. He was a short, stout fellow, with a big face, capable of expressing a good deal of astonishment. He seemed to be a peasant or farmer. "What do you here?" he continued, his guttural phrases tolerably intelligible to me.

I explained as clearly as I could that we were on the way to Wesel. Then I awoke the Duchess and her husband, and stretching our chilled and aching limbs, we went outside, the man still gazing at us. Alas! the day was not much better than the night. We could see but a very little way, a couple of hundred yards round us only. The rest was mist--all mist. We appealed to the man for food and shelter, and he nodded, and, obeying his signs rather than his words, we kicked up our starved beasts and plodded out into the fog by his side. Anne mounted silently and without objection, but it was plain that something strange had happened to her. Her condition was unnatural. The Duchess gazed at her very anxiously, and, getting no answers, or very scanty ones, to her questions, shook her head gravely.

But we were on the verge of one pleasure at least. When we reached the hospitable kitchen of the farmhouse it was joy indeed to stand before the great turf fire, and feel the heat stealing into our half-frozen bodies; to turn and warm back and front, while the good wife set bread and hot milk before us. How differently we three felt in half an hour! How the Duchess's eyes shone once more! How easily rose the laugh to our lips! Joy had indeed come with the morning. To be warm and dry and well fed after being cold and wet and hungry--what a thing this is!

But on one neither food nor warmth seemed to have any effect. Mistress Anne did, indeed, in obedience to my lady's sharp words, raise her bowl to her lips. But she set it down quickly and sat looking in dull apathy at the glowing peat. What had come over her?

Master Bertie went out with the farmer to attend to the horses, and when he came back he had news.

"There is a lad here," he said in some excitement, "who has just seen three foreigners ride past on the road, along with two Germans on pack-horses; five in all. They must be three of the party who followed us yesterday."

I whistled. "Then Clarence got himself out," I said, shrugging my shoulders. "Well! well!"

"I expect that is so," Master Bertie answered, the Duchess remaining silent. "The question arises again, what is to be done?" he continued. "We may follow them to Wesel, but the good man says the floods are deep between here and the town, and we shall have Clarence and his party before us all the way--shall perhaps run straight into their arms."

"But what else can we do?" I said. "It is impossible to go back."

We held a long conference, and by much questioning of our host learned that half a league away was a ferry-boat, which could carry as many as two horses over the river at a time. On the farther side we might hit a road leading to Santon, three leagues distant. Should we go to Santon after all? The farmer thought the roads on that side of the river might not be flooded. We should then be in touch once more with our Dutch friends and might profit by Master Lindstrom's advice, on which I for one was now inclined to set a higher value.

"The river is bank full. Are you sure the ferry-boat can cross?" I asked.

Our host was not certain. And thereupon an unexpected voice struck in.

"Oh, dear, do not let us run any more risks!" it said. It was Mistress Anne's. She was herself again, trembling, excited, bright-eyed; as different as possible from the Anne of a few minutes before. A great change had come over her. Perhaps the warmth had done it.

A third course was suggested, to stay quietly where we were. The farmhouse stood at some little distance from the road; and though it was rough--it was very rough, consisting only of two rooms, in one of which a cow was stalled--still it could furnish food and shelter. Why not stay there?

But the Duchess wisely, I think, decided against this. "It is unpleasant to go wandering again," she said with a shiver. "But I shall not rest until we are within the walls of a town. Master Lindstrom laid so much stress on that. And I fancy that the party who overtook us last night are not the main body. Others will have gone to Wesel by boat perhaps, or along the other bank. There they will meet, and, learning we have not arrived, they will probably return this way and search for us."

"Clarence----"

"Yes, if we have Clarence to deal with," Master Bertie assented gravely, "we cannot afford to lose a point. We will try the ferry."

It was something gained to start dry and warm. But the women's pale faces--for little by little the fatigue, the want of rest, the fear, were telling even on the Duchess--were sad to see. I was sore and stiff myself. The wound I had received so mysteriously had bled afresh, probably during last night's fight. We needed all our courage to put a brave face on the matter, and bear up and go out again into the air, which for the first week in May was cold and nipping. Suspense and anxiety had told in various ways on all of us. While I felt a fierce anger against those who were driving us to these straits, Master Bertie was nervous and excited, alarmed for his wife and child, and inclined to see an enemy in every bush.

However, we cheered up a little when we reached the ferry and found the boat could cross without much risk. We had to go over in two detachments, and it was nearly an hour past noon before we all stood on the farther bank and bade farewell to the honest soul whose help had been of so much importance to us. He told us we had three leagues to go, and we hoped to be at rest in Santon by four o'clock.

But the three leagues turned out to be more nearly five, while the road was so founderous that we had again and again to quit it.

The evening came on, the light waned, and still we were feeling our way, so to speak--the women tired and on the verge of tears; the men muddy to the waist, savage, and impatient. It was eight o'clock, and dusk was well upon us before we caught sight of the first lights of Santon, and in fear lest the gates might be shut, pressed forward at such speed as our horses could compass.

"Do you go on!" the Duchess adjured us. "Anne and I will be safe enough behind you. Let me take the child, and do you ride on. We cannot pass the night in the fields."

The importance of securing admission was so great that Master Bertie and I agreed; and cantered on, soon outstripping our companions, and almost in the gloom losing sight of them. Dark masses of woods, the last remnants, apparently, of a forest, lay about the road we had to traverse. We were passing one of these, scarcely three hundred paces short of the town, and I was turning in the saddle to see that the ladies were following safely, when I heard Master Bertie, who was a bow-shot in front of me, give a sudden cry.

I wheeled round hastily to learn the reason, and was just in time to see three horsemen sweep into the road before him from the cover of the trees. They were so close to him--and they filled the road--that his horse carried him amongst them almost before he could check it, or so it seemed to me. I heard their loud challenge, saw his arm wave, and guessed that his sword was out. I spurred desperately to join him, giving a wild shout of encouragement as I did so. But before I could come up, or indeed cross half the distance, the scuffle was over. One man fell headlong from his saddle, one horse fled riderless down the road, and at sight of this, or perhaps of me, the others turned tail without more ado and made off, leaving Master Bertie in possession of the field. The whole thing had passed in the shadow of the wood in less than half a minute. When I drew rein by him he was sheathing his sword. "Is it Clarence?" I cried eagerly.

"No, no; I did not see him. I think not," he answered. He was breathing hard and was very much excited. "They were poor swordsmen, for Spaniards," he added--"very poor, I thought."

I jumped off my horse, and, kneeling beside the man, turned him over. He was badly hurt, if not dying, cut across the neck. He looked hard at him by such light as there was, and did not recognize him as one of our assailants of the night before.

"I do not think he is a Spaniard," I said slowly. Then a certain suspicion occurred to my mind, and I stooped lower over him.

"Not a Spaniard?" Master Bertie said stupidly. "How is that?"

Before I answered I raised the man in my arms, and, carrying him carefully to the side of the road, set him with his back to a tree. Then I got quickly on my horse. The women were just coming up. "Master Bertie," I said in a low voice, as I looked this way and that to see if the alarm had spread, "I am afraid there is a mistake. But say nothing to them. It is one of the town-guard you have killed!"

"One of the town-guard!" he cried, a light bursting in on him, and the reins dropping from his hand. "What shall we do? We are lost, man!"

CHAPTER XIV.

AT BAY IN THE GATEHOUSE.

What was to be done? That was the question, and a terrible question it was. Behind us we had the inhospitable country, dark and dreary, the night wind sweeping over it. In front, where the lights twinkled and the smoke of the town went up, we were like to meet with a savage reception. And it was no time for weighing alternatives. The choice had to be made, made in a moment; I marvel to this day at the quickness with which I made it for good or ill.

"We must get into the town!" I cried imperatively. "And before the alarm is given. It is hopeless to fly, Master Bertie, and we cannot spend another night in the fields. Quick, madam!" I continued to the Duchess, as she came up. I did not wait to hear his opinion, for I saw he was stunned by the catastrophe. "We have hurt one of the town-guard through a mistake. We must get through the gate before it is discovered!"

I seized her rein and flogged up her horse, and gave her no time to ask questions, but urged on the party at a hand gallop until the gate was reached. The attempt, I knew, was desperate, for the two men who had escaped had ridden straight for the town; but I saw no other resource, and it seemed to me to be better to surrender peaceably, if that were possible, than to expose the women to another night of such cold and hunger as the last. And fortune so far favored us that when we reached the gate it was open. Probably, the patrol having ridden through to get help, no one had thought fit to close it; and, no one withstanding us, we spurred our sobbing horses under the archway and entered the street.

It was a curious entry, and a curious scene we came upon. I remember now how strange it all looked. The houses, leaning forward in a dozen quaint forms, clear cut against the pale evening sky, caused a darkness as of a cavern in the narrow street below. Here and there in the midst of this darkness hung a lantern, which, making the gloom away from it seem deeper, lit up the things about it, throwing into flaring prominence some barred window with a scared face peering from it, some corner with a puddle, a slinking dog, a broken flight of steps. Just within the gate stood a brazier full of glowing coal, and beside it a halbert rested against the wall. I divined that the watchman had run into the town with the riders, and I drew rein in doubt, listening and looking. I think if we had ridden straight on then, all might have been well; or, at least, we might have been allowed to give ourselves up.

But we hesitated a moment, and were lost. No doubt, though we saw but one, there were a score of people watching us, who took us for four men, Master Bertie and I being in front; and these, judging from the boldness of our entry that there were more behind, concluded that this was a foray upon the town. At any rate, they took instant advantage of our pause. With a swift whir an iron pot came hurtling past me, and, missing the Duchess by a hand's-breadth, went clanking under the gatehouse. That served for a signal. In a moment an alarm of hostile cries rose all round us. An arrow whizzed between my horse's feet. Half a dozen odd missiles, snatched up by hasty hands, came raining in on us out of the gloom. The town seemed to be rising as one man. A bell began to ring, and a hundred yards in front, where the street branched off to right and left, the way seemed suddenly alive from wall to wall with lights and voices and brandished arms, the gleam of steel, and the babel of a furious crowd--a crowd making down toward us with a purpose we needed no German to interpret.

It was a horrible moment; the more horrible that I had not expected this fury, and was unnerved as well as taken aback by it. Remembering that I had brought my companions here, and that two were women, one was a child, I quailed. How could I protect them? There was no mistaking the stern meaning of those cries, of that rage so much surpassing anything I had feared. Though I did not know that the man we had struck down was a bridegroom, and that there were those in the crowd in whose ears the young wife's piercing scream still rang, I yet quailed before their yells and curses.

As I glanced round for a place of refuge, my eyes lit on an open doorway close to me, and close also to the brazier and halbert. It was a low stone doorway, beetle-browed, with a coat of arms carved over it. I saw in an instant that it must lead to the tower above us--the gatehouse; and I sprang from my horse, a fresh yell from the houses hailing the act. I saw that, if we were to gain a moment for parleying, we must take refuge there. I do not know how I did it, but somehow I made myself understood by the others and got the women off their horses and dragged Mistress Anne inside, where at once we both fell in the darkness over the lower steps of a spiral staircase. This hindered the Duchess, who was following, and I heard a scuffle taking place behind us. But in that confined space--the staircase was very narrow--I could give no help. I could only stumble upward, dragging the fainting girl after me, until we emerged through an open doorway at the top into a room. What kind of room I did not notice then, only that it was empty. Notice! It was no time for taking notice. The bell was clanging louder and louder outside. The mob were yelling like hounds in sight of their quarry. The shouts, the confused cries, and threats, and questions deafened me. I turned to learn what was happening behind me. The other two had not come up.

I felt my way down again, one hand on the central pillar, my shoulder against the outside wall. The stair-foot was faintly lit by the glow from outside, and on the bottom step I came on some one, hurt or dead, just a dark mass at my feet. It was Master Bertie. I gave a cry and leaped over his body. The Duchess, brave wife, was standing before him, the halbert which she had snatched up presented at the doorway and the howling mob outside.

Fortunately the crowd had not yet learned how few we were; nor saw, I think, that it was but a woman who confronted them. To rush into the low doorway and storm the narrow winding staircase in the face of unknown numbers was a task from which the bravest veterans might have flinched, and the townsfolk, furious as they were, hung back. I took advantage of the pause. I grasped the halbert myself and pushed the Duchess back. "Drag him up!" I muttered. "If you cannot manage it, call Anne!"

But grief and hard necessity gave her strength, and, despite the noise in front of me, I heard her toil panting up with her burden. When I judged she had reached the room above, I too turned and ran up after her, posting myself in the last angle just below the room. There I was sheltered from missiles by the turn in the staircase, and was further protected by the darkness. Now I could hold the way with little risk, for only one could come up at a time, and he would be a brave man who should storm the stairs in my teeth.

All this, I remember, was done in a kind of desperate frenzy, in haste and confusion, with no plan or final purpose, but simply out of the instinct of self-preservation, which led me to do, from moment to moment, what I could to save our lives. I did not know whether there was another staircase to the tower, nor whether there were enemies above us; whether, indeed, enemies might not swarm in on us from a dozen entrances. I had no time to think of more than just this; that my staircase, of which I did know, must be held.

I think I had stood there about a minute, breathing hard and listening to the din outside, which came to my ears a little softened by the thick walls round me--so much softened, at least, that I could hear my heart beating in the midst of it--when the Duchess came back to the door above. I could see her, there being a certain amount of light in the room behind her, but she could not see me. "What can I do?" she asked softly.

I answered by a question. "Is he alive?" I muttered.

"Yes; but hurt," she answered, struggling with a sob, with a fluttering of the woman's heart she had repressed so bravely. "Much hurt, I fear! Oh, why, why did we come here?"

She did not mean it as a reproach, but I took it as one, and braced myself more firmly to meet this crisis--to save her at least if it should be any way possible. When she asked again "Can I do anything?" I bade her take my pike and stand where I was for a moment. Since no enemy had yet made his appearance above, the strength of our position seemed to hold out some hope, and it was the more essential that I should understand it and know exactly what our chances were.

I sprang up the stairs into the room and looked round, my eyes seeming to take in everything at once. It was a big bare room, with signs of habitation only in one corner. On the side toward the town was a long, low window, through which--a score of the diamond panes were broken already--the flare of the besiegers' torches fell luridly on the walls and vaulted roof. By the dull embers of a wood fire, over which hung a huge black pot, Master Bertie was lying on the boards, breathing loudly and painfully, his head pillowed on the Duchess's kerchief. Beside him sat Mistress Anne, her face hidden, the child wailing in her lap. A glance round assured me that there was no other staircase, and that on the side toward the country, the wall was pierced with no window bigger than a loophole or an arrow-slit; with no opening which even a boy could enter. For the present, therefore, unless the top of the tower should be escaladed from the adjacent houses--and I could do nothing to provide against that--we had nothing to fear except from the staircase and the window I have mentioned. Every moment, however, a missile or a shot crashed through the latter, adding the shiver of falling glass to the general din. No wonder the child wailed and the girl sank over it in abject terror. Those savage yells might well make a woman blench. They carried more fear and dread to my heart than did the real danger of our position, desperate as it was.

And yet it was so desperate that, for a moment, I leant against the wall dazed and hopeless, listening to the infernal tumult without and within. Had Bertie been by my side to share the responsibility and join in the risk, I could have borne it better. I might have felt then some of the joy of battle, and the stern pleasure of the one matched against the many. But I was alone. How was I to save these women and that poor child from the yelling crew outside? How indeed? I did not know the enemy's language; I could not communicate with him, could not explain, could not even cry for quarter for the women.

A stone which glanced from one of the mullions and grazed my shoulder roused me from this fit of cowardice, which, I trust and believe, had lasted for a few seconds only. At the same moment an unusual volley of missiles tore through the window as if discharged at a given signal. We were under cover, and they did us no harm, rolling for the most part noisily about the floor. But when the storm ceased and a calm as sudden followed, I heard a dull, regular sound close to the window--a thud! thud! thud!--and on the instant divined the plan and the danger. My courage came back and with it my wits. I remembered an old tale I had heard, and, dropping my sword where I stood, I flew to the hearth, and unhooked the great pot. It was heavy; half full of something--broth, most likely; but I recked nothing of that, I bore it swiftly to the window, and just as the foremost man on the ladder had driven in the lead work before him with his ax, flung the whole of the contents--they were not scalding, but they were very hot--in his face. The fellow shrieked loudly, and, blinded and taken by surprise, lost his hold and fell against his supporter, and both tumbled down again more quickly than they had come up.

Sternly triumphant, I poised the great pot itself in my hands, thinking to fling it down upon the sea of savage upturned faces, of which I had a brief view, as the torches flared now on one, now on another. But prudence prevailed. If no more blood were shed it might still be possible to get some terms. I laid the pot down by the side of the window as a weapon to be used only in the last resort.

Meanwhile the Duchess, posted in the dark, had heard the noise of the window being driven in, and cried out pitifully to know what it was. "Stand firm!" I shouted loudly. "Stand firm. We are safe as yet."

Even the uproar without seemed to abate a little as the first fury of the mob died down. Probably their leaders were concerting fresh action. I went and knelt beside Master Bertie and made a rough examination of his wound. He had received a nasty blow on the back of the head, from which the blood was still oozing, and he was insensible. His face looked very long and thin and deathlike. But, so far as I could ascertain, the bones were uninjured, and he was now breathing more quietly. "I think he will recover," I said, easing his clothes.

Anne was crouching on the other side of him. As she did not answer I looked up at her. Her lips were moving, but the only word I caught was "Clarence!" I did not wonder she was distraught; I had work enough to keep my own wits. But I wanted her help, and I repeated loudly, "Anne! Anne!" trying to rouse her.

She looked past me shuddering. "Heaven forgive you!" she muttered. "You have brought me to this! And now I must die! I must die here. In the net they have set for others is their own foot taken!"

She was quite beside herself with terror. I saw that she was not addressing me; and I had not time to make sense of her wanderings. I left her and went out to speak to the Duchess. Poor woman! even her brave spirit was giving way. I felt her cold hands tremble as I took the halbert from her. "Go into the room a while," I said softly. "He is not seriously hurt, I am sure. I will guard this. If any one appears at the window, scream."

She went gladly, and I took her place, having now to do double duty. I had been there a few minutes only, listening, with my soul in my ears, to detect the first signs of attack, either below me or in the room behind, when I distinguished a strange rustling sound on the staircase. It appeared to come from a point a good deal below me, and probably, whoever made it was just within the doorway. I peered into the gloom, but could see no one as yet. "Stand!" I cried in a tone of warning. "Who is that?"

The sound ceased abruptly, but it left me uneasy. Could they be going to blow us up with gunpowder? No! I did not think so. They would not care to ruin the gateway for the sake of capturing so small a party. And the tower was strong. It would not be easy to blow it up.

Yet in a short time the noise began again; and my fears returned with it. "Stand!" I cried savagely, "or take care of yourself."

The answer was a flash of bright light--which for a second showed the rough stone walls winding away at my feet--a stunning report, and the pattering down of half a dozen slugs from the roof. I laughed, my first start over. "You will have to come a little higher up!" I cried tauntingly, as I smelt the fumes. My eyes had become so accustomed to the darkness that I felt sure I should detect an assailant, however warily he might make his approach. And my halbert was seven feet long, so that I could reach as far as I could see. I had had time, too, to grow cool.

After this there was comparative quiet for another space. Every now and then a stone or, more rarely, the ball of an arquebuse would come whizzing into the room above. But I did not fear this. It was easy to keep under cover. And their shouting no longer startled me. I began to see a glimpse of hope. It was plain that the townsfolk were puzzled how to come at us without suffering great loss. They were unaware of our numbers, and, as it proved, believed that we had three uninjured men at least. The staircase was impracticable as a point of assault, and the window, being only three feet in height and twenty from the ground, was not much better, if defended, as they expected it would be, by a couple of desperate swordsmen.

I was not much astonished, therefore, when the rustling sound, beginning again at the foot of the staircase, came this time to no more formidable issue than a hail in Spanish. "Will you surrender?" the envoy cried.

"No!" I said roundly.

"Who are you?" was the next question.

"We are English!" I answered.

He went then; and there for the time the negotiations ended. But, seeing the dawn of hope, I was the more afraid of any trap or surprise, and I cried to the Duchess to be on her guard. For this reason, too, the suspense of the next few minutes was almost more trying than anything which had gone before. But the minutes came at last to an end. A voice below cried loudly in English, "Holloa! are you friends?"

"Yes, yes," I replied joyfully, before the words had well ceased to rebound from the walls. For the voice and accent were Master Lindstrom's. A cry of relief from the room behind me showed that there, too, the speaker was recognized. The Duchess came running to the door, but I begged her to go back and keep a good lookout. And she obeyed.

"How come you here? How has it happened?" Master Lindstrom asked, his voice, though he still remained below, betraying his perplexity and unhappiness. "Can I not do something? This is terrible, indeed."

"You can come up, if you like," I answered, after a moment's thought. "But you must come alone. And I cannot let even you, friend as you are, see our defenses."

As he came up I stepped back and drew the door of the room toward me, so that, though a little light reached the head of the stairs, he could not, standing there, see into the room or discern our real weakness. I did not distrust him--Heaven forbid! but he might have to tell all he saw to his friends below, and I thought it well, for his sake as well as our own, that he should be able to do this freely, and without hurting us. As he joined me I held up a finger for silence and listened keenly. But all was quiet below. No one had followed him. Then I turned and warmly grasped his hands, and we peered into one another's faces. I saw he was deeply moved; that he was thinking of Dymphna, and how I had saved her. He held my hands as though he would never loose them.

"Well!" I said, as cheerfully as I could, "have you brought us an offer of terms? But let me tell you first," I continued, "how it happened." And I briefly explained that we had mistaken the captain of the guard and his two followers for Clarence and the two Spaniards. "Is he dead?" I continued.

"No, he is still alive," Master Lindstrom answered gravely. "But the townsfolk are furious, and the seizure of the tower has still further exasperated them. Why did you do it?"

"Because we should have been torn to pieces if we had not done it," I answered dryly. "You think we are in a strait place?"

"Do you not think so yourself?" he said, somewhat astonished.

I laughed. "That is as may be," I answered with an affectation of recklessness. "The staircase is narrow and the window low. We shall sell our lives dearly, my friend. Yet, for the sake of the women who are with us, we are willing to surrender if the citizens offer us terms. After all, it was an accident. Cannot you impress this on them?" I added eagerly.

He shook his head. "They will not hear reason," he said.

"Then," I replied, "impress the other thing upon them. Tell them that our swords are sharp and we are desperate."

"I will see what I can do," he answered slowly. "The Duke of Cleves is expected here to-morrow, and the townsfolk feel they would be disgraced forever if he should find their gate held by a party of marauders, as they consider you."

"The Duke of Cleves?" I repeated. "Perhaps he may be better affected toward us."

"They will overpower you before he comes," Master Lindstrom answered despondently. "I would put no trust in him if I were you. But I will go to them, and, believe me, I will do all that man can do."

"Of that I am sure," I said warmly. And then, cautioning me to remain strictly on the defensive, he left me.

Before his footsteps had ceased to echo on the stairs the door beside me opened, and Mistress Anne appeared at it. I saw at once that his familiar voice had roused her from the stupor of fear in which I had last seen her. Her eyes were bright, her whole frame was thrilling with excitement, hope, suspense. I began to understand her; to discern beneath the disguise thrown over it in ordinary times by a strong will, the nervous nature which was always confident or despairing, which felt everything so keenly-- everything, that is, which touched itself. "Well?" she cried, "well?"

"Patience! patience!" I replied rather sharply. I could not help comparing her conduct with that of the Duchess, and blaming her, not for her timidity, but for the selfishness which she had betrayed in her fear. I could fancy Petronilla trembling and a coward, but not despairing nor utterly cast down, nor useless when others needed her, nor wrapped in her own terrors to the very exclusion of reason. "Patience!" I said; "he is coming back. He and his friends will do all they can for us. We must wait a while and hope, and keep a good lookout."

She had her hand on the door, and by an abrupt movement, she slipped out to me and closed it behind her. This made the staircase so dark that I could no longer distinguish her face, but I judged from her tone that her fears were regaining possession of her. "Clarence," she muttered, her voice low and trembling. "Have you thought of him? Could not he help us? He may have followed us here, and may be here now. Now! And perhaps he does not know in what danger we are."

"Clarence!" I said, astonished and almost angry. "Clarence help us? Go back, girl, go back. You are mad. He would be more likely to complete our ruin. Go in and nurse the baby!" I added bitterly.

What could she mean, I asked myself, when she had gone in. Was there anything in her suggestion? Would Clarence follow us hither? If so, and if he should come in time, would he have power to help us, using such mysterious influence, Spanish or English, as he seemed to possess? And if he could help us, would it be better to fall into his hands than into those of the exasperated Santonese? I thought the Duchess would say "No!"

So it mattered not what I answered myself. I hoped, now Master Lindstrom had appeared, that the women would be allowed to go free; and it seemed to me that to surrender to Clarence would be to hand over the Duchess to her enemy simply that the rest of us might escape.

Master Lindstrom returned while I was still considering this, and, observing the same precautions as before, I bade him join me. "Well?" I said, not so impetuously, I hope, as Mistress Anne, yet I dare say with a good deal of eagerness. "Well, what do they say?" For he was slow to speak.

"I have bad news," he answered gently.

"Ah!" I ejaculated, a lump which was due as much to rage as to any other emotion rising in my throat. "So they will give us no terms? Then so be it! Let them come and take us."

"Nay," he hastened to answer. "It is not so bad as that, lad. They are fathers and husbands themselves, and not lanzknechts. They will suffer the women to go free, and will even let me take charge of them if necessary."

"They will!" I exclaimed, overjoyed. I wondered why on earth he had hesitated to tell me this. "Why, that is the main point, friend."

"Yes," he said gravely, "perhaps so. More, the men may go too, if the tower be surrendered within an hour. With one exception, that is. The man who struck the blow must be given up."

"The man who struck the blow!" I repeated slowly. "Do you mean--you mean the man who cut the patrol down?"

"Yes," he said. He was peering very closely at me, as though he would learn from my face who it was. And I stood thinking. This was as much as we could expect. I divined, and most truly, that but for the honest Dutchman's influence, promises, perhaps bribes, such terms would never have been offered to us by the men who hours before had driven us to hold as if we had been vermin. Yet give up Master Bertie? "What," I said, "will be done to him? The man who must be given up, I mean?" Master Lindstrom shook his head. "It was an accident," I urged, my eyes on his.

He grasped my hand firmly, and, turning away his face, seemed for a while unable to speak. At last he whispered, "He must suffer for the others, lad. I fear so. It is a hard fate, a cruel fate. But I can do no more. They will not hear me on this. It is true he will be first tried by the magistrate, but there is no hope. They are very hard."

My heart sank. I stood irresolute, pondering on what we ought to do, pondering on what I should say to the wife who so loved the man who must die. What could I say? Yet, somehow I must break the news. I asked Master Lindstrom to wait where he was while I consulted the others, adding, "You will answer for it that there will be no attack while you are here, I suppose?"

"I will," he said. I knew I could trust him, and I went in to the Duchess, closing the door behind me. A change had come over the room since I had left it. The moon had risen and was flinging its cold white light through the twisted and shattered framework of the window, to fall in three bright panels on the floor. The torches in the street had for the most part burned out, or been extinguished. In place of the red glare, the shouts and the crash of glass, the atmosphere of battle and strife I had left, I found this silvery light and a stillness made more apparent by the distant hum of many voices.

Mistress Anne was standing just within the threshold, her face showing pale against the gloom, her hands clasped. The Duchess was kneeling by her husband, but she looked up as I entered.

"They will let us all go," I said bluntly; it was best to tell the tale at once--"except the one who hurt the patrol, that is."

It was strange how differently the two women received the news; while Mistress Anne flung her hands to her face with a sobbing cry of thankfulness, and leaned against the wall crying and shaking, my lady stood up straight and still, breathing hard but saying nothing. I saw that she did not need to ask what would be done to the one who was excepted. She knew. "No," she murmured at last, her hands pressed to her bosom, "we cannot do it! Oh, no, no!"

"I fear we must," I said gently--calmly, too, I think. Yet in saying it I was not quite myself. An odd sensation was growing upon me in the stillness of the room. I began on a sudden, I did not know why, to thrill with excitement, to tremble with nervousness, such as would rather have become one of the women than a man. My head grew hot, my heart began to beat quickly. I caught myself looking out, listening, waiting for something to happen, something to be said. It was something more terrible, as it seemed to me, than the din and crash of the worst moments of the assault. What was it? What was it that was threatening my being? An instant and I knew.

"Oh, no, never!" cried the Duchess again, her voice quivering, her face full of keenest pain. "We will not give you up. We will stand or fall together, friend."

Give *you* up! Give *you* up! Ha! The veil was lifted now, and I saw what the something with the cold breath going before it was. I looked quietly from her to her husband; and I asked--I fancy she thought my question strangely irrelevant at that moment, "How is he? Is he better?"

"Much better. He knew me for a moment," she answered. "Then he seemed to sink away again. But his eyes were quite clear."

I stood gazing down at his thin face, which had ever looked so kindly into mine. My fingers played idly with the knot of my sword. "He will live?" I asked abruptly, harshly.

She started at the sudden question. But, brutal as it must have sounded, she was looking at me in pity so great and generous that it did not wound her. "Oh, yes," she said, her eyes still clinging to me. "I think he will live, thank Heaven!"

Thank Heaven! Ah, yes, thank Heaven!

I turned and went slowly toward the door. But before I reached it she was at my side, nay, was on her knees by me, clasping my hand, looking up to me with streaming eyes. "What are you going to do?" she cried, reading, I suppose, something in my face.

"I will see if Master Lindstrom cannot get better terms for us," I answered.

She rose, still detaining me. "You are sure?" she said, still eying me jealously.

"Quite sure," I answered, forcing a smile. "I will come back and report to you."

She let me go then, and I went out and joined Lindstrom on the staircase.

"Are you certain," I asked, speaking in a whisper, "that they will--that the town will keep its word and let the others go?"

"I am quite sure of it," he replied nodding. "They are Germans, and hard and pitiless, but you may trust them. So far I will answer for them."

"Then we accept," I said gravely. "I give myself up. Let them take me."

CHAPTER XV.

BEFORE THE COURT.

I had not seen the first moonbeams pierce the broken casement of the tower-room, but I was there to watch the last tiny patch of silver glide aslant from wall to sill, and sill to frame, and so pass out. Near the fire, which had been made up, and now glowed and crackled bravely on the hearthstone at my elbow, my three jailers had set a mattress for me; and on this I sat, my back to the wall and my face to the window. The guards lounged on the other side of the hearth round a lantern, playing at dice and drinking. They were rough, hard men, whose features, as they leaned over the table and the light played strongly on their faces, blazoning them against a wall of shadow, were stern and rugged enough. But they had not shown themselves unkindly. They had given me a share of their wine, and had pointed to the window and shrugged their shoulders, as much as to say that it was my own fault if I suffered from the draught. Nay, from time to time, one of them would turn from his game and look at me--in pity, I think--and utter a curse that was meant for encouragement.

Even when the first excitement had passed away, I felt none of the stupefaction which I have heard that men feel in such a position. My brain was painfully active. In vain I longed to sleep, if it were only that I might not be thought to fear death. But the fact that I was to be tried first, though the sentence was a certainty, distracted and troubled me. My thoughts paced from thing to thing; now dwelling on the Duchess and her husband, now flitting to Petronilla and Sir Anthony, to the old place at home and the servants; to strange petty things, long familiar--a tree in the chase at Coton, an herb I had planted. Once a great lump rose in my throat, and I had to turn away to hide the hot tears that would rise at the thought that I must die in this mean German town, in this unknown corner, and be buried and forgotten! And once, too, to torment me, there rose a doubt in my mind whether Master Bertie would recover; whether, indeed, I had not thrown my life away for nothing. But it was too late to think of that! And the doubt, which the Evil One himself must have suggested, so terrible was it passed away quickly.

My thoughts raced, but the night crawled. We had surrendered about ten, and the magistrates, less pitiful than the jailers, had forbidden my friends to stay with me. An hour or more after midnight, two of the men lay down and the other sat humming a drinking-song, or at intervals rose to yawn and stretch himself and look out of the window. From time to time, the cry of the watchman going his rounds came drearily to my ears, recalling to me the night I had spent behind the boarding in Moorgate Street, when the adventure which was to end to-morrow--nay, to-day--in a few hours--had lured me away. To-day? Was I to die to-day? To perish with all my plans, hopes, love? It seemed impossible. As I gazed at the window, whose shape began to be printed on my brain, it seemed impossible. My soul so rose in rebellion against it, that the perspiration stood on my brow, and I had to clasp my hands about my knees, and strain every muscle to keep in the cry I would have uttered! a cry, not of fear, but of rage and remonstrance and revolt.

I was glad to see the first streaks of dawn, to hear the first cock-crowings, and, a few minutes later, the voices of men in the street and on the stairs. The sounds of day and life acted magically upon me. The horror of the night passed off as does the horror of a dream. When a man, heavily cloaked and with his head covered, came in, the door being shut behind him by another hand, I looked up at him bravely. The worst was past.

He replied by looking down at me for a few moments without disclosing himself, the collar of his cloak being raised so high that I could see nothing of his features. My first notion that he must be Master Lindstrom passed away; and, displeased by his silent scrutiny, and thinking him a stranger, I said sharply, "I hope you are satisfied, sir."

"Satisfied?" he replied, in a voice which made me start so that the irons clanked on my feet, "Well, I think I should be--seeing you so, my friend!"

It was Clarence! Of all men, Clarence! I knew his voice, and he, seeing himself recognized, lowered his cloak. I stared at him in stupefied silence, and he at me in a grim curiosity. I was not prepared for the blunt abruptness with which he continued--using almost the very words he had used when face to face with me in the flood: "Now tell me who you are, and what brought you into this company?"

I gave him no answer. I still stared at him in silence.

"Come!" he continued, his hawk's eyes bent on my face, "make a clean breast of it, and perhaps--who knows? I may help you yet, lad. You have puzzled and foiled me, and I want to understand you. Where did my lady pick you up just when she wanted you? I had arranged for every checker on the board except you. Who are you?"

This time I did answer him--by a question. "How many times have we met?" I asked.

"Three," he said readily, "and the last time you nearly rid the world of me. Now the luck is against you. It generally is in the end against those who thwart me, my friend." He chuckled at the conceit, and I read in his face at once his love of intrigue and his vanity. "I come uppermost, as always."

I only nodded.

"What do you want?" I asked. I felt a certain expectation. He wanted something.

"First, to know who you are."

"I shall not tell you!" I answered.

He smiled dryly, sitting opposite to me. He had drawn up a stool, and made himself comfortable. He was not an uncomely man as he sat there playing with his dagger, a dubious smile on his lean, dark face. Unwarned, I might have been attracted by the masterful audacity, the intellect as well as the force which I saw stamped on his features. Being warned, I read cunning in his bold eyes, and cruelty in the curl of his lip. "What do you want next?" I asked.

"I want to save your life," he replied lightly.

At that I started--I could not help it.

"Ha! ha!" he laughed, "I thought the stoicism did not go quite down to the bottom, my lad. But there, it is true enough, I have come to help you. I have come to save your life if you will let me."

I strove in vain to keep entire mastery over myself. The feelings to which he appealed were too strong for me. My voice sounded strange, even in my own ears, as I said hoarsely, "It is impossible! What can you do?"

"What can I do?" he answered with a stern smile. "Much! I have, boy, a dozen strings in my hands, and a neck--a life at the end of each!"

He raised his hand, and extending the fingers, moved them to and fro.

"See! see! A life, a death!" he exclaimed. "And for you, I can and will save your life--on one condition."

"On one condition?" I murmured.

"Ay, on one condition; but it is a very easy one. I will save your life on my part; and you, on yours, must give me a little assistance. Do you see? Then we shall be quits."

"I do not understand," I said dully. I did not. His words had set my heart fluttering so that I could for the moment take in only one idea--that here was a new hope of life.

"It is very simple," he resumed, speaking slowly. "Certain plans of mine require that I should get your friend the Duchess conveyed back to England. But for you I should have succeeded before this. In what you have hindered me, you can now help me. You have their confidence and great influence with them. All I ask is that you will use that influence so that they may be at a certain place at a certain hour. I will contrive the rest. It shall never be known, I promise you, that you----"

"Betrayed them!"

"Well, gave me some information," he said lightly, puffing away my phrase.

"No. Betrayed them!" I persisted.

"Put it so, if you please," he replied, shrugging his shoulders and raising his eyebrows. "What is in a word?"

"You are the tempter himself, I think!" I cried in bitter rage--for it *was* bitter--bitter, indeed, to feel that new-born hope die out. "But you come to me in vain. I defy you!"

"Softly! softly!" he answered with calmness.

Yet I saw a little pulse beating in his cheek that seemed to tell of some emotion kept in subjection.

"It frightens you at first," he said. "But listen. You will do them no harm, and yourself good. I shall get them anyway, both the Duchess and her husband; though, without your aid, it will be more difficult. Why, help of that kind is given every day. They need never know it. Even now there is one of whom you little dream who has----"

"Silence!" I cried fiercely. "I care not. I defy you!"

I could think of only one thing. I was wild with rage and disappointment. His words had aggravated the pain of every regret, every clinging to life I felt.

"Go!" I cried. "Go and leave me, you villain!"

"If I do leave you," he said, fixing his eyes on me, "it will be, my friend--to death."

"Then so be it!" I answered wildly. "So be it! I will keep my honor."

"Your honor!" The mask dropped from his face, and he sneered as he rose from his seat. A darker scowl changed and disfigured his brow, as he lost hope of gaining me. "Your honor? Where will it be by to-night?" he hissed, his eyes glowering down at me. "Where a week hence, when you will be cast into a pit and forgotten? Your honor, fool? What is the honor of a dead man? Pah! But die, then, if you will have it so! Die, like the brainless brute you are! And rot, and be forgotten!" he concluded passionately.

They were terrible words; more terrible I know now than either he or I understood then. They so shook me that when he was gone I crouched trembling on my pallet, hiding my face in a fit of horror--taking no heed of my jailers or of appearances. "Die and be forgotten! Die and be forgotten!" The doom rang in my ears.

Something which seemed to me angelic roused me from this misery. It was the sound of a kindly, familiar voice speaking English. I looked up and found the Dutchman bending over me with a face of infinite distress. With him, but rather behind him, stood Van Tree, pale and vicious-eyed, tugging his scanty chin-beard and gazing about him like a dog seeking some one to fasten upon. "Poor lad! poor lad!" the old man said, his voice shaking as he looked at me.

I sprang to my feet, the irons rattling as I dashed my hand across my eyes.

"It is all right!" I said hurriedly. "I had a--but never mind that. It was like a dream. Only tell the Duchess to look to herself," I continued, still rather vehemently. "Clarence is here. He is in Santon. I have seen him."

"You have seen him?" both the Dutchmen cried at once.

"Ay!" I said, with a laugh that was three parts hysterical--indeed, I was still tingling all over with excitement. "He has been here to offer me my life if I would help him in his schemes. I told him he was the tempter, and defied him. And he--he said I should die and be forgotten!" I added, trembling, yet laughing wildly at the same time.

"I think he *is* the tempter!" said Master Lindstrom solemnly, his face very grim. "And therefore a liar and the father of lies! You may die, lad, to-day; perhaps you must. But forgotten you shall not be, while we live, or one of us lives, or one of the children who shall come after us. He is a liar!"

I got my hands, with a struggle, from the old man, and turning my back upon him, went and looked out of the window. The sun was rising. The tower of the great minster, seen row for the first time, rose in stately brightness above the red roofs and quaint gables and the rows of dormer windows. Down in the streets the grayness and chill yet lingered. But above was a very glory of light and warmth and color--the rising of the May sun. When I turned round I was myself again. The calm beauty of that sight had stolen into my soul. "Is it time?" I said cheerfully. For the crowd was gathering below, and there were voices and feet on the stairs.

"I think it is," Master Lindstrom answered. "We have obtained leave to go with you. You need fear no violence in the streets, for the man who was hurt is still alive and may recover. I have been with the magistrates this morning," he continued, "and found them better disposed to you; but the Sub-dean has joint jurisdiction with them, as the deputy of the Bishop of Arras, who is dean of the minster; and he is, for some reason, very bitter against you."

"The Bishop of Arras? Granville, do you mean?" I asked. I knew the name of the Emperor's shrewd and powerful minister, by whose advice the Netherlands were at this time ruled.

"The same. He, of course, is not here, but his deputy is. Were it not for him---- But there, it is no good talking of that!" the Dutchman said, breaking off and rubbing his head in his chagrin.

One of the guards who had spent the night with me brought me at this moment a bowl of broth with a piece of bread in it. I could not eat the bread, but I drank the broth and felt the better for it. Having in my pocket a little money with which the Duchess had furnished me, I put a silver piece in the bowl and handed it back to him. The man seemed astonished, and muttered something in German as he turned away.

"What did he say?" I asked the Dutchman.

"Oh, nothing, nothing," he answered.

"But what was it? It was something," I persisted, seeing him confused.

"He--well, he said he would have a mass said for you!" Lindstrom answered in despair. "It will do no harm."

"No, why should it?" I replied mechanically.

We were in the street by this time, Master Lindstrom and Van Tree walking beside me in the middle of a score of soldiers, who seemed to my eyes fantastically dressed. I remarked, as we passed out, a tall man clothed in red and black, who was standing by the door as if waiting to fall in behind me. He carried on his shoulder a long broad-bladed sword, and I guessed who he was, seeing how Master Lindstrom strove to intercept my view of him. But I was not afraid of *that*. I had heard long ago--perhaps six months in time, but it seemed long ago--how bravely Queen Jane had died. And if a girl had not trembled, surely a man should not. So I looked steadfastly at him, and took great courage, and after that was able to gaze calmly on the people, who pressed to stare at me, peeping over the soldiers' shoulders, and clustering in every doorway and window to see me go past. They were all silent, and it even seemed to me that some--but this may have been my fancy--pitied me.

I saw nothing of the Duchess, and might have wondered, had not Master Lindstrom explained that he had contrived to keep her in ignorance of the hour fixed for the proceedings. Her husband was better, he said, and conscious; but, for fear of exciting him, they were keeping the news from him also. I remember I felt for a moment very sore at this, and then I tried to persuade myself that it was right.

The distance through the streets was short, and almost before I was aware of it I was in the court-house, the guard had fallen back, and I was standing before three persons who were seated behind a long table. Two of them were grave, portly men wearing flat black caps and scarlet robes, with gold chains about their necks. The third, dressed as an ecclesiastic, wore a huge gem ring upon his thumb. Behind them stood three attendants holding a sword, a crosier, and a ducal cap upon a cushion; and above and behind all was a lofty stained window, whose rich hues, the sun being low as yet, shot athwart the corbels of the roof. At the end of the table sat a black-robed man with an ink-horn and spectacles, a grave, still, down-looking man; and the crowd being behind me, and preserving a dead silence, and the attendants standing like statues, I seemed indeed to be alone with these four at the table, and the great stained window and the solemn hush. They talked to one another in low tones for a minute, gazing at me the while. And I fancied they were astonished to find me so young.

At length they all fell back into their chairs. "Do you speak German?" the eldest burgher said, addressing me gravely. He sat in the middle, with the Sub-dean on his right.

"No; but I speak and understand Spanish," I answered in that language, feeling chilled already by the stern formality which like an iron hand was laying its grip upon me.

"Good! Your name?" replied the president.

"I am commonly called Francis Carey, and I am an Englishman." The Sub-dean--he was a pale, stout man, with gloomy eyes--had hitherto been looking at me in evident doubt. But at this he nodded assent, and, averting his eyes from me, gazed meditatively at the roof of the hall, considering apparently what he should have for breakfast.

"You are charged," said the president slowly, consulting a document, "with having assaulted and wounded in the highway last night one Heinrich Schröder, a citizen of this town, acting at the time as Lieutenant of the Night Guard. Do you admit this, prisoner, or do you require proof?"

"He was wounded," I answered steadily, "but by mistake, and in error. I supposed him to be one of three persons who had unlawfully waylaid me and my party on the previous night between Emmerich and Wesel."

The Sub-dean, still gazing at the roof, shook his head with a faint smile. The other magistrates looked doubtfully at me, but made no comment, and my words seemed to be wasted on the silence. The president consulted his document again, and continued: "You are also charged with having by force of arms, in time of peace, seized a gate of this town, and maintained it, and declined to surrender it when called upon so to do. What do you say to that?"

"It is true in part," I answered firmly. "I seized not the gate, but part of the tower, in order to preserve my life and to protect certain ladies traveling with me from the violence of a crowd which, under a misapprehension, was threatening to do us a mischief."

The priest again shook his head, and smiled faintly at the carved roof. His colleagues were perhaps somewhat moved in my favor, for a few words passed between them. However, in the end they shook their heads, and the president mechanically asked me if I had anything further to say.

"Nothing!" I replied bitterly. The ecclesiastic's cynical heedlessness, his air of one whose mind is made up, seemed so cruel to me whose life was at stake, that I lost patience. "Except what I have said," I continued--"that for the wounding, it was done in error; and for the gate-seizing, I would do it again to save the lives of those with me. Only that and this: that I am a foreigner ignorant of your language and customs, desiring only to pass peacefully through your country."

"That is all?" the president asked impassively.

"All," I answered, yet with a strange tightening at my throat. Was it all? All I could say for my life?

I was waiting, sore and angry and desperate, to hear the sentence, when there came an interruption. Master Lindstrom, whose presence at my side I had forgotten, broke suddenly into a torrent of impassioned words, and his urgent voice, ringing through the court, seemed in a moment to change its aspect--to infuse into it some degree of life and sympathy. More than one guttural exclamation, which seemed to mark approval, burst from the throng at the back of the hall. In another moment, indeed, the Dutchman's courage might have saved me. But there was one who marked the danger. The Sub-dean, who had at first only glowered at the speaker in rude astonishment, now cut him short with a harsh question.

"One moment, Master Dutchman!" he cried. "Are you one of the heretics who call themselves Protestants?"

"I am. But I understand that there is here liberty of conscience," our friend answered manfully, nothing daunted in his fervor at finding the attack turned upon himself.

"That depends upon the conscience," the priest answered with a scowl. "We will have no Anabaptists here, nor foreign praters to bring us into feud with our neighbors. It is enough that such men as you are allowed to live. We will not be bearded by you, so take warning! Take heed, I say, Master Dutchman, and be silent!" he repeated, leaning forward and clapping his hand upon the table.

I touched Master Lindstrom's sleeve--who would of himself have persisted--and stayed him. "It is of no use," I muttered. "That dog in a crochet has condemned me. He will have his way!"

There was a short debate between the three judges, while in the court you might have heard a pin drop. Master Lindstrom had fallen back once more. I was alone again, and the stained window seemed to be putting forth its mystic influence to enfold me, when, looking up, I saw a tiny shadow flit across the soft many-hued rays which streamed from it athwart the roof. It passed again, once, twice, thrice. I peered upward intently. It was a swallow flying to and fro amid the carved work.

Yes, a swallow. And straightway I forgot the judges; forgot the crowd. The scene vanished and I was at Coton End again, giving Martin Luther the nest for Petronilla--a sign, as I meant it then, that I should return. I should never return now. Yet my heart was on a sudden so softened that, instead of this reflection giving me pain, as one would have expected, it only filled me with a great anxiety to provide for the event. She must not wait and watch for me day after day, perhaps year after year. I must see to it somehow; and I was thinking with such intentness of this, that it was only vaguely I heard the sentence pronounced. It might have been some other person who was to be beheaded at the east gate an hour before noon. And so God save the Duke!

CHAPTER XVI.

IN THE DUKE'S NAME.

They took me back to the room in the tower, it being now nearly ten o'clock. Master Lindstrom would fain have stayed with me constantly to the end, but having the matter I have mentioned much in my mind, I begged him to go and get me writing materials. When he returned Van Tree was with him. With a particularity very curious at that moment, I remarked that the latter was carrying something.

"Where did you get that?" I said sharply and at once.

"It is your haversack," he answered, setting it down quietly. "I found the man who had taken possession of your horse, and got it from him. I thought there might be something in it you might like."

"It is my haversack," I assented. "But it was not on my horse. I have not seen it since I left it in Master Lindstrom's house by the river. I left it on the pallet in my room there, and it was forgotten. I searched for it at Emmerich, you remember."

"I only know," he replied, "that I discovered it behind the saddle of the horse you were riding yesterday."

He thought that I had become confused and was a little wrong-headed from excitement. Master Lindstrom also felt troubled, as he told me afterward, at seeing me taken up with a trifle at such a time.

But there was nothing wrong with my wits, as I promptly showed them.

"The horse I was riding yesterday?" I continued. "Ah! then, I understand. I was riding the horse which I took from the Spanish trooper. The Spaniard must have annexed the haversack when he and his companions searched the house after our departure."

"That is it, no doubt," Master Lindstrom said. "And in the hurry of yesterday's ride you failed to notice it."

It was a strange way of recovering one's property--strange that the enemy should have helped one to it. But there are times--and this to me was one--when the strange seems the ordinary and commonplace. I took the sack and slipped my hand through a well-known slit in the lining. Yes, the letter I had left there was there still--the letter to Mistress Clarence. I drew it out. The corners of the little packet were frayed, and the parchment was stained and discolored, no doubt by the damp which had penetrated to it. But the seal was whole. I placed it, as it was, in Master Lindstrom's hands.

"Give it," I said, "to the Duchess afterward. It concerns her. You have heard us talk about it. Bid her make what use she pleases of it."

I turned away then and sat down, feeling a little flurried and excited, as one about to start upon a journey might feel; not afraid nor exceedingly depressed, but braced up to make a brave show and hide what sadness I did feel by the knowledge that many eyes were upon me, and that more would be watching me presently. At the far end of the room a number of people had now gathered, and were conversing together. Among them were not only my jailers of the night, but two or three officers, a priest who had come to offer me his services, and some inquisitive gazers who had obtained admission. Their curiosity, however, did not distress me. On the contrary, I was glad to hear the stir and murmur of life about me to the last.

I will not set down the letter I wrote to the Duchess, though it were easy for me to do so, seeing that her son has it now. It contains some things very proper to be said by a dying man, of which I am not ashamed-- God forbid! but which it would not be meet for me to repeat here. Enough that I told her in a few words who I was, and entreated her, in the name of whatever services I had rendered her, to let Petronilla and Sir Anthony know how I had died. And I added something which would, I thought, comfort her and her husband--namely, that I was not afraid, or in any suffering of mind or body.

The writing of this shook my composure a little. But as I laid down the pen and looked up and found that the time was come, I took courage in a marvelous manner. The captain of the guard--I think that out of a compassionate desire not to interrupt me they had allowed me some minutes of grace--came to me, leaving the group at the other end, and told me gravely that I was waited for. I rose at once and gave the letter to Master Lindstrom with some messages in which Dymphna and Anne were not forgotten. And then, with a smile--for I felt under all those eyes as if I were going into battle--I said: "Gentlemen, I am ready if you are. It is a fine day to die. You know," I added gayly, "in England we have a proverb, 'The better the day, the better the deed!' So it is well to have a good day to have a good death, Sir Captain."

"A soldier's death, sir, is a good death;" he answered gravely, speaking in Spanish and bowing.

Then he pointed to the door.

As I walked toward it, I paused momentarily by the window, and looked out on the crowd below. It filled the sunlit street--save where a little raised platform strewn with rushes protruded itself--with heads from wall to wall, with faces all turned one way--toward me. It was a silent crowd standing in hushed awe and expectation, the consciousness of which for an instant sent a sudden chill to my heart, blanching my cheek, and making my blood run slow for a moment. The next I moved on to the door, and bowing to the spectators as they stood aside, began to descend the narrow staircase.

There were guards going down before me, and behind me were Master Lindstrom and more guards. The Dutchman reached forward in the gloom, and clasped my hand, holding it, as we went down, in a firm, strong grip.

"Never fear," I said to him cheerily, looking back. "It is all right."

He answered in words which I will not write here; not wishing, as I have said, to make certain things common.

I suppose the doorway at the bottom was accidentally blocked, for a few steps short of it we came to a standstill; and almost at the same moment I started, despite myself, on hearing a sudden clamor and a roar of many voices outside.

"What is it?" I asked the Dutchman.

"It is the Duke of Cleves arriving, I expect," he whispered. "He comes in by the other gate."

A moment later we moved on and passed out into the light, the soldiers before me stepping on either side to give me place. The sunshine for an instant dazzled me, and I lowered my eyes. As I gradually raised them again I saw before me a short lane formed by two rows of spectators kept back by guards; and at the end of this, two or three rough wooden steps leading to a platform on which were standing a number of people. And above and beyond all only the bright blue sky, the roofs and gables of the nearer houses showing dark against it.

I advanced steadily along the path left for me, and would have ascended the steps. But at the foot of them I came to a standstill, and looked round for guidance. The persons on the scaffold all had their backs turned to me, and did not make way, while the shouting and uproar hindered them from hearing that we had come out. Then it struck me, seeing that the people at the windows were also gazing away, and taking no heed of me, that the Duke was passing the farther end of the street, and a sharp pang of angry pain shot through me. I had come out to die, but that which was all to me was so little to these people that they turned away to see a fellow-mortal ride by!

Presently, as we stood there, in a pit, as it were, getting no view, I felt Master Lindstrom's hand, which still clasped mine, begin to shake; and turning to him, I found that his face had changed to a deep red, and that his eyes were protruding with a kind of convulsive eagerness which instantly infected me.

"What is it?" I stammered. I began to tremble also. The air rang, it seemed to me, with one word, which a thousand tongues took up and reiterated. But it was a German word, and I did not understand it.

"Wait! wait!" Master Lindstrom exclaimed. "Pray God it be true!"

He seized my other hand and held it as though he would protect me from something. At the same moment Van Tree pushed past me, and, bounding up the steps, thrust his way through the officials on the scaffold, causing more than one fur-robed citizen near the edge to lose his balance and come down as best he could on the shoulders of the guards.

"What is it?" I cried. "What is it?" I cried in impatient wonder.

"Oh! my lad, my lad!" Master Lindstrom answered, his face close to mine, and the tears running down his cheeks. "It is cruel if it be not true! Cruel! They cry a pardon!"

"A pardon?" I echoed.

"Ay, lad, a pardon. But it may not be true," he said, putting his arm about my shoulder. "Do not make too sure of it. It is only the mob cry it out."

My heart made a great bound, and seemed to stand still. There was a loud surging in my brain, and a mist rose before my eyes and hid everything. The clamor and shouting of the street passed away, and sounded vague and distant. The next instant, it is true, I was myself again, but my knees were trembling under me, and I stood flaccid and unnerved, leaning on my friend.

"Well?" I said faintly.

"Patience! patience a while, lad!" he answered.

But, thank Heaven! I had not long to wait. The words were scarcely off his tongue, when another hand sought mine and shook it wildly; and I saw Van Tree before me, his face radiant with joy, while a man whom he had knocked down in his hasty leap from the scaffold was rising beside me with a good-natured smile. As if at a signal, every face now turned toward me. A dozen friendly hands passed me up the steps amid a fresh outburst of cheering. The throng on the scaffold opened somehow, and I found myself in a second, as it seemed, face to face with the president of the court. He smiled on me gravely and kindly--what smiles there seemed to be on all those faces--and held out a paper.

"In the name of the Duke!" he said, speaking in Spanish, in a clear, loud voice. "A pardon!"

I muttered something, I know not what; nor did it matter, for it was lost in a burst of cheering. When this was over and silence obtained, the magistrate continued, "You are required, however, to attend the Duke at the courthouse. Whither we had better proceed at once."

"I am ready, sir," I muttered.

A road was made for us to descend, and, walking in a kind of beautiful dream, I passed slowly up the street by the side of the magistrate, the crowd everywhere willingly standing aside for us. I do not know whether all those thousands of faces really looked joyfully and kindly on me as I passed, or whether the deep thankfulness which choked me, and brought the tears continually to my eyes, transfigured them and gave them a generous charm not their own. But this I do know: that the sunshine seemed brighter and the air softer than ever before; that the clouds trailing across the blue expanse were things of beauty such as I had never met before; that to draw breath was a joy, and to move, delight; and that only when the dark valley was left behind did I comprehend its full gloom--by Heaven's mercy. So may it be with all!

At the door of the court-house, whither numbers of the people had already run, the press was so great that we came to a standstill, and were much buffeted about, though in all good humor, before, even with the aid of the soldiers, we could be got through the throng. When I at last emerged I found myself again before the table, and saw--but only dimly, for the light now fell through the stained window directly on my head--a commanding figure standing behind it. Then a strange thing happened. A woman passed swiftly round the table, and came to me and flung her arms round my neck and kissed me. It was the Duchess, and for a moment she hung upon me, weeping before them all.

"Madam," I said softly, "then it is you who have done this!"

"Ah!" she exclaimed, holding me off from her and looking at me with eyes which glowed through her tears, "and it was you who did that!"

She drew back from me then, and took me by the hand, and turned impetuously to the Duke of Cleves, who stood behind smiling at her in frank amusement. "This," she said, "is the man who gave his life for my husband, and to whom your highness has given it back."

"Let him tell his tale," the Duke answered gravely. "And do you, my cousin, sit here beside me."

She left me and walked round the table, and he came forward and placed her in his own chair amid a great hush of wonder, for she was still meanly clad, and showed in a hundred places the marks and stains of travel. Then he stood by her with his hand on the back of the seat. He was a tall, burly man, with bold, quick-glancing eyes, a flushed face, and a loud manner; a fierce, blusterous prince, as I have heard. He was plainly dressed in a leather hunting-suit, and wore huge gauntlets and brown boots, with a broad-leaved hat pinned up on one side. Yet he looked a prince.

Somehow I stammered out the tale of the surrender.

"But why? why? why, man?" he asked, when I had finished; "why did you let them think it was you who wounded the burgher, if it was not?"

"Your highness," I answered, "I had received nothing but good from her grace, I had eaten her bread and been received into her service. Besides, it was through my persuasion that we came by the road which led to this misfortune instead of by another way. Therefore it seemed to me right that I should suffer, who stood alone and could be spared--and not her husband."

"It was a great deed!" cried the prince loudly. "I would I had such a servant. Are you noble, lad?"

I colored high, but not in pain or mortification. The old wound might reopen, but amid events such as those of this morning it was a slight matter. "I come of a noble family, may it please your highness," I answered modestly; "but circumstances prevent me claiming kinship with it."

He was about, I think, to question me further, when the Duchess looked up, and said something to him and he something to her. She spoke again and he answered. Then he nodded assent. "You would fain stand on your own feet?" he cried to me. "Is that so?"

"It is, sire," I answered.

"Then so be it!" he replied loudly, looking round on the throng with a frown. "I will ennoble you. You would have died for your lord and friend, and therefore I give you a rood of land in the common graveyard of Santon to hold of me, and I name you Von Santonkirch. And I, William, Duke of Cleves, Julich and Guelders, prince of the Empire, declare you noble, and give you for your arms three swords of justice; and the motto you may buy of a clerk! Further, let this decree be enrolled in my Chancery. Are you satisfied?"

As I dropped on my knees, my eyes sparkling, there was a momentary disturbance behind me. It was caused by the abrupt entrance of the Sub-dean. He took in part of the situation at a glance; that is, he saw me kneeling before the Duke. But he could not see the Duchess of Suffolk, the Duke's figure being interposed. As he came forward, the crowd making way for him, he cast an angry glance at me, and scarcely smoothed his brow even to address the prince. "I am glad that your highness has not done what was reported to me," he said hastily, his obeisance brief and perfunctory. "I heard an uproar in the town, and was told that this man was pardoned."

"It is so!" said the Duke curtly, eying the ecclesiastic with no great favor. "He is pardoned."

"Only in part, I presume," the priest rejoined urgently. "Or, if otherwise, I am sure that your highness has not received certain information with which I can furnish you."

"Furnish away, sir," quoth the Duke, yawning.

"I have had letters from my Lord Bishop of Arras respecting him."

"Respecting him!" exclaimed the prince, starting and bending his brows in surprise.

"Respecting those in whose company he travels," the priest answered hastily. "They are represented to me as dangerous persons, pestilent refugees from England, and obnoxious alike to the Emperor, the Prince of Spain, and the Queen of England."

"I wonder you do not add also to the King of France and the Soldan of Turkey!" growled the Duke. "Pish! I am not going to be dictated to by Master Granvelle--no, nor by his master, be he ten times Emperor! Go to! Go to! Master Sub-dean! You forget yourself, and so does your master the Bishop. I will have you know that these people are not what you think them. Call you my cousin, the widow of the consort of the late Queen of France, an obnoxious person? Fie! Fie! You forget yourself!"

He moved as he stopped speaking, so that the astonished churchman found himself confronted on a sudden by the smiling, defiant Duchess. The Sub-dean started and his face fell, for, seeing her seated in the Duke's presence, he discerned at once that the game was played out. Yet he rallied himself, bethinking him, I fancy, that there were many spectators. He made a last effort. "The Bishop of Arras----" he began.

"Pish!" scoffed the Duke, interrupting him.

"The Bishop of Arras----" the priest repeated firmly.

"I would he were hung with his own tapestry!" retorted the Duke, with a brutal laugh.

"Heaven forbid!" replied the ecclesiastic, his pale face reddening and his eyes darting baleful glances at me. But he took the hint, and henceforth said no more of the Bishop. Instead, he continued smoothly, "Your highness has, of course, considered the danger--the danger, I mean, of provoking neighbors so powerful by shielding this lady and making her cause your own. You will remember, sir----"

"I will remember Innspruck!" roared the Duke, in a rage, "where the Emperor, ay, and your everlasting Bishop too, fled before a handful of Protestants, like sheep before wolves. A fig for your Emperor! I never feared him young, and I fear him less now that he is old and decrepit and, as men say, mad. Let him get to his watches, and you to your prayers. If there were not this table between us, I would pull your ears, Master Churchman!"

*   *   *   *   *

"But tell me," I asked Master Bertie as I stood beside his couch an hour later, "how did the Duchess manage it? I gathered from something you or she said, a short time back, that you had no influence with the Duke of Cleves."

"Not quite that," he answered. "My wife and the late Duke of Suffolk had much to do with wedding the Prince's sister to King Henry, thirteen--fourteen years back, is it? And so far we might have felt confident of his protection. But the marriage turned out ill, or turned out short, and Queen Anne of Cleves was divorced. And--well, we felt a little less confident on that account, particularly as he has the name of a headstrong, passionate man."

"Heaven keep him in it!" I said, smiling. "But you have not told me yet what happened."

"The Duchess was still asleep this morning, fairly worn out, as you may suppose, when a great noise awoke her. She got up and went to Dymphna, and learned it was the Duke's trumpets. Then she went to the window, and, seeing few people in the streets to welcome him, inquired why this was. Dymphna broke down at that, and told her what was happening to you, and that you were to die at that very hour. She went out straightway, without covering her head,--you know how impetuous she is,--and flung herself on her knees in the mud before the Duke's horse as he entered. He knew her, and the rest you can guess."

Can guess? Ah, what happiness it was! Outside, the sun fell hotly on the steep red roofs, with their rows of casements, and on the sleepy square, in which knots of people still lingered, talking of the morning's events. I could see below me the guard which Duke William, shrewdly mistrusting the Sub-dean, had posted in front of the house, nominally to do the Duchess honor. I could hear in the next room the cheerful voices of my friends. What happiness it was to live! What happiness to be loved! How very, very good and beautiful and glorious a world, seemed the world to me on that old May morning in that quaint German town which we had entered so oddly!

As I turned from the window full of thankfulness, my eyes met those of Mistress Anne, who was sitting on the far side of the sick man's couch, the baby in a cradle beside her. The risk and exposure of the last week had made a deeper mark upon her than upon any of us. She was paler, graver, older, more of a woman and less, much less, of a girl. And she looked very ill. Her eyes, in particular, seemed to have grown larger, and as they dwelt on me now there was a strange and solemn light in them, under which I grew uneasy.

"You have been wonderfully preserved," she said presently, speaking dreamily, and as much to herself as to me.

"I have, indeed," I answered, thinking she referred only to my escape of the morning.

But she did not.

"There was, firstly, the time on the river when you were hurt with the oar," she continued, gazing absently at me, her hands in her lap; "and then the night when you saw Clarence with Dymphna."

"Or, rather, saw him without her," I interposed, smiling. It was strange that she should mention it as a fact, when at the time she had so scolded me for making the statement.

"And then," she continued, disregarding my interruption, "there was the time when you were stabbed in the passage; and again when you had the skirmish by the river; and then to-day you were within a minute of death. You have been wonderfully preserved!"

"I have," I assented thoughtfully. "The more as I suspect that I have to thank Master Clarence for all these little adventures."

"Strange--very strange!" she muttered, removing her eyes from me that she might fix them on the floor.

"What is strange?"

The abrupt questioner was the Duchess, who came bustling in at the moment. "What is strange?" she repeated, with a heightened color and dancing eyes. "Shall I tell you?" She paused and looked brightly at me, holding something concealed behind her. I guessed in a moment, from the aspect of her face, what it was: the letter which I had given to Master Lindstrom in the morning, and which, with a pardonable forgetfulness, I had failed to reclaim.

I turned very red. "It was not intended for you now," I said shyly. For in the letter I had told her my story.

"Pooh! pooh!" she cried. "It is just as I thought. A pretty piece of folly! No," she continued, as I opened my mouth, "I am not going to keep your secret, sir. You may go down on your knees. It will be of no use. Richard, you remember Sir Anthony Cludde of Coton End in Warwickshire?"

"Oh, yes," her husband said, rising on his elbow, while his face lit up, and I stood bashfully, shifting my feet.

"I have danced with him a dozen times, years ago!" she continued, her eyes sparkling with mischief. "Well, sir, this gentleman, Master Francis Carey, otherwise Von Santonkirch, is Francis Cludde, his nephew!"

"Sir Anthony's nephew?"

"Yes, and the son of Ferdinand Cludde, whom you also have heard of, of whom the less----"

She stopped, and turned quickly, interrupted by a half-stifled scream. It was a scream full of sudden horror and amazement and fear; and it came from Mistress Anne. The girl had risen, and was gazing at me with distended eyes and blanched cheeks, and hands stretched out to keep me off--gazing, indeed, as if she saw in me some awful portent or some dreadful threat. She did not speak, but she began, without taking her eyes from me, to retreat toward the door.

"Hoity toity!" cried my lady, stamping her foot in anger. "What has happened to the girl? What----"

What, indeed? The Duchess stopped, still more astonished. For, without uttering a word of explanation or apology, Mistress Anne had reached the door, groped blindly for the latch, found it, and gone out, her eyes, with the same haunted look of horror in them, fixed on me to the last.

CHAPTER XVII.

A LETTER THAT HAD MANY ESCAPES.

"Hoity, toity!" the Duchess cried again, looking from one to another of us when Anne had disappeared. "What has come to the little fool? Has she gone crazy?"

I shook my head, too completely at sea even to hazard a conjecture. Master Bertie shook his head also, keeping his eyes glued to the door, as if he could not believe Anne had really gone.

"I said nothing to frighten her!" my lady protested.

"Nothing at all," I answered. For how should the announcement that my real name was Cludde terrify Mistress Anne Brandon nearly out of her senses?

"Well, no," Master Bertie agreed, his thoughtful face more thoughtful than usual; "so far as I heard, you said nothing. But I think, my dear, that you had better follow her and learn what it is. She must be ill."

The Duchess sat down. "I will go by-and-by," she said coolly, at which I was not much surprised, for I have always remarked that women have less sympathy with other women's ailments, especially of the nerves, than have men.

"For the moment I want to scold this brave, silly boy here!" she continued, looking so kindly at me that I blushed again, and forgot all about Mistress Anne. "To think of him leaving his home to become a wandering squire of dames merely because his father was a--well, not quite what he would have liked him to be! I remember something about him," she continued, pursing up her lips, and nodding her head at us. "I fancied him dead, however, years ago. But there! if every one whose father were not quite to his liking left home and went astraying, Master Francis, all sensible folk would turn innkeepers, and make their fortunes."

"It was not only that which drove me from home," I explained. "The Bishop of Winchester gave me clearly to understand----"

"That Coton was not the place for you!" exclaimed my lady scornfully. "He is a sort of connection of yours, is he not? Oh, I know. And he thinks he has a kind of reversionary interest in the property! With you and your father out of the way, and only your girl cousin left, his interest is much more likely to come to hand. Do you see?"

I recalled what Martin Luther had said about the cuckoo. But I have since thought that probably they both wronged Stephen Gardiner in this. He was not a man of petty mind, and his estate was equal to his high place. I think it more likely that his motive in removing me from Coton was chiefly the desire to use my services abroad, in conjunction perhaps with some remoter and darker plan for eventually devoting the Cludde property to the Church. Such an act of piety would have been possible had Sir Anthony died leaving his daughter unmarried, and would certainly have earned for the Chancellor Queen Mary's lasting favor. I think it the more likely to have been in his mind because his inability to persuade the gentry to such acts of restitution--King Harry had much enriched us--was always a sore point with the Queen, and more than once exposed him to her resentment.

"The strangest thing of all," the Duchess continued with alacrity, "seems to me to be this: that if he had not meddled with you, he would not have had his plans in regard to us thwarted. If he had not driven you from home, you would never have helped me to escape from London, nor been with us to foil his agents."

"A higher power than the Chancellor arranged that!" said Master Bertie emphatically.

"Well, at any rate, I am glad that you are you!" the Duchess answered, rising gayly. "A Cludde? Why, one feels at home again. And yet," she continued, her lips trembling suddenly, and her eyes filling with tears as she looked at me, "there was never house raised yet on nobler deed than yours."

"Go! go! go!" cried her husband, seeing my embarrassment. "Go and look to that foolish girl!"

"I will! Yet stop!" cried my lady, pausing when she was half way across the floor, and returning, "I was forgetting that I have another letter to open. It is very odd that this letter was never opened before," she continued, producing that which had lain in my haversack. "It has had several narrow escapes. But this time I vow I will see inside it. You give me leave?"

"Oh, yes," I said, smiling. "I wash my hands of it. Whoever the Mistress Clarence to whom it is addressed may be, it is enough that her name is Clarence! We have suffered too much at his hands."

"I open it, then!" my lady cried dramatically. I nodded. She took her husband's dagger and cut the green silk which bound the packet, and opened and read.

Only a few words. Then she stopped, and looking off the paper, shivered. "I do not understand this," she murmured. "What does it mean?"

"No good! I'll be sworn!" Master Bertie replied, gazing at her eagerly. "Read it aloud, Katherine."

"'To Mistress A---- B----. I am advertised by my trusty agent, Master Clarence, that he hath benefited much by your aid in the matter in which I have employed him. Such service goeth always for much, and never for naught, with me. In which belief confirm yourself. For the present, working with him as heretofore, be secret, and on no account let your true sentiments come to light. So you will be the more valuable to me, even as it is more easy to unfasten a barred door from within than from without.'"

Here the Duchess broke off abruptly, and turned on us a face full of wonder. "What does it mean?" she asked.

"Is that all?" her husband said.

"Not quite," she answered, returning to it, and reading:

"'Those whom you have hitherto served have too long made a mockery of sacred things, but their cup is full and the business of seeing that they drink it lieth with me, who am not wont to be slothful in these matters. Be faithful and secret. Good speed and fare you well.--Ste. Winton."

"One thing is quite clear!" said Master Bertie slowly. "That you and I are the persons whose cup is full. You remember how you once dressed up a dog in a rochet, and dandled it before Gardiner? And it is our matter in which Clarence is employed. Then who is it who has been cooperating with him, and whose aid is of so much value to him?"

"'Even as it is easier,'" I muttered thoughtfully, "'to unfasten a barred door from within than from without." What was it of which that strange sentence reminded me? Ha! I had it. Of the night on which we had fled from Master Lindstrom's house, when Mistress Anne had been seized with that odd fit of perverseness, and had almost opened the door looking upon the river in spite of all I could say or do. It was of that the sentence reminded me. "To whom is it addressed?" I asked abruptly.

"To Mistress Clarence," my lady answered.

"No; inside, I mean."

"Oh! to Mistress A---- B----. But that gives us no clew," she added. "It is a disguise. You see they are the two first letters of the alphabet."

So they were. And the initial letters of Anne Brandon! I wondered that the Duchess did not see it, that she did not at once turn her suspicions toward the right quarter. But she was, for a woman, singularly truthful and confiding. And she saw nothing.

I looked at Master Bertie. He seemed puzzled, discerning, I fancy, how strangely the allusions pointed to Mistress Anne, but not daring at once to draw the inference. She was his wife's kinswoman by marriage--albeit a distant one--and much indebted to her. She had been almost as his own sister. She was young and fair, and to associate treachery and ingratitude such as this with her seemed almost too horrible.

Then why was I so clear sighted as to read the riddle? Why was I the first to see the truth? Because I had felt for days a vague and ill-defined distrust of the girl. I had seen more of her odd fits and caprices than had the others. Looking back now I could find a confirmation of my idea in a dozen things which had befallen us. I remembered how ill and stricken she had looked on the day when I had first brought out the letter, and how strangely she had talked to me about it. I remembered Clarence's interview with, not Dymphna,--as I had then thought,--but, as I now guessed, Anne, wearing her cloak. I recalled the manner in which she had used me to persuade Master Bertie to take the Wesel instead of the Santon road; no doubt she had told Clarence to follow in that direction, if by any chance we escaped him on the island. And her despair when she heard in the church porch that I had killed Clarence at the ford! And her utter abandonment to fear--poor guilty thing!--when she thought that all her devices had only led her with us to a dreadful death! These things, in the light in which I now viewed them, were cogent evidences against her.

"It must have been written to some one about us!" said the Duchess at length. "To some one in our confidence. 'On our side of the door,' as he calls it."

"Yes, that is certain," I said.

"And on the wrapper he styles her Mistress Clarence. Now who----"

"Who could it have been? That is the question we have to answer," Master Bertie replied dryly. Hearing his voice, I knew he had come at last to the same conclusion to which I had jumped. "I think you may dismiss the servants from the inquiry," he continued. "The Bishop of Winchester would scarcely write to them in that style."

"Dismiss the servants? Then who is left?" she protested.

"I think----" He lost courage, hesitated, and broke off. She looked at him wonderingly. He turned to me, and, gaining confirmation from my nod, began again. "I think I should ask A---- B----," he said.

"A---- B----?" she cried, still not seeing one whit.

"Yes. Anne Brandon," he answered sternly.

She repeated his words softly and stood a moment gazing at him. In that moment she saw it all. She sat down suddenly on the chair beside her and shuddered violently, as if she had laid her hand unwittingly upon a snake. "Oh, Richard," she whispered, "it is too horrible!"

"I fear it is too true," he answered gloomily.

I shrank from looking at them, from meeting her eyes or his. I felt as if this shame had come upon us all. The thought that the culprit might walk into the room at any moment filled me with terror. I turned away and looked through the window, leaving the husband and wife together.

"Is it only the name you are thinking of?" she muttered.

"No," he answered. "Before I left England to go to Calais I saw something pass between them--between her and Clarence--which, surprised me. Only in the confusion of those last days it slipped from my memory for the time."

"I see," she said quietly. "The villain!"

Looking back on the events of the last week, I found many things made plain by the lurid light now cast upon them. I understood how Master Lindstrom's vase had come to be broken when we were discussing the letter, which in my hands must have been a perpetual terror to the girl. I discerned that she had purposely sown dissension between myself and Van Tree, and recalled how she had striven to persuade us not to leave the island; then, how she had induced us to take that unlucky road; finally, how on the road her horse had lagged and lagged behind, detaining us all when every minute was precious. The things all dovetailed into one another; each by itself was weak, but together they formed a strong scaffold--a scaffold strong enough for the hanging of a man, if she had been a man! The others appealed to me, the Duchess feverishly anxious to be assured one way or the other. The very suspicion of the existence of such treachery at her side seemed to stifle her. Still looking out of the window I detailed the proofs I have mentioned, not gladly, Heaven knows, or in any spirit of revenge. But my duty was rather to my companions who had been true to me, than to her. I told them the truth as far as I knew it. The whole wretched, miserable truth was only to become known to me later.

"I will go to her," the Duchess said presently, rising from her seat.

"My dear!" her husband cried. He stretched out his hand, and grasping her skirt detained her. "You will not----"

"Do not be afraid!" she replied sadly, as she stooped over him and kissed his forehead. "It is a thing past scolding, Richard; past love and even hope, and all but past pity. I will be merciful as we hope for mercy, but she can never be friend of ours again, and some one must tell her. I will do so and return. As for that man!" she continued, obscuring suddenly the fair and noble side of her character which she had just exhibited, and which I confess had surprised me, for I had not thought her capable of a generosity so uncommon; "as for that man," she repeated, drawing herself up to her full height, while her eyes sparkled and her cheek grew red, "who has turned her into a vile schemer and a shameless hypocrite, as he would fain have turned better women, I will show him no mercy nor grace if I ever have him under my feet. I will crush him as I would an adder, though I be crushed next moment myself!"

She was sweeping with that word from the room, and had nearly reached the door before I found my voice. Then I called out "Stay!" just in time. "You will do no good, madam, by going!" I said, rising. "You will not find her. She is gone."

"Gone?"

"Yes," I said quietly. "She left the house twenty minutes ago. I saw her cross the market-place, wearing her cloak and carrying a bag. I do not think she will return."

"Not return? But whither has she gone?" they both cried at once.

I shook my head.

"I can only guess," I said in a low voice. "I saw no more than I have told you."

"But why did you not tell me'" the Duchess cried reproachfully. "She shall be brought back."

"It would be useless," Master Bertie answered. "Yet I doubt if it be as Carey thinks. Why should she go just at this time? She does not know that she is found out. She does not know that this letter has been recovered. Not a word, mind, was said of it before she left the room."

"No," I allowed; "that is true."

I was puzzled on this point myself, now I came to consider it. I could not see why she had taken the alarm so opportunely; but I maintained my opinion nevertheless.

"Something frightened her," I said; "though it may not have been the letter."

"Yes," said the Duchess, after a moment's silence. "I suppose you are right. I suppose something frightened her, as you say. I wonder what it was, poor wretch!"

It turned out that I was right. Mistress Anne had gone indeed, having stayed, so far as we could learn from an examination of the room which she had shared with Dymphna, merely to put together the few things which our adventures had left her. She had gone out from among us in this foreign land without a word of farewell, without a good wish given or received, without a soul to say God speed! The thought made me tremble. If she had died it would have been different. Now, to feel sorrow for her as for one who had been with us in heart as well as in body, seemed a mockery. How could we grieve for one who had moved day by day and hour by hour among us, only that with each hour and day she might plot and scheme and plan our destruction? It was impossible!

We made inquiries indeed, but without result; and so, abruptly and terribly she passed--for the time--out of our knowledge, though often afterward I recalled sadly the weary, hunted look which I had sometimes seen in her eyes when she sat listless and dreamy. Poor girl! Her own acts had placed her, as the Duchess said, beyond love or hope, but not beyond pity.

So it is in life. The day which sees one's trial end sees another's begin. We--the Duchess and her child, Master Bertie and I--stayed with our good and faithful friends the Lindstroms a while, resting and recruiting our strength; and during this interval, at the pressing instance of the Duchess, I wrote letters to Sir Anthony and Petronilla, stating that I was abroad, and was well, and looked presently to return; but not disclosing my refuge or the names of my companions. At the end of five days, Master Bertie being fairly strong again and Santon being considered unsafe for us as a permanent residence, we went under guard to Wesel, where we were received as people of quality, and lodged, there being no fitting place, in the disused church of St. Willibrod. Here the child was christened Peregrine--a wanderer; the governor of the city and I being godfathers. And here we lived in peace--albeit with hearts that yearned for home--for some months.

During this time two pieces of news came to us from England: one, that the Parliament, though much pressed to it, had refused to acquiesce in the confiscation of the Duchess's estates; the other, that our joint persecutor, the great Bishop of Winchester, was dead. This last we at first disbelieved. It was true, nevertheless. Stephen Gardiner, whose vast schemes had enmeshed people so far apart in station, and indeed in all else, as the Duchess and myself, was dead at last; had died toward the end of

1555, at the height of his power, with England at his feet, and gone to his Maker. I have known many worse men.

We trusted that this might open the way for our return, but we found on the contrary that fresh clouds were rising. The persecution of the Reformers, which Queen Mary had begun in England, was carried on with increasing rigor, and her husband, who was now King of Spain and master of the Netherlands, freed from the prudent checks of his father, was inclined to pleasure her in this by giving what aid he could abroad. His Minister in the Netherlands, the Bishop of Arras, brought so much pressure to bear upon our protector to induce him to give us up, that it was plain the Duke of Cleves must sooner or later comply. We thought it better, therefore, to remove ourselves, and presently did so, going to the town of Winnheim in the Rhine Palatinate.

We found ourselves not much more secure here, however, and all our efforts to discover a safe road into France failing, and the stock of money which the Duchess had provided beginning to give out, we were in great straits whither to go or what to do.

At this time of our need, however, Providence opened a door in a quarter where we least looked for it. Letters came from Sigismund, the King of Poland, and from the Palatine of Wilna in that country, inviting the Duchess and Master Bertie to take up their residence there, and offering the latter an establishment and honorable employment. The overture was unlooked for, and was not accepted without misgivings, Wilna being so far distant, and there being none of our race in that country. However, assurance of the Polish King's good faith reached us--I say us, for in all their plans I was included--through John Alasco, a nobleman who had visited England. And in due time we started on this prodigious journey, and came safely to Wilna, where our reception was such as the letters had led us to expect.

I do not propose to set down here our adventures, though they were many, in that strange country of frozen marshes and endless plains, but to pass over eighteen months which I spent not without profit to myself in the Pole's service, seeing something of war in his Lithuanian campaigns, and learning much of men and the world, which here, to say nothing of wolves and bears, bore certain aspects not commonly visible in Warwickshire. I pass on to the early autumn of 1558, when a letter from the Duchess, who was at Wilna, was brought to me at Cracovy. It was to this effect:

"Dear Friend: Send you good speed! Word has come to us here of an enterprise Englandward, which promises, if it be truly reported to us, to so alter things at home that there may be room for us at our own firesides.

Heaven so further it, both for our happiness and the good of the religion. Master Bertie has embarked on it, and I have taken upon myself to answer for your aid and counsel, which have never been wanting to us. Wherefore, dear friend, come, sparing neither horse nor spurs, nor anything which may bring you sooner to Wilna, and your assured and loving friend, Katherine Suffolk."

In five days after receiving this I was at Wilna, and two months later I saw England again, after an absence of three years. Early in November, 1558, Master Bertie and I landed at Lowestoft, having made the passage from Hamburg in a trading vessel of that place. We stopped only to sleep one night, and then, dressed as traveling merchants, we set out on the road to London, entering the city without accident or hindrance on the third day after landing.

CHAPTER XVIII.

THE WITCH'S WARNING.

"One minute!" I said. "That is the place."

Master Bertie turned in his saddle, and looked at it. The light was fading into the early dusk of a November evening, but the main features of four cross streets, the angle between two of them filled by the tall belfry of a church, were still to be made out. The east wind had driven loiterers indoors, and there was scarcely any one abroad to notice us. I pointed to a dead wall ten paces down one street. "Opposite that they stopped," I said. "There was a pile of boards leaning against it then."

"You have had many a worse bedchamber since, lad," he said, smiling.

"Many," I answered. And then by a common impulse we shook up the horses, and trotting gently on were soon clear of London and making for Islington. Passing through the latter we began to breast the steep slope which leads to Highgate, and coming, when we had reached the summit, plump upon the lights of the village, pulled up in front of a building which loomed darkly across the road.

"This is the Gatehouse Tavern," Master Bertie said in a low voice. "We shall soon know whether we have come on a fool's errand--or worse!"

We rode under the archway into a great courtyard, from which the road issued again on the other side through another gate. In one corner two men were littering down a line of packhorses by the light of the lanterns, which brought their tanned and rugged faces into relief. In another, where the light poured ruddily from an open doorway, an ostler was serving out fodder, and doing so, if we might judge from the travelers' remonstrances, with a niggardly hand. From the windows of the house a dozen rays of light shot athwart the darkness, and disclosed as many pigs wallowing asleep in the middle of the yard. In all we saw a coarse comfort and welcome. Master Bertie led the way across the yard, and accosted the ostler. "Can we have stalls and beds?" he asked.

The man stayed his chaffering, and looked up at us. "Every man to his business," he replied gruffly. "Stalls, yes; but of beds I know nothing. For women's work go to the women."

"Right!" said I, "so we will. With better luck than you would go, I expect, my man!"

Bursting into a hoarse laugh at this--he was lame and one-eyed and not very well-favored--he led us into a long, many-stalled stable, feebly lit by lanterns which here and there glimmered against the walls. "Suit yourselves," he said; "first come is first served here."

He seemed an ill-conditioned fellow, but the businesslike way in which we went about our work, watering, feeding, and littering down in old campaigners' fashion, drew from him a grunt of commendation. "Have you come from far, masters?" he asked.

"No, from London," I answered curtly. "We come as linen-drapers from Westcheap, if you want to know."

"Ay, I see that," he said chuckling. "Never were atop of a horse before nor handled anything but a clothyard; oh, no!"

"We want a merchant reputed to sell French lace," I continued, looking hard at him. "Do you happen to know if there is a dealer here with any?"

He nodded rather to himself than to me, as if he had expected the question. Then in the same tone, but with a quick glance of intelligence, he answered, "I will show you into the house presently, and you can see for yourselves. A stable is no place for French lace." He pointed with a wink over his shoulder toward a stall in which a man, apparently drunk, lay snoring. "That is a fine toy!" he ran on carelessly, as I removed my dagger from the holster and concealed it under my cloak--"a fine plaything--for a linen draper!"

"Peace, peace, man! and show us in," said Master Bertie impatiently.

With a shrug of his shoulders the man obeyed. Crossing the courtyard behind him, we entered the great kitchen, which, full of light and warmth and noise, presented just such a scene of comfort and bustle, of loud talking, red-faced guests, and hurrying bare-armed serving-maids, as I remembered lighting upon at St. Albans three years back. But I had changed much since then, and seen much. The bailiff himself would hardly have recognized his old antagonist in the tall, heavily cloaked stranger, whose assured air, acquired amid wild surroundings in a foreign land, gave him a look of age to which I could not fairly lay claim. Master Bertie had assigned the lead to me as being in less danger of recognition, and I followed the ostler toward the hearth without hesitation. "Master Jenkin!" the man cried, with the same rough bluntness he had shown without, "here are two travelers want the lace-seller who was here to-day. Has he gone?"

"Who gone?" retorted the host as loudly.

"The lace merchant who came this morning."

"No; he is in No. 32," returned the landlord. "Will you sup first, gentlemen?"

We declined, and followed the ostler, who made no secret of our destination, telling those in our road to make way, as the gentlemen were for No. 32. One of the crowd, however, who seemed to be crossing from the lower end of the room, failed apparently to understand, and, interposing between us and our guide, brought me perforce to a halt.

"By your leave, good woman!" I said, and turned to pass round her.

But she foiled me with unexpected nimbleness, and I could not push her aside, she was so very old. Her gums were toothless and her forehead was lined and wrinkled. About her eyes, which under hideous red lids still shone with an evil gleam--a kind of reflection of a wicked past--a thousand crows' feet had gathered. A few wisps of gray hair struggled from under the handkerchief which covered her head. She was humpbacked, and stooped over a stick, and whether she saw or not my movement of repugnance, her voice was harsh when she spoke.

"Young gentleman," she croaked, "let me tell your fortune by the stars. A fortune for a groat, young gentleman!" she continued, peering up into my face and frustrating my attempts to pass.

"Here is a groat," I answered peevishly, "and for the fortune, I will hear it another day. So let us by!"

But she would not. My companion, seeing that the attention of the room was being drawn to us, tried to pull me by her. But I could not use force, and short of force there was no remedy. The ostler, indeed, would have interfered on our behalf, and returned to bid her, with a civility he had not bestowed on us, "give us passage." But she swiftly turned her eyes on him in a sinister fashion, and he retreated with an oath and a paling face, while those nearest to us--and half a dozen had crowded round--drew back, and crossed themselves in haste almost ludicrous.

"Let me see your face, young gentleman," she persisted, with a hollow cough. "My eyes are not so clear as they were, or it is not your cloak and your flap-hat that would blind me."

Thinking it best to get rid of her, even at a slight risk--and the chance that among the travelers present there would be one able to recognize me was small indeed--I uncovered. She shot a piercing glance at my face, and looking down on the floor, traced hurriedly a figure with her stick. She studied the phantom lines a moment, and then looked up.

"Listen!" she said solemnly, and waving her stick round me, she quavered out in tones which filled me with a strange tremor:

"The man goes east, and the wind blows west,
Wood to the head, and steel to the breast!
The man goes west, and the wind blows east,
The neck twice doomed the gallows shall feast!

"Beware!" she went on more loudly, and harshly, tapping with her stick on the floor, and snaking her palsied head at me. "Beware, unlucky shoot of a crooked branch! Go no farther with it! Go back! The sword may miss or may not fall, but the cord is sure!"

If Master Bertie had not held my arm tightly, I should have recoiled, as most of those within hearing had already done. The strange allusions to my past, which I had no difficulty in detecting, and the witch's knowledge of the risks of our present enterprise, were enough to startle and shake the most constant mind; and in the midst of enterprises secret and dangerous, few minds are so firm or so reckless as to disdain omens. That she was one of those unhappy beings who buy dark secrets at the expense of their souls, seemed certain; and had I been alone, I should have, I am not ashamed to say it, given back.

But I was lucky in having for my companion a man of rare mind, and besides of so single a religious belief that to the end of his life he always refused to put faith in a thing of the existence of which I have no doubt myself--I mean witchcraft.

He showed at this moment the courage of his opinions. "Peace, peace, woman!" he said compassionately. "We shall live while God wills it, and die when he wills it. And neither live longer nor die earlier! So let us by."

"Would you perish?" she quavered.

"Ay! If so God wills," he answered undaunted.

At that she seemed to shake all over, and hobbled aside, muttering, "Then go on! Go on! God wills it!"

Master Bertie gave me no time for hesitation, but, holding my arm, urged me on to where the ostler stood awaiting the event with a face of much discomposure. He opened the door for us, however, and led the way up a narrow and not too clean staircase. On the landing at the head of this he paused, and raised his lantern so as to cast the light on our faces. "She has overlooked me, the old witch!" he said viciously; "I wish I had never meddled in this business."

"Man!" Master Bertie replied sternly; "do you fear that weak old woman?"

"No; but I fear her master," retorted the ostler, "and that is the devil!"

"Then I do not," Master Bertie answered bravely. "For my Master is as good a match for him as I am for that old woman. When he wills it, man, you will die, and not before. So pluck up spirit."

Master Bertie did not look at me, though I needed his encouragement as much as the ostler, having had better proofs of the woman's strange knowledge. But, seeing that his exhortation had emboldened this ignorant man, I was ashamed to seem to hesitate. When the ostler knocked at the door--not of 32, but of 15--and it presently opened, I went in without more ado.

The room was a bare inn-chamber. A pallet without coverings lay in one corner. In the middle were a couple of stools, and on one of them a taper.

The person who had opened to us stood eying us attentively; a bluff, weather-beaten man with a thick beard and the air of a sailor. "Well," he said, "what now?"

"These gentlemen want to buy some lace," the ostler explained.

"What lace do they want?" was the retort.

"French lace," I answered.

"You have come to the right shop, then," the man answered briskly. Nodding to our conductor to depart, he carefully let him out. Then, barring the door behind him, he as rapidly strode to the pallet and twitched it aside, disclosing a trap door. He lifted this, and we saw a narrow shaft descending into darkness. He brought the taper and held it so as to throw a faint light into the opening. There was no ladder, but blocks of wood nailed alternately against two of the sides, at intervals of a couple of feet or so, made the descent pretty easy for an active man. "The door is on this side," he said, pointing out the one. "Knock loudly once and softly twice. The word is the same."

We nodded and while he held the taper above, we descended, one by one, without much difficulty, though I admit that half-way down the old woman's words "Go on and perish" came back disquietingly to my mind. However, my foot struck the bottom before I had time to digest them, and a streak of light which seemed to issue from under a door forced my thoughts the next moment into a new channel. Whispering to Master Bertie to pause a minute, for there was only room for one of us to stand at the bottom of the shaft, I knocked in the fashion prescribed.

The sound of loud voices, which I had already detected, ceased on a sudden, and I heard a shuffling on the other side of the boards. This was followed by silence, and then the door was flung open, and, blinded for the moment by a blaze of light, I walked mechanically forward into a room. I made out as I advanced a group of men standing round a rude table, their figures thrown into dark relief by flares stuck in sconces on the walls behind them. Some had weapons in their hands and others had partly risen from their seats and stood in postures of surprise. "What do you seek?" cried a threatening voice from among them.

"Lace," I answered.

"What lace?"

"French lace."

"Then you are welcome--heartily welcome!" was the answer given in a tone of relief. "But who comes with you?"

"Master Richard Bertie, of Lincolnshire," I answered promptly; and at that moment he emerged from the shaft.

A still more hearty murmur of welcome hailed his name and appearance, and we were borne forward to the table amid a chorus of voices, the greeting given to Master Bertie being that of men who joyfully hail unlooked-for help. The room, from its vaulted ceiling and stone floor, and the trams of casks which lay here and there or near the table serving for seats, appeared to be a cellar. Its dark, gloomy recesses, the flaring lights, and the weapons on the table, seemed meet and fitting surroundings for the anxious faces which were gathered about the board; for there was a something in the air which was not so much secrecy as a thing more unpleasant--suspicion and mistrust. Almost at the moment of our entrance it showed itself. One of the men, before the door had well closed behind us, went toward it, as if to go out. The leader--he who had questioned me--called sharply to him, bidding him come back. And he came back, but reluctantly, as it seemed to me.

I barely noticed this, for Master Bertie, who was known personally to many and by name to all, was introducing me to two who were apparently the leaders: Sir Thomas Penruddocke, a fair man as tall as myself, loose-limbed and untidily dressed, with a reckless eye and a loud tongue; and Master Walter Kingston, a younger brother, I was told, of that Sir Anthony Kingston who had suffered death the year before for conspiracy against the queen--the same in which Lord Devon had showed the white feather. Kingston was a young man of moderate height and slender; of a brown complexion, and delicate, almost womanish beauty, his sleepy dark eyes and dainty mustache suggesting a temper rather amiable than firm. But the spirit of revenge had entered into him, and I soon learned that not even Penruddocke, a Cornish knight of longer lineage than purse, was so vehement a plotter or so devoted to the cause. Looking at the others my heart sank; it needed no greater experience than mine to discern that, except three or four whom I identified as stout professors of religion, they were men rather of desperate fortunes than good estate. I learned on the instant that conspiracy makes strange bedfellows, and that it is impossible to do dirty work even with the purest intentions--in good company! Master Bertie's face indicated to one who knew him as well as I did something of the same feeling; and could the clock have been put back awhile, and we placed with free hands and uncommitted outside the Gatehouse, I think we should with one accord have turned our backs on it, and given up an attempt which in this company could scarcely fare any way but ill. Still, for good or evil, the die was cast now, and retreat was out of the question.

We had confronted too many dangers during the last three years not to be able to face this one with a good courage; and presently Master Bertie, taking a seat, requested to be told of the strength and plans of our associates, his businesslike manner introducing at once some degree of order and method into a conference which before our arrival had--unless I was much mistaken--been conspicuously lacking in both.

"Our resources?" Penruddocke replied confidently. "They lie everywhere, man! We have but to raise the flag and the rest will be a triumphal march. The people, sick of burnings and torturings, and heated by the loss of Calais last January, will flock to us. Flock to us, do I say? I will answer for it they will!"

"But you have some engagements, some promises from people of standing?"

"Oh, yes! But the whole nation will join us. They are weary of the present state of things."

"They may be as weary of it as you say," Master Bertie answered shrewdly; "but is it equally certain that they will risk their necks to amend it? You have fixed upon some secure base from which we can act, and upon which, if necessary, we may fall back to concentrate our strength?"

"Fall back?" cried Penruddocke, rising from his seat in heat. "Master Bertie, I hope you have not come among us to talk of falling back! Let us have no talk of that. If Wyatt had held on at once London would have been his! It was falling back ruined him."

Master Bertie shook his head. "If you have no secure base, you run the risk of being crushed in the first half hour," he said. "When a fire is first lighted the breeze puts it out which afterward but fans it."

"You will not say that when you hear our plans. There are to be three risings at once. Lord Delaware will rise in the west."

"But will he?" said Master Bertie pointedly, disregarding the threatening looks which were cast at him by more than one. "The late rebellion there was put down very summarily, and I should have thought that countryside would not be prone to rise again. *Will* Lord Delaware rise?"

"Oh, yes, he will rise fast enough!" Penruddocke replied carelessly. "I will answer for him. And on the same day, while we do the London business, Sir Richard Bray will gather his men in Kent."

"Do not count on him!" said Master Bertie. "A prisoner, muffled and hoodwinked, was taken to the Tower by water this afternoon. And rumor says it was Sir Richard Bray."

There was a pause of consternation, during which one looked at another, and swarthy faces grew pale. Penruddocke was the first to recover himself. "Bah!" he exclaimed, "a fig for rumor! She is ever a lying jade! I will bet a noble Richard Bray is supping in his own house at this minute."

"Then you would lose," Master Bertie rejoined sadly, and with no show of triumph. "On hearing the report I sent a messenger to Sir Richard's house. He brought word back that Sir Richard Bray had been fetched away unexpectedly by four men, and that the house was in confusion."

A murmur of dismay broke out at the lower end of the table. But the Cornishman rose to the situation. "What matter?" he cried boisterously. "What we have lost in Bray we have gained in Master Bertie. He will raise Lincolnshire for us, and the Duchess's tenants. There should be five hundred stout men of the latter, and two-thirds of them Protestants at heart. If Bray has been seized there is the more call for haste that we may release him."

This appeal was answered by an outburst of cries. One or two even rose, and waving their weapons swore a speedy vengeance. But Master Bertie sat silent until the noise had subsided. Then he spoke. "You must not count on them either, Sir Thomas," he said firmly. "I cannot find it in my conscience to bring my wife's tenants into a plan so desperate as this appears to be. To appeal to the people generally is one thing; to call on those who are bound to us and who cannot in honor refuse is another. And I will not risk in a hopeless struggle the lives of men whose fathers looked for guidance to me and mine."

A silence, the silence of utter astonishment, fell upon the plotters round the table. In every face--and they were all turned upon my companion--I read rage and distrust and dismay. They had chafed under his cold criticisms and his calm reasonings. But this went beyond all, and there were hands which stole instinctively to daggers, and eyes which waited scowling for a signal. But Penruddocke, sanguine by nature and rendered reckless by circumstances, had still the feelings of a gentleman, and something in him responded to the appeal which underlay Master Bertie's words. He remained silent, gazing gloomily at the table, his eyes perhaps opened at this late hour to the hopelessness of the attempt he meditated.

It was Walter Kingston who came to the fore, and put into words the thoughts of the coarser and more selfish spirits round him. Leaping from his seat he dashed his slender hand on the table. "What does this mean?" he sneered, a dangerous light in his dark eyes. "Those only are here or should be here who are willing to stake all--all, mind you--on the cause. Let us have no sneaks! Let us have no men with a foot on either bank! Let us have no Courtenays nor cowards! Such men ruined Wyatt and hanged my brother! A curse on them!" he cried, his voice rising almost to a scream.

"Master Kingston! do you refer to me?" Bertie rejoined in haughty surprise.

"Ay, I do!" cried the young man hotly.

"Then I must beg leave of these gentlemen to explain my position."

"Your position? So! More words?" quoth the other mockingly.

"Ay! as many words as I please," retorted Master Bertie, his color rising. "Afterward I will be as ready with deeds, I dare swear, as any other! My tenants and my wife's I will not draw into an almost hopeless struggle. But my own life and my friend's, since we have obtained your secrets, I must risk, and I will do so in honor to the death. For the rest, who doubts my courage may test it below ground or above."

The young man laughed rudely. "You will risk your life, but not your lands, Master Bertie? That is the position, is it?"

My companion was about to utter a rejoinder, fierce for him, when I, who had hitherto sat silent, interposed. "The old witch told the truth," I cried bitterly. "She said if we came hither we should perish. And perish we shall, through being linked to a dozen men as brave as I could wish, but the biggest fools under heaven!"

"Fools?" shouted Kingston.

"Ay, fools!" I repeated. "For who but fools, being at sea in a boat in which all must sink or swim, would fall a-quarreling? Tell me that!" I cried, slapping the table.

"You are about right," Penruddocke said, and half a dozen voices muttered assent.

"About right, is he?" shrieked Kingston. "But who knows we are in a boat together? Who knows that, I'd like to hear?"

"I do!" I said, standing up and overtopping him by eight inches. "And if any man hints that Master Bertie is here for any other purpose or with any other intent than to honestly risk his life in this endeavor as becomes a gentleman, let him stand out--let him stand out, and I will break his neck! Fie, gentlemen, fie!" I continued, after a short pause, which I did not make too long lest Master Kingston's passion should get the better of his prudence. "Though I am young I have seen service. But I never saw battle won yet with dissension in the camp. For shame! Let us to business, and make the best dispositions we may."

"You talk sense, Master Carey!" Penruddocke cried, with a great oath. "Give me your hand. And do you, Kingston, hold your peace. If Master Bertie will not raise his men to save his own skin, he will hardly do it for ours. Now, Sir Richard Bray being taken, what is to be done, my lads? Come, let us look to that."

So the storm blew over. But it was with heavy hearts that two of us fell to the discussion which followed, counting over weapons and assigning posts, and debating this one's fidelity and that one's lukewarmness. Our first impressions had not deceived us. The plot was desperate, and those engaged in it were wanting in every element which should command success--in information, forethought, arrangement--everything save sheer audacity. When after a prolonged and miserable sitting it was proposed that all should take the oath of association on the Gospels, Master Bertie and I assented gloomily. It would make our position no worse, for already we were fully committed. The position was indeed bad enough. We had only persuaded the others to a short delay; and even this meant that we must remain in hiding in England, exposed from day to day to all the chances of detection and treachery.

Sir Thomas brought out from some secret place about him a tiny roll of paper wrapped in a quill, and while we stood about him looking over his shoulders, he laboriously added, letter by letter, three or four names. The stern, anxious faces which peered the while at the document or scanned each other only to find their anxiety reflected, the flaring lights behind us, the recklessness of some and the distrust of others, the cloaks in which many were wrapped to the chin, and the occasional gleam of hidden weapons, made up a scene very striking. The more as it was no mere show, but some of us saw only too distinctly behind it the figure of the headsman and the block.

"Now," said Penruddocke, who himself I think took a certain grim pleasure in the formality, "be ready to swear, gentlemen, in pairs, as I call the names. Kingston and Matthewson!"

Lolling against the wall under one of the sconces I looked at Master Bertie, expecting to be called up with him. He smiled as our eyes met; and I thought with a rush of tenderness how lightly I could have dared the worst had all my associates been like him. But repining came too late, and in a moment Penruddocke surprised me by calling out "Crewdson and Carey!"

So Master Bertie was not to be my companion! I learned afterward that men who were strangers to one another were purposely associated, the theory being that each should keep an eye upon his oath-fellow. I went forward to the end of the table, and took the book.

There was a slight pause.

"Crewdson!" called Penruddocke sharply; "did you not hear, man?"

There was a little stir at the farther end of the room, and he came forward, moving slowly and reluctantly. I saw that he was the man whom Penruddocke had called back when we entered, a man of great height, though slender, and closely cloaked. A drooping gray mustache covered his mouth, and that was almost all I made out before Sir Thomas, with some sharpness, bade him uncover. He did so with an abrupt gesture, and reaching out his hand grasped the other end of the book as though he would take it from me. His manner was so strange that I looked hard at him, and he, jerking up his head with a gesture of defiance, looked at me too, his face very pale.

I heard Penruddocke's voice droning the words of the oath, but I paid no attention to them--I was busied with something else. Where had I seen the sinister gleam in those eyes before, and that forehead high and narrow, and those lean, swarthy cheeks? Where had I before confronted that very face which now glared into mine across the book? Its look was bold and defiant, but low down in the cheek I saw a little pulse beating furiously, a pulse which told of anxiety, and the jaws, half veiled by the ragged mustache, were set in an iron grip. Where? Ha! I knew. I dropped my end of the book and stepped back.

"Look to the door!" I cried, my voice sounding harsh and strange in my own ears. "Let no one leave! I denounce that man!" And raising my hand I pointed pitilessly at my oath-fellow. "I denounce him--he is a spy and traitor!"

"I a spy?" the man shouted fiercely--with the fierceness of despair.

"Ay, you! you! Clarence, or Crewdson, or whatever you call yourself, I denounce you! My time has come!"

"... HE IS A SPY AND A TRAITOR!"

CHAPTER XIX.

FERDINAND CLUDDE.

The bitterness of that hour long past, when he had left me for death, when he had played with the human longing for life, and striven without a thought of pity to corrupt me by hopes and fears the most awful that mortals know, was in my voice as I spoke. I rejoiced that vengeance had come upon him at last, and that I was its instrument. I saw the pallor of a great fear creep into his dark cheek, and read in his eyes the vicious passion of a wild beast trapped, and felt no pity. "Master Clarence!" I said, and laughed--laughed mockingly. "You do not look pleased to see your friends. Or perhaps you do not remember me. Stand forward, Master Bertie! Maybe he will recognize you."

But though Master Bertie came forward and stood by my side gazing at him, the villain's eyes did not for an instant shift from mine. "It is the man!" my companion said after a solemn pause--for the other, breathing fast, made no answer. "He was a spy in the pay of Bishop Gardiner, when I knew him. At the Bishop's death I heard that he passed into the service of the Spanish Ambassador, the Count de Feria. He called himself at that time Clarence. I recognize him."

The quiet words had their effect. From full one-half of the savage crew round us a fierce murmur rose more terrible than any loud outcry. Yet this seemed a relief to the doomed man; he forced himself to look away from me and to confront the dark ring of menacing faces which hemmed him in. The moment he did so he appeared to find courage and words. "They take me for another man!" he cried in hoarse accents. "I know nothing of them!" and he added a fearful oath. "He knows me. Ask him!"

He pointed to Walter Kingston, who was sitting moodily on a tram outside the ring, and who alone had not risen under the excitement of my challenge. On being thus appealed to he looked up suddenly. "If I am to choose between you," he said bitterly, "and say which is the true man, I know which I shall pick."

"Which?" Clarence murmured. "Which?" This time his tone was different. In his voice was the ring of hope.

"I should give my vote for you," Kingston replied, looking contemptuously at him. "I know something about you, but of the other gentleman I know nothing!"

"And not much of the person you call Crewdson," I retorted fiercely, "since you do not know his real name."

"I know this much," the young man answered, tapping his boot with his scabbard with studied carelessness, "that he lent me some money, and seemed a good fellow and one that hated a mass priest. That is enough for me. As for his name, it is his fancy perhaps. You call yourself Carey. Well, I know a good many Careys, but I do not know you, nor ever heard of you!"

I swung round on him with a hot cheek. But the challenge which was upon my tongue was anticipated by Master Bertie, who drew me forcibly back. "Leave this to me, Francis," he said, "and do you watch that man. Master Kingston and gentlemen," he continued, turning again to them, and drawing himself to his full height as he addressed them, "listen, if you please! You know me, if you do not know my friend. The honor of Richard Bertie has never been challenged until to-night, nor ever will be with impunity. Leave my friend out of the question and put me in it. I, Richard Bertie, say that that man is a paid spy and informer, come here in quest of blood-money! And he, Crewdson, a nameless man, says that I lie. Choose between us. Or look at him and judge! Look!"

He was right to bid them look. As the savage murmur rose again and took from the wretched man his last hope, as the ugliness of despair and wicked, impotent passion distorted his face, he was indeed the most deadly witness against himself.

The lights which shone on treacherous weapons half hidden, or on the glittering eyes of cruel men whose blood was roused, fell on nothing so dangerous as the livid, despairing face which, unmasked and eyed by all with aversion, still defied us. Traitor and spy as he was, he had the merit of courage at least; he would die game. And even as I, with a first feeling of pity for him, discerned this, his sword was out, and with a curse he lunged at me.

Penruddocke saved me by a buffet which sent me reeling against the wall, so that the villain's thrust was spent on air. Before he could repeat it, four or five men flung themselves upon him from behind. For a moment there was a great uproar, while the group surrounding him swayed to and fro as he dragged his captors up and down with a strength I should not have expected. But the end was certain, and we stood looking on quietly. In a minute or two they had him down, and disarming him, bound his hands.

For me he seemed to have a special hatred. "Curse you!" he panted, glaring at me as he lay helpless. "You have been my evil angel! From the first day I saw you, you have thwarted me in every plan, and now you have brought me to this!"

"Not I, but yourself," I answered.

"My curse upon you!" he cried again, the rage and hate in his face so terrible that I turned away shuddering and sick at heart. "If I could have killed you," he cried, "I would have died contented."

"Enough!" interposed Penruddocke briskly. "It is well for us that Master Bertie and his friend came here to-night. Heaven grant it be not too late! We do not need," he added, looking round, "any more evidence, I think?"

The dissent was loud, and, save for Kingston, who still sat sulking apart, unanimous.

"Death?" said the Cornishman quietly.

No one spoke, but each man gave a brief stern nod.

"Very well," the leader continued; "then I propose----"

"One moment," said Master Bertie, interrupting him. "A word with you apart, with our friends' permission. You can repeat it to them afterward."

He drew Sir Thomas aside, and they retired into the corner by the door, where they stood talking in whispers. I had small reason to feel sympathy for the man who lay there tied and doomed to die like a calf. Yet even I shuddered--yes, and some of the hardened men round me shuddered also at the awful expression in his eyes as, without moving his head, he followed the motions of the two by the door. Some faint hope springing into being wrung his soul, and brought the perspiration in great drops to his forehead. I turned away, thinking gravely of the early morning three years ago when he had tortured me by the very same hopes and fears which now racked his own spirit.

Penruddocke came back, Master Bertie following him.

"It must not be done to-night," he announced quietly, with a nod which meant that he would explain the reason afterward. "We will meet again to-morrow at four in the afternoon instead of at eight in the evening. Until then two must remain on guard with him. It is right he should have some time to repent, and he shall have it."

This did not at once find favor.

"Why not run him through now?" said one bluntly. "And meet to-morrow at some place unknown to him? If we come here again we shall, likely enough, walk straight into the trap."

"Well, have it that way, if you please," answered Sir Thomas, shrugging his shoulders. "But do not blame me afterward if you find we have let slip a golden opportunity. Be fools if you like. I dare say it will not make much difference in the end!"

He spoke at random, but he knew how to deal with his crew, it seemed, for on this those who had objected assented reluctantly to the course he proposed. "Barnes and Walters are here in hiding, so they had better be the two to guard him," he continued. "There is no fear that they will be inclined to let him go!" I looked at the men whom the glances of their fellows singled out, and found them to belong to the little knot of fanatics I had before remarked: dark, stern men, worth, if the matter ever came to fighting, all the rest of the band put together.

"At four, to-morrow, then, we meet," Sir Thomas concluded lightly. "Then we will deal with him, never fear! Now it is near midnight, and we must be going. But not all together, or we shall attract attention."

Half an hour later Master Bertie and I rode softly out of the courtyard and turned our faces toward the city. The night wind came sweeping across the valley of the Thames, and met us full in the face as we reached the brow of the hill. It seemed laden with melancholy whispers. The wretched enterprise, ill-conceived, ill-ordered, and in its very nature desperate, to which we were in honor committed, would have accounted of itself for any degree of foreboding. But the scene through which we had just passed, and on my part the knowledge that I had given up a fellow-being to death, had their depressing influences. For some distance we rode in silence, which I was the first to break.

"Why did you put off his punishment?" I asked.

"Because I think he will give us information in the interval," Bertie answered briefly. "Information which may help us. A spy is generally ready to betray his own side upon occasion."

"And you will spare him if he does?" I asked. It seemed to me neither justice nor mercy.

"No," he said, "there is no fear of that. Those who go with ropes round their necks know no mercy. But drowning men will catch at straws; and ten to one he will babble!"

I shivered. "It is a bad business," I said.

He thought I referred to the conspiracy, and he inveighed bitterly against it, reproaching himself for bringing me into it, and for his folly in believing the rosy accounts of men who had all to win, and nothing save their worthless lives to lose. "There is only one thing gained," he said. "We are likely to pay dearly for that, so we may think the more of it. We have been the means of punishing a villain."

"Yes," I said, "that is true. It was a strange meeting and a strange recognition. Strangest of all that I should be called up to swear with him."

"Not strange," Master Bertie answered gravely. "I would rather call it providential. Let us think of that, and be of better courage, friend. We have been used; we shall not be cast away before our time."

I looked back. For some minutes I had thought I heard behind us a light footstep, more like the pattering of a dog than anything else. I could see nothing, but that was not wonderful, for the moon was young and the sky overcast. "Do you hear some one following us?" I said.

Master Bertie drew rein suddenly, and turning in the saddle we listened. For a second I thought I still heard the sound. The next it ceased, and only the wind toying with the November leaves and sighing away in the distance, came to our ears. "No," he said, "I think it must have been your fancy. I hear nothing."

But when we rode on the sound began again, though at first more faintly, as if our follower had learned prudence and fallen farther behind. "Do not stop, but listen!" I said softly. "Cannot you hear the pattering of a naked foot now?"

"I hear something," he answered. "I am afraid you are right, and that we are followed."

"What is to be done?" I said, my thoughts busy.

"There is Caen wood in front," he answered, "with a little open ground on this side of it. We will ride under the trees and then stop suddenly. Perhaps we shall be able to distinguish him as he crosses the open behind us." We made the experiment; but as if our follower had divined the plan, his footstep ceased to sound before we had stopped our horses. He had fallen farther behind. "We might ride quickly back," I suggested, "and surprise him."

"It would be useless," Bertie answered. "There is too much cover close to the road. Let us rather trot on and outstrip him."

We did trot on; and what with the tramp of our horses as they swung along the road, and the sharp passage of the wind by our ears, we heard no more of the footstep behind. But when we presently pulled up to breathe our horses--or rather within a few minutes of our doing so--there it was behind us, nearer and louder than before. I shivered as I listened; and presently, acting on a sudden impulse, I wheeled my horse round and spurred him back a dozen paces along the road.

I pulled up.

There was a movement in the shadow of the trees on my right, and I leaned forward, peering in that direction. Gradually, I made out the lines of a figure standing still as though gazing at me; a strange, distorted figure, crooked, short, and in some way, though no lineament of the face was visible, expressive of a strange and weird malevolence. It was the witch! The witch whom I had seen in the kitchen at the Gatehouse. How, then, had she come hither? How had she, old, lame, decrepit, kept up with us?

I trembled as she raised her hand, and, standing otherwise motionless, pointed at me out of the gloom. The horse under me was trembling too, trembling violently, with its ears laid back, and, as she moved, its terror increased, it plunged wildly. I had to give for a moment all my attention to it, and though I tried, in mere revolt against the fear which I felt was overcoming me, to urge it nearer, my efforts were vain. After nearly unseating me, the beast whirled round and, getting the better of me, galloped down the road toward London.

"What is it?" cried Master Bertie, as I came speedily up with him; he had ridden slowly on. "What is the matter?"

"Something in the hedge startled it," I explained, trying to soothe the horse. "I could not clearly see what it was."

"A rabbit, I dare say," he remarked, deceived by my manner.

"Perhaps it was," I answered. Some impulse, not unnatural, led me to say nothing about what I had seen. I was not quite sure that my eyes had not deceived me. I feared his ridicule, too, though he was not very prone to ridicule. And above all I shrank from explaining the medley of superstitious fear, distrust, and abhorrence in which I held the creature who had shown so strange a knowledge of my life.

We were already near Holborn, and reaching without further adventure a modest inn near the Bars, we retired to a room we had engaged, and lay down with none of the gallant hopes which had last night formed the subject of our talk. Yet we slept well, for depression goes better with sleep than does the tumult of anticipation; and I was up early, and down in the yard looking to the horses before London was well awake. As I entered the stable a man lying curled up in the straw rolled lazily over and, shading his eyes, glanced up. Apparently he recognized me, for he got slowly to his feet. "Morning!" he said gruffly.

I stood staring at him, wondering if I had made a mistake.

"What are you doing here, my man?" I said sharply, when I had made certain I knew him, and that he was really the surly ostler from the

Gatehouse tavern at Highgate. "Why did you come here? Why have you followed us?"

"Come about your business," he answered. "To give you that."

I took the note he held out to me. "From whom?" I said. "Who sent it by you?"

"Cannot tell," he replied, shaking his head.

"Cannot, or will not?" I retorted.

"Both," he said doggedly. "But there, if you want to know what sort of a kernel is in a nut, you don't shake the tree, master--you crack the nut."

I looked at the note he had given me. It was but a slip of paper folded thrice. The sender had not addressed, or sealed, or fastened it in anyway; had taken no care either to insure its reaching its destination or to prevent prying eyes seeing the contents. If one of our associates had sent it, he had been guilty of the grossest carelessness. "You are sure it is for me?" I said.

"As sure as mortal can be," he answered. "Only that it was given me for a man, and not a mouse! You are not afraid, master?"

I was not; but he edged away as he spoke, and looked with so much alarm at the scrap of paper that it was abundantly clear he was very much afraid himself, even while he derided me. I saw that if I had offered to return the note he would have backed out of the stable and gone off there and then as fast as his lame foot would let him. This puzzled me. However, I read the note. There was nothing in it to frighten me. Yet, as I read, the color came into my face, for it contained one name to which I had long been a stranger.

"To Francis Cludde," it ran. "If you would not do a thing of which you will miserably repent all your life, and which will stain you in the eyes of all Christian men, meet me two hours before noon at the cross street by St. Botolph's, where you first saw Mistress Bertram. And tell no one. Fail not to come. In Heaven's name, fail not!"

The note had nothing to do with the conspiracy, then, on the face of it; mysterious as it was, and mysteriously as it came. "Look here!" I said to the man. "Tell me who sent it, and I will give you a crown."

"I would not tell you," he answered stubbornly, "if you could make me King of England! No, nor King of Spain too! You might rack me and you would not get it from me!"

His one eye glowed with so obstinate a resolve that I gave up the attempt to persuade him, and turned to examine the message itself. But here I fared no better. I did not know the handwriting, and there was no peculiarity in the paper. I was no wiser than before. "Are you to take back any answer?" I said.

"No," he replied, "the saints be thanked for the same! But you will bear me witness," he went on anxiously, "that I gave you the letter. You will not forget that, or say that you have not had it? But there!" he added to himself as he turned away, speaking in a low voice, so that I barely caught the sense of the words, "what is the use? she will know!"

She will know! It had something to do with a woman then, even if a woman were not the writer. I went in to breakfast in two minds about going. I longed to tell Master Bertie and take his advice, though the unknown had enjoined me not to do so. But for the time I refrained, and explaining my absence of mind as well as I could, I presently stole away on some excuse or other, and started in good time, and on foot, into the city. I reached the rendezvous a quarter of an hour before the time named, and strolling between the church and the baker's shop, tried to look as much like a chance passer-by as I could, keeping the while a wary lookout for any one who might turn out to be my correspondent.

The morning was cold and gray. A drizzling rain was falling. The passers were few, and the appearance of the streets dirty and, with littered kennels, was dreary indeed. I found it hard at once to keep myself warm and to avoid observation as I hung about. Ten o'clock had rung from more than one steeple, and I was beginning to think myself a fool for my pains, when a woman of middle height, slender and young in figure, but wearing a shabby brown cloak, and with her head muffled in a hood, as though she had the toothache or dreaded the weather more than ordinary, turned the corner of the belfry and made straight toward me. She drew near, and seemed about to pass me without notice. But when abreast of me she glanced up suddenly, her eyes the only features I could see.

"Follow me to the church!" she murmured gently. And she swept on to the porch.

I obeyed reluctantly; very reluctantly, my feet seeming like lead. For I knew who she was. Though I had only seen her eyes, I had recognized them, and guessed already what her business with me was. She led the way resolutely to a quiet corner. The church was empty and still, with only the scent of incense in the air to tell of a recent service. It was no surprise to me when she turned abruptly, and, removing her hood, looked me in the face.

"What have you done with him?" she panted, laying her hand on my arm. "Speak! Tell me what you have done with him?"

The question, the very question, I had foreseen! Yet I tried to fence with her. I said, "With whom?"

"With whom?" she repeated bitterly. "You know me! I am not so changed in three years that you do not recognize me?"

"No; I know you," I said.

There was a hectic flush on her cheeks, and it seemed to me that the dark hair was thinner on her thin temples than when I had seen her last. But the eyes were the same.

"Then why ask with whom?" she cried passionately. "What have you done with the man you called Clarence?"

"Done with him?" I said feebly.

"Ay, done with him? Come, speak and tell me!" she repeated in fierce accents, her hand clutching my wrist, her eyes probing my face with merciless glances. "Have you killed him? Tell me!"

"Killed him, Mistress Anne?" I said sullenly. "No, I have not killed him."

"He is alive?" she cried.

"For all I know, he is alive."

She glared at me for some seconds to assure herself that I was telling the truth. Then she heaved a great sigh; her hands fell from my wrists, the color faded out of her face, and she lowered her eyes. I glanced round with a momentary idea of escape--I so shrank from that which was to come. But before I had well entertained the notion she looked up, her face grown calm.

"Then what have you done with him?" she asked.

"I have done nothing with him," I answered.

She laughed; a mirthless laugh. "Bah!" she said, "do not tell me lies! That is your honor, I suppose--your honor to your friends down in the cellar there! Do you think that I do not know all about them? Shall I give you the list? He is a very dangerous conspirator, is Sir Thomas Penruddocke, is he not? And that scented dandy Master Kingston! Or Master Crewdson--tell me of him! Tell me of him, I say!" she exclaimed, with a sudden return from irony to a fierce eagerness, a breathless impatience. "Why did he not come up last night? What have you done with him?"

I shook my head, sick and trembling. How could I tell her?

"I see," she said. "You will not tell me. But you swear he is yet alive, Master Cludde? Good. Then you are holding him for a hostage? Is that it?" with a piercing glance at my face. "Or, you have condemned him, but for some reason the sentence has not been executed!" She drew a long, deep breath, for I fear my face betrayed me. "That is it, is it? Then there is still time."

She turned from me and looked toward the end of the aisle, where a dull red lamp hanging before the altar glowed feebly in the warm scented air. She seemed so to turn and so to look in thankfulness, as if the news she had learned were good instead of what it was. "What is the hour fixed?" she asked suddenly.

I shook my head.

"You will not tell me? Well, it matters not," she answered briskly. "He must be saved. Do you hear? He must be saved, Master Cludde. That is your business."

I shook my head.

"You think it is not?" she said. "Well, I can show you it is! Listen!"

She raised herself on a step of the font, and looked me harshly in the face. "If he be not given up to me safe and sound by sunset this evening, I will betray you all! All! I have the list here," she muttered sternly, touching her bosom. "You, Master Bertie, Penruddocke, Fleming, Barnes--all. All, do you hear? Give him up or you shall hang!"

"You would not do it!" I cried aghast, peering into her burning eyes.

"Would not do it? Fool!" she hissed. "If all the world but he had one head, I would cut it off to save his! He is my husband! Do you hear? He is my husband--my all! Do you think I have given up everything, friends and honor and safety, for him, to lose him now? No! You say I would not do it? Do you know what I have done? You have a scar there."

She touched me lightly on the breast. "I did it," she said.

"You?" I muttered.

"Yes, I, you blind fool! I did it," she answered. "You escaped then, and I was glad of it, since the wound answered my purpose. But you will not escape again. The cord is surer."

Something in her last words crossed my memory and enlightened me.

"You were the woman I saw last night," I said. "You followed us from High gate."

"What matter! What matter!" she exclaimed impatiently. "Better be footsore than heartsore. Will you do now what I want? Will you answer for his life?"

"I can do nothing without the others," I said.

"But the others know nothing," she answered. "They do not know their own danger. Where will you find them?"

"I shall find them," I replied resolutely. "And in any case I must consult Master Bertie. Will you come and see him?"

"And be locked up too?" she said sternly, and in a different tone. "No. It is you must do this, and you must answer for it, Francis Cludde. You, and no one else."

"I can do nothing by myself," I repeated.

"Ay, but you can--you must!" she retorted, "or Heaven's curse will be upon you! You think me mad to say that. Listen! Listen, fool! The man whom you have condemned, whom you have left to die, is not only my husband, wedded to me these three years, but your father--your father, Ferdinand Cludde!"

CHAPTER XX.

THE COMING QUEEN.

I stood glaring at her.

"You were a blind bat or you would have found it out for yourself," she continued scornfully. "A babe would have guessed it, knowing as much of your father as you did."

"Does he know himself?" I muttered hoarsely, looking anywhere but at her now. The shock had left me dull and confused. I did not doubt her word, rather I wondered with her that I had not found this out for myself. But the possibility of meeting my father in that wide world into which I had plunged to escape from the knowledge of his existence, had never occurred to me. Had I thought of it, it would have seemed too unlikely; and though I might have seen in Gardiner a link between us, and so have identified him, the greatness of the Chancellor's transactions, and certain things about Clarence which had seemed, or would have seemed, had I ever taken the point into consideration, at variance with my ideas of my father, had prevented me getting upon the track.

"Does he know that you are his son, do you mean?" she said. "No, he does not."

"You have not told him?"

"No," she answered with a slight shiver.

I understood. I comprehended that even to her the eagerness with which, being father and son, we had sought one another's lives during those days on the Rhine, had seemed so dreadful that she had concealed the truth from him.

"When did you learn it?" I asked, trembling too.

"I knew his right name before I ever saw you," she answered. "Yours I learned on the day I left you at Santon." Looking back I remembered the strange horror, then inexplicable, which she had betrayed; and I understood it. So it was that knowledge which had driven her from us! "What will you do now?" she said. "You will save him? You must save him! He is your father."

Save him? I shuddered at the thought that I had destroyed him! that I, his son, had denounced him! Save him! The perspiration sprang out in beads on my forehead. If I could not save him I should live pitied by my friends and loathed by my enemies!

"If it be possible," I muttered, "I will save him."

"You swear it?" she cried. Before I could answer she seized my arm and dragged me up the dim aisle until we stood together before the Figure and the Cross. The chimes above us rang eleven. A shaft of cold sunshine pierced a dusty window, and, full of dancing motes, shot athwart the pillars.

"Swear!" she repeated with trembling eagerness, turning her eyes on mine, and raising her hand solemnly toward the Figure. "Swear by the Cross!"

"I swear," I said.

She dropped her hand. Her form seemed to shrink and grow less. Making a sign to me to go, she fell on her knees on the step, and drew her hood over her face. I walked away on tiptoe down the aisle, but glancing back from the door of the church I saw the small, solitary figure still kneeling in prayer. The sunshine had died away. The dusty window was colorless. Only the red lamp glowed dully above her head. I seemed to see what the end would be. Then I pushed aside the curtain, and slipped out into the keen air. It was hers to pray. It was mine to act.

I lost no time, but on my return I could not find Master Bertie either in the public room or in the inn yard, so I sought him in his bedroom, where I found him placidly reading a book; his patient waiting in striking contrast with the feverish anxiety which had taken hold of me. "What is it, lad?" he said, closing the volume, and laying it down on my entrance. "You look disturbed?"

"I have seen Mistress Anne," I answered. He whistled softly, staring at me without a word. "She knows all," I continued.

"How much is all?" he asked after a pause.

"Our names--all our names, Penruddocke's, Kingston's, the others; our meeting-place, and that we hold Clarence a prisoner. She was that old woman whom we saw at the Gatehouse tavern last night."

He nodded, appearing neither greatly surprised nor greatly alarmed. "Does she intend to use her knowledge?" he said. "I suppose she does."

"Unless we let him go safe and unhurt before sunset."

"They will never consent to it," he answered, shaking his head.

"Then they will hang!" I cried.

He looked hard at me a moment, discerning something strange in the bitterness of my last words. "Come, lad," he said, "you have not told me all. What else have you learned?"

"How can I tell you?" I cried wildly, waving him off, and going to the lattice that my face might be hidden from him. "Heaven has cursed me!" I added, my voice breaking.

He came and laid his hand on my shoulder. "Heaven curses no one," he said. "Most of our curses we make for ourselves. What is it, lad?"

I covered my face with my hands. "He--he is my father," I muttered. "Do you understand? Do you see what I have done? He is my father!"

"Ha!" Master Bertie uttered that one exclamation in intense astonishment; then he said no more. But the pressure of his hand told me that he understood, that he felt with me, that he would help me. And that silent comprehension, that silent assurance, gave the sweetest comfort. "He must be allowed to go, then, for this time," he resumed gravely, after a pause in which I had had time to recover myself. "We will see to it. But there will be difficulties. You must be strong and brave. The truth must be told. It is the only way."

I saw that it was, though I shrank exceedingly from the ordeal before me. Master Bertie advised, when I grew more calm, that we should be the first at the rendezvous, lest by some chance Penruddocke's orders should be anticipated; and accordingly, soon after two o'clock, we mounted, and set forth. I remarked that my companion looked very carefully to his arms, and, taking the hint, I followed his example.

It was a silent, melancholy, anxious ride. However successful we might be in rescuing my father--alas! that I should have to-day and always to call that man father--I could not escape the future before me. I had felt shame while he was but a name to me; how could I endure to live, with his infamy always before my eyes? Petronilla, of whom I had been thinking so much since I returned to England, whose knot of velvet had never left my breast nor her gentle face my heart--how could I go back to her now? I had thought my father dead, and his name and fame old tales. But the years of foreign life which yesterday had seemed a sufficient barrier between his past and myself--of what use were they now? Or the foreign service I had fondly regarded as a kind of purification?

Master Bertie broke in on my reverie much as if he had followed its course. "Understand one thing, lad!" he said, laying his hand on the withers of my horse. "Yours must not be the hand to punish your father. But after to-day you will owe him no duty. You will part from him to-day and he will be a stranger to you. He deserted you when you were a child; and if you owe reverence to any one, it is to your uncle and not to him. He has himself severed the ties between you."

"Yes," I said. "I will go abroad. I will go back to Wilna."

"If ill comes of our enterprise--as I fear ill will come--we will both go back, if we can," he answered. "If good by any chance should come of it, then you shall be my brother, our family shall be your family. The Duchess is rich enough," he added with a smile, "to allow you a younger brother's portion."

I could not answer him as I desired, for we passed at that moment under the archway, and became instantly involved in the bustle going forward in the courtyard. Near the principal door of the inn stood eight or nine horses gayly caparisoned and in the charge of three foreign-looking men, who, lounging in their saddles, were passing a jug from hand to hand. They turned as we rode in and looked at us curiously, but not with any impertinence. Apparently they were waiting for the rest of their party, who were inside the house. Civilly disposed as they seemed, the fact that they were armed, and wore rich liveries of black and gold, caused me, and I think both of us, a momentary alarm.

"Who are they?" Master Bertie asked in a low voice, as he rode to the opposite door and dismounted with his back to them.

"They are Spaniards, I fancy," I said, scanning them over the shoulders of my horse as I too got off. "Old friends, so to speak."

"They seem wonderfully subdued for them," he answered, "and on their best behavior. If half the tales we heard this morning be true, they are not wont to carry themselves like this."

Yet they certainly were Spanish, for I overheard them speaking to one another in that language; and before we had well dismounted, their leader-- whom they received with great respect, one of them jumping down to hold his stirrup--came out with three or four more and got to horse again. Turning his rein to lead the way out through the north gate he passed near us, and as he settled himself in his saddle took a good look at us. The look passed harmlessly over me, but reaching Master Bertie became concentrated. The rider started and smiled faintly. He seemed to pause, then he raised his plumed cap and bowed low--covered himself again and rode on. His train all followed his example and saluted us as they passed. Master Bertie's face, which had flushed a fiery red under the other's gaze, grew pale again. He looked at me, when they had gone by, with startled eyes.

"Do you know who that was?" he said, speaking like one who had received a blow and did not yet know how much he was hurt.

"No," I said.

"It was the Count de Feria, the Spanish Ambassador," he answered. "And he recognized me. I met him often, years ago. I knew him again as soon as he came out, but I did not think he would by any chance recognize me in this dress."

"Are you sure," I asked in amazement, "that it was he?"

"Quite sure," he answered.

"But why did he not have you arrested, or at least detained? The warrants are still out against you."

Master Bertie shook his head. "I cannot tell," he said darkly. "He is a Spaniard. But come, we have the less time to lose. We must join our friends and take their advice; we seem to be surrounded by pitfalls."

At this moment the lame ostler came up, and grumbling at us as if he had never seen us in his life before, and never wished to see us again, took our horses. We went into the kitchen, and taking the first chance of slipping upstairs to No. 15, we were admitted with the same precautions as before, and descending the shaft gained the cellar.

Here we were not, as we had looked to be, the first on the scene. I suppose a sense of the insecurity of our meeting-place had led every one to come early, so as to be gone early. Penruddocke indeed was not here yet, but Kingston and half a score of others were sitting about conversing in low tones. It was plain that the distrust and suspicion which we had remarked on the previous day had not been allayed by the discovery of Clarence's treachery.

Indeed, it was clear that the distrust and despondency had to-day become a panic. Men glared at one another and at the door, and talked in whispers and started at the slightest sound. I glanced round. The one I sought for with eager yet shrinking eyes was not to be seen. I turned to Master Bertie, my face mutely calling on him to ask the question. "Where is the prisoner?" he said sharply.

A moment I hung in suspense. Then one of the men said, "He is in there. He is safe enough!" He pointed, as he spoke, to a door which seemed to lead to an inner cellar.

"Right," said Master Bertie, still standing. "I have two pieces of bad news for you nevertheless. Firstly I have just been recognized by the Spanish Ambassador, whom I met in the courtyard above."

Half the men rose to their feet. "What is he doing here?" they cried, one boldly, the others with the quaver very plain in their voices.

"I do not know; but he recognized me. Why he took no steps to detain or arrest me I cannot tell. He rode away by the north road."

They gazed at one another and we at them. The wolfish look which fear brings into some faces grew stronger in theirs.

"What is your other bad news?" said Kingston, with an oath.

"A person outside, a friend of the prisoner, has a list of our names, and knows our meeting-place and our plans. She threatens to use the knowledge unless the man Clarence or Crewdson be set free."

There was a loud murmur of wrath and dismay, amid which Kingston alone preserved his composure. "We might have been prepared for that," he said quietly. "It is an old precaution of such folk. But how did you come to hear of it?"

"My friend here saw the messenger and heard the terms. The man must be set free by sunset."

"And what warranty have we that he will not go straight with his plans and his list to the Council?"

Master Bertie could not answer that, neither could I; we had no surety, and if we set him free could take none save his word. *His word!* Could even I ask them to accept that? To stake the life of the meanest of them on it?

I saw the difficulties of the position, and when Master Kingston pronounced coolly that this was a waste of time, and that the only wise course was to dispose of the principal witness, both in the interests of justice and our own safety, and then shift for ourselves before the storm broke, I acknowledged in my heart the wisdom of the course, and felt that yesterday it would have received my assent.

"The risk is about the same either way," Master Bertie said.

"Not at all," Kingston objected, a sparkle of malice in his eye. Last night we had thwarted him. To-night it was his turn; and the dark lowering looks of those round him showed that numbers were with him. "This fellow can hang us all. His accomplice who escapes can know nothing save through him, and could give only vague and uncertain evidence. No, no. Let us cast lots who shall do it, get it done quickly, and begone."

"We must wait at least," Bertie urged, "until Sir Thomas comes."

"No!" retorted Kingston, with heat. "We are all equal here. Besides the man was condemned yesterday, with the full assent of all. It only remains to carry out the sentence. Surely this gentleman," he continued, turning suddenly upon me, "who was so ready to accuse him yesterday, does not wish him spared to-day?"

"I do wish it," I said, in a low tone.

"Ho! ho!" he cried, folding his arms and throwing back his head, astonished at the success of his own question. "Then may we ask for your reasons, sir? Last night you could not lay your tongue to words too bad for him. Tonight you wish to spare him, and let him go?"

"I do," I said. I felt that every eye was upon me, and that, Master Bertie excepted, not one there would feel sympathy with me in my humiliation. They were driven to the wall. They had no time for fine feeling, for sympathy, for appreciation of the tragic, unless it touched themselves. What chance had I with them, though I was a son pleading for a father? Nay, what argument had I save that I was his son, and that I had brought him to this? No argument. Only the appeal to them that they would not make me a parricide! And I felt that at this they would mock.

And so, in view of those stern, curious faces, a new temptation seized me--the temptation to be silent. Why should I not stand by and let things take their course? Why should I not spare myself the shame which I already saw would be fruitless? When Master Kingston, with a cynical bow, said, "Your reasons, sir?" I stood mute and trembling. If I kept silence, if I refused to give my reasons, if I did not acknowledge the prisoner, but merely begged his life, he would die, and the connection between us would be known only to one or two. I should be freed from him and might go my own way. The sins of Ferdinand Cludde were well-nigh forgotten--why take to myself the sins of Clarence, which would otherwise never stain my name, would never be associated with my father or myself?

Why, indeed? It was a great and sore temptation, as I stood there before all those eyes. He had deserved death. I had given him up in perfect innocence. Had I any right to call on them to risk their lives that I might go harmless in conscience, and he in person? Had I----

What, was there after all some taint in my blood? Was I going to become like him--to take to myself a shame of my own earning, in the effort to escape from the burden of his ill-fame? I remembered in time the oath I had sworn, and when Kingston repeated his question, I answered him quickly. "I did not know yesterday who he was," I said. "I have discovered since that he is my father. I ask nothing on his account. Were he only my father I would not plead for him. I plead for myself," I murmured. "If you show no pity, you make me a parricide."

I had done them wrong. There was something in my voice, I suppose, as I said the words which cost me so much, which wrought with almost all of them in a degree. They gazed at me with awed, wondering faces, and murmured "His father!" in low tones. They were recalling the scene of last night, the moment when I had denounced him, the curse he had hurled at me, the half-told story of which that had seemed the climax. I had wronged them. They did see the tragedy of it.

Yes, they pitied me; but they showed plainly that they would still do what perhaps I should have done in their place--justice. "He knows too much!" said one. "Our lives are as good as his," muttered another--the first to become thoroughly himself again--"why should we all die for him?" The wolfish glare came back fast to their eyes. They handled their weapons impatiently. They were longing to be away. At this moment, when I saw I had indeed made my confession in vain, Master Bertie struck in. "What," he said, "if Master Carey and I take charge of him, and escorting him to his agent without, be answerable for both of them?"

"You would be only putting your necks into the noose!" said Kingston.

"We will risk that!" replied my friend--and what a friend and what a man he seemed amid that ignoble crew!--"I will myself promise you that if he refuse to remain with us until midnight, or tries wherever we are to raise an alarm or communicate with any one, I will run him through with my own hand? Will not that satisfy you?"

"No," Master Kingston retorted, "it will not! A bird in the hand is worth two in the bush!"

"But the woman outside?" said one timidly.

"We must run that risk!" quoth he. "In an hour or two we shall be in hiding. Come, the lot must be drawn. For this gentleman, let him stand aside."

I leaned against the wall, dazed and horror-stricken. Now that I had identified myself with him I felt a great longing to save him. I scarcely noticed the group drawing pieces of paper at the table. My every thought was taken up with the low door over there, and the wretched man lying bound in the darkness behind it. What must be the horror, the black despair, the hate and defiance of his mind as he lay there, trapped at last like any beast of prey? It was horrible! horrible! horrible!

I covered my face and could not restrain the cry of unutterable distress which rose to my lips. They looked round, two or three of them, from the table. But the impression my appeal had made upon them had faded away already, and they only shrugged their shoulders and turned again to their task. Master Bertie alone stood apart, his arms folded, his face grave and dark. He too had abandoned hope. There seemed no hope, when suddenly there came a knocking at the door. The papers were dropped, and while some stood as if stiffened into stone, others turned and gazed at their neighbors. It was a knocking more hasty and imperative than the usual summons, though given in the same fashion. At last a man found tongue. "It is Sir Thomas," he suggested, with a sigh of relief. "He is in a hurry and brings news. I know his knock."

"Then open the door, fool," cried Kingston. "If you can see through a two-inch plank, why do you stand there like a gaby?"

Master Bertie anticipated the man, and himself opened the door and admitted the knocker. Penruddocke it was; he came in, still drumming on the door with his fist, his eyes sparkling, his ruddy cheeks aglow. He crossed the threshold with a swagger, and looking at us all burst into a strange peal of laughter. "Yoicks! Gone to earth!" he shouted, waving his hand as if he had a whip in it. "Gone to earth--gone forever! Did you think it was the Lords of the Council, my lads?"

He had left the door wide open behind him, and we now saw in the doorway the seafaring man who usually guarded the room above. "What does this mean, Sir Thomas?" Kingston said sternly. He thought, I fancy, as many of us did, that the knight was drunk. "Have you given that man permission to leave his post?"

"Post? There are no more posts," cried Sir Thomas, with a strange jollity. He certainly was drunk, but perhaps not with liquor. "Except good fat posts," he continued, smacking Master Bertie on the shoulder, "for loyal men who have done the state service, and risked their lives in evil times! Posts? I shall get so drunk to-night that the stoutest post on Ludgate will not hold me up!"

"You seem to have gone far that way already," my friend said coldly.

"So will you, when you hear the news!" Penruddocke replied more soberly. "Lads, the Queen is dying!"

In the vaulted room his statement was received in silence; a silence dictated by no feeling for the woman going before her Maker--how should we who were plotting against her feel for her, we who were for the most part homeless and proscribed through her?--but the silence of men in doubt, in doubt whether this might mean all that from Sir Thomas's aspect it seemed to mean.

"She cannot live a week!" Penruddocke continued. "The doctors have given up hope, and at the palace all is in confusion. She has named the

Princess Elizabeth her successor, and even now Cecil is drawing up the proclamations. To show that the game is really up, the Count de Feria, the Spanish Ambassador, has gone this very day to Hatfield to pay his respects to the coming queen."

Then indeed the vaulted roof did ring--ring and ring again with shouts of "The Coming Queen!" Men over whom the wings of death had seemed a minute ago to be hovering, darkening all things to them, looked up and saw the sun. "The Coming Queen!" they cried.

"You need fear nothing!" continued Penruddocke wildly. "No one will dare to execute the warrants. The Bishops are shaking in their miters. Pole is said to be dying. Bonner is more likely to hang himself than burn others. Up and out and play the man! Away to your counties and get ready your tar-barrels! Now we will give them a taste of the Cujus Regio! Ho! drawer, there! A cup of ale!"

He turned, and shouting a scrap of a song, swaggered back into the shaft and began to ascend. They all trooped after him, talking and laughing, a reckless, good-natured crew, looking to a man as if they had never known fear or selfishness--as if distrust were a thing impossible to them. Master Kingston alone, whom his losses had soured and who still brooded over his revenge, went off moodily.

I was for stopping one of them; but Master Bertie directed my eyes by a gesture of his hand to the door at the far end of the cellar, and I saw that the key was in the lock. He wrung my hand hard. "Tell him all," he muttered. "I will wait above."

CHAPTER XXI.

MY FATHER.

Tell him all? I stood thinking, my hand on the key. The voices of the rearmost of the conspirators sounded more and more faintly as they passed up the shaft, until their last accents died in the room above, and silence followed; a silence in strange contrast with the bright glare of the torches which burned round me and lit up the empty cellar as for a feast. I was wondering what he would say when I told him all--when I said "I am your son! I, whom Providence has used to thwart your plans, whose life you sought, whom, without a thought of pity, you left to perish! I am your son!"

Infinitely I dreaded the moment when I should tell him this, and hear his answer; and I lingered with my hand on the key until an abrupt knocking on the other side of the door brought the blood to my face. Before I could turn the key the hasty summons was repeated, and grew to a frantic, hurried drumming on the boards--a sound which plainly told of terror suddenly conceived and in an instant full-grown. A hoarse cry followed, coming dully to my ears through the thickness of the door, and the next moment the stout planks shook as a heavy weight fell against them.

I turned the key, and the door was flung open from within. My father stumbled out.

The strong light for an instant blinded him, and he blinked as an owl does brought to the sunshine. Even in him the long hours passed in solitude and the blackness of despair had worked changes. His hair was grayer; in patches it was almost white, and then again dark. He had gnawed his lower lip, and there were bloodstains on it. His mustache, too, was ragged and torn, as if he had gnawed that also. His eyes were bloodshot, his lean face was white and haggard and fierce.

"Ha!" he cried, trembling, as he peered round, "I thought they had left me to starve! There were rats in there! I thought----"

He stopped. He saw me standing holding the edge of the door. He saw that otherwise the room was empty, the farther door leading to the shaft open. An open door! To him doubtless it seemed of all sights the most wonderful, the most heavenly! His knees began to shake under him.

"What is it?" he muttered. "What were they shouting about? I heard them shouting."

"The queen is dying," I answered simply, "or dead, and you can do us no more harm. You are free."

"Free?" He repeated the word, leaning against the wall, his eyes wild and glaring, his lips parted.

"Yes, free," I answered, in a lower voice--"free to go out into the air of heaven a living man!" I paused. For a moment I could not continue. Then I added solemnly, "Sir, Providence has saved you from death, and me from a crime."

He leaned still against the wall, dazed, thunderstruck, almost incredulous, and looked from me to the open door and back again as if without this constant testimony of his eyes he could not believe in his escape.

"It was not Anne?" he murmured. "She did not----"

"She tried to save your life," I answered; "but they would not listen to her."

"Did she come here?"

As he spoke, he straightened himself with an effort and stood up. He was growing more like himself.

"No," I answered. "She sent for me and told me her terms. But Kingston and the others would not listen to them. You would have been dead now, though I did all I could to save you, if Penruddocke had not brought this news of the queen."

"She is dead?"

"She is dying. The Spanish Ambassador," I added, to clinch the matter, for I saw he doubted, "rode through here this afternoon to pay his court to the Princess Elizabeth at Hatfield."

He looked down at the ground, thinking deeply. Most men would have been unable to think at all, unable to concentrate their thoughts on anything save their escape from death. But a life of daily risk and hazard had so hardened this man that I was certain, as I watched him, that he was not praying nor giving thanks. He was already pondering how he might make the most out of the change; how he might to the best advantage sell his knowledge of the government whose hours were numbered to the government which soon would be. The life of intrigue had become second nature to him.

He looked up and our eyes met. We gazed at one another.

"Why are you here?" he said curiously. "Why did they leave you? Why were you the one to stop to set me free, Master Carey?"

"My name is not Carey," I answered.

"What is it, then?" he asked carelessly.

"Cludde," I answered softly.

"Cludde!" He called it out. Even his self-mastery could not cope with this surprise. "Cludde," he said again--said it twice in a lower voice.

"Yes, Cludde," I answered, meeting and yet shrinking from his questioning eyes, "my name is Cludde. So is yours. I tried to save your life, because I learned from Mistress Anne----"

I paused. I shrank from telling him that which, as it seemed to me, would strike him to the ground in shame and horror. But he had no fear.

"What?" he cried. "What did you learn?"

"That you are my father," I answered slowly. "I am Francis Cludde, the son whom you deserted many years ago, and to whom Sir Anthony gave a home at Coton."

I expected him to do anything except what he did. He stared at me with astonished eyes for a minute, and then a low whistle issued from his lips.

"My son, are you! My son!" he said coolly. "And how long have you known this, young sir?"

"Since yesterday," I murmured. The words he had used on that morning at Santon, when he had bidden me die and rot, were fresh in my memory--in my memory, not in his. I recalled his treachery to the Duchess, his pursuit of us, his departure with Anne, the words in which he had cursed me. He remembered apparently none of these things, but simply gazed at me with a thoughtful smile.

"I wish I had known it before," he said at last. "Things might have been different. A pretty dutiful son you have been!"

The sneer did me good. It recalled to my mind what Master Bertie had said.

"There can be no question of duty between us," I answered firmly. "What duty I owe to any one of my family, I owe to my uncle."

"Then why have you told me this?"

"Because I thought it right you should know it," I answered, "were it only that, knowing it, we may go different ways. We have nearly done one another a mischief more than once," I added gravely.

He laughed. He was not one whit abashed by the discovery, nor awed, nor cast down. There was even in his cynical face a gleam of kindliness and pride as he scanned me. We were almost of a height--I the taller by an inch or two; and in our features I believe there was a likeness, though not such as to invite remark.

"You have grown to be a chip of the old block," he said coolly. "I would as soon have you for a son as another. I think on the whole I am pleased. You talked of Providence just now"--this with a laugh of serene amusement--"and perhaps you were right. Perhaps there is such a thing. For I am growing old, and lo! it gives me a son to take care of me."

I shook my head. I could never be that kind of son to him.

"Wait a bit," he said, frowning slightly. "You think your side is up and mine is down, and I can do you no good now, but only harm. You are ashamed of me. Well, wait," he continued, nodding confidently. "Do not be too sure that I cannot help you. I have been wrecked a dozen times, but I never yet failed to find a boat that would take me to shore."

Yes, he was so arrogant in the pride of his many deceits that an hour after Heaven had stretched out its hand to save him, he denied its power and took the glory to himself. I did not know what to say to him, how to undeceive him, how to tell him that it was not the failure of his treachery which shamed me, but the treachery itself. I could only remain silent.

And so he mistook me; and, after pondering a moment with his chin in his hand, he continued:

"I have a plan, my lad. The Queen dies. Well--I am no bigot--long live the Queen and the Protestant religion! The down will be up and the up down, and the Protestants will be everything. It will go hard then with those who cling to the old faith."

He looked at me with a crafty smile, his head on one side.

"I do not understand," I said coldly.

"Then listen. Sir Anthony, will hold by his religion. He used to be a choleric gentleman, and as obstinate as a mule. He will need but to be pricked up a little, and he will get into trouble with the authorities as sure as eggs are eggs. I will answer for it. And then----"

"Well?" I said grimly. How was I to observe even a show of respect for him when I was quivering with fierce wrath and abhorrence? "Do you think that will benefit *you?*" I cried. "Do you think that you are so high in favor with Cecil and the Protestants that they will set you in Sir Anthony's place? You!"

He looked at me still more craftily, not put out by my indignation, but rather amused by it.

"No, lad, not me," he replied, with tolerant good-nature. "I am somewhat blown upon of late. But Providence has not given me back my son for nothing. I am not alone in the world now. I must remember my family. I must think a little of others as well as of myself."

"What do you mean?" I said, recoiling.

He scanned me for a moment, with his eyes half-shut, his head on one side. Then he laughed, a cynical, jarring laugh.

"Good boy!" he said. "Excellent boy! He knows no more than he is told. His hands are clean, and he has friends upon the winning side who will not see him lose a chance, should a chance turn up. Be satisfied. Keep your hands clean if you like, boy. We understand one another."

He laughed again and turned away; and, much as I dreaded and disliked him, there was something in the indomitable nature of the man which wrung from me a meed of admiration. Could the best of men have recovered more quickly from despair? Could the best of men, their plans failing, have begun to spin fresh webs with equal patience? Could the most courageous and faithful of those who have tried to work the world's bettering, have faced the downfall of their hopes with stouter hearts, with more genuine resignation? Bad as he was, he had courage and endurance beyond the common.

He came back to me when he had gone a few paces.

"Do you know where my sword is?" he asked in a matter-of-fact tone, as one might ask a question of an old comrade.

I found it cast aside behind the door. He took it from me, grumbling over a nick in the edge, which he had caused by some desperate blow when he was seized. He fastened it on with an oath. I could not look at the sword without remembering how nearly he had taken my life with it. The recollection did not trouble him in the slightest.

"Now farewell!" he said carelessly, "I am going to turn over a new leaf, and begin returning good for evil. Do you go to your friends and do your work, and I will go to my friends and do mine."

Then with a nod he walked briskly away, and I heard him climb the ladder and depart.

What was he going to do? I was so deeply amazed by the interview that I did not understand. I had thought him a wicked man, but I had not conceived the hardness of his nature. As I stood alone looking round the vault, I could hardly believe that I had met and spoken to my father, and told him I was his son--and this was all! I could hardly believe that he had gone away with this knowledge, unmoved and unrepentant; alike unwarned by the Providence which had used me to thwart his schemes, and untouched by the beneficence which had thrice held him back from the crime of killing me--ay, proof even against the long-suffering which had plucked him from the abyss and given him one more chance of repentance.

I found Master Bertie in the stables waiting for me with some impatience. Of which, upon the whole, I was glad. For I had no wish to be closely questioned, and the account I gave him of the interview might at another time have seemed disjointed and incoherent. He listened to it, however, without remark; and his next words made it clear that he had other matters in his mind.

"I do not know what to do about fetching the Duchess over," he said. "This news seems to be true, and she ought to be here."

"Certainly," I agreed.

"The country in general is well affected to the Princess Elizabeth," he continued. "Yet the interests of the Bishops, of the Spanish faction, and of some of the council, will lie in giving trouble. To avoid this, we should show our strength. Therefore I want the Duchess to come over with all speed. Will you fetch her?" he added sharply, turning to me.

"Will I?" I cried in surprise.

"Yes, you. I cannot well go myself at this crisis. Will you go instead?"

"Of course I will," I answered.

And the prospect cheered me wonderfully. It gave me something to do, and opened my eyes to the great change of which Penruddocke had been the herald, a change which was even then beginning. As we rode down Highgate Hill that day, messengers were speeding north and south and east and west, to Norwich and Bristol and Canterbury and Coventry and York, with the tidings that the somber rule under which England had groaned for five years and more was coming to an end. If in a dozen towns of England they roped their bells afresh; if in every county, as Penruddocke had prophesied, they got their tar-barrels ready; if all, save a few old-fashioned folk and a few gloomy bigots and hysterical women, awoke as from an evil dream; if even sensible men saw in the coming of the young queen a panacea for all their ills--a quenching of Smithfield fires, a Calais recovered, a cure for the worthless coinage which hampered trade, and a riddance of worthless foreigners who plundered it--with better roads, purer justice, a fuller Exchequer, more favorable seasons--if England read all this in that news of Penruddocke's, was it not something to us also?

It was indeed. We were saved at the last moment from the dangerous enterprise on which we had rashly embarked. We had now such prospects before us as only the success of that scheme could have ordinarily opened. Ease and honor instead of the gallows, and to lie warm instead of creaking in the wind! Thinking of this, I fell into a better frame of mind as I jogged along toward London. For what, after all, was my father to me, that his existence should make me unhappy, or rob mine of all pleasure? I had made a place for myself in the world. I had earned friends for myself. He might take away my pride in the one, but he could never rob me of the love of the others--of those who had eaten and drunk and fought and suffered beside me, and for whom I too had fought and suffered!

*　　　*　　　*　　　*　　　*

"A strange time for the swallows to come back," said my lady, turning to smile at me, as I rode on her off-side.

It would have been strange, indeed, if there had been swallows in the air. For it was the end of December. The roads were frost-bound and the trees leafless. The east wind, gathering force in its rush across the Essex marshes, whirled before it the last trophies of Hainault Forest, and seemed, as it whistled by our ears and shaved our faces, to grudge us the shelter to which we were hastening. The long train behind us--for the good times of which we had talked so often had come--were full of the huge fire we expected to find at the inn at Barking--our last stage on the road to London. And if the Duchess and I bore the cold more patiently, it was probably because we had more food for thought--and perhaps thicker raiment.

"Do not shake your head," she continued, glancing at me with mischief in her eyes, "and flatter yourself you will not go back, but will go on making yourself and some one else unhappy. You will do nothing of the kind, Francis. Before the spring comes you and I will ride over the drawbridge at Coton End, or I am a Dutchwoman!"

"I cannot see that things are changed," I said.

"Not changed?" she replied. "When you left, you were nobody. Now you are somebody, if it be only in having a sister with a dozen serving-men in her train. Leave it to me. And now, thank Heaven, we are here! I am so stiff and cold, you must lift me down. We have not to ride far after dinner, I hope."

"Only seven miles," I answered, as the host, who had been warned by an outrider to expect us, came running out with a tail at his heels.

"What news from London, Master Landlord?" I said to him as he led us through the kitchen, where there was indeed a great fire, but no chimney, and so to a smaller room possessing both these luxuries. "Is all quiet?"

"Certainly, your worship," he replied, bowing and rubbing his hands. "There never was such an accession, nor more ale drunk, nor powder burned--and I have seen three--and there was pretty shouting at old King Harry's, but not like this. Such a fair young queen, men report, with a look of the stout king about her, and as prudent and discreet as if she had changed heads with Sir William Cecil. God bless her, say I, and send her a wise husband!"

"And a loving one," quoth my lady prettily. "Amen."

"I am glad all has gone off well," I continued, speaking to the Duchess, as I turned to the blazing hearth. "If there had been blows, I would fain have been here to strike one."

"Nay, sir, not a finger has wagged against her," the landlord answered, kicking the logs together--"to speak of, that is, your worship. I do hear to-day of a little trouble down in Warwickshire. But it is no more than a storm in a wash-tub, I am told."

"In Warwickshire?" I said, arrested, in the act of taking off my cloak, by the familiar name. "In what part, my man?"

"I am not clear about that, sir, not knowing the country," he replied. "But I heard that a gentleman there had fallen foul of her Grace's orders about church matters, and beaten the officers sent to see them carried out; and that, when the sheriff remonstrated with him, he beat him too. But I warrant they will soon bring him to his senses."

"Did you hear his name?" I asked. There was a natural misgiving in my mind. Warwickshire was large; and yet something in the tale smacked of Sir Anthony.

"I did hear it," the host answered, scratching his head, "but I cannot call it to mind. I think I should know it if I heard it."

"Was it Sir Anthony Cludde?"

"It was that very same name!" he exclaimed, clapping his hands in wonder. "To be sure! Your worship has it pat!"

I slipped back into my cloak again, and snatched up my hat and whip. But the Duchess was as quick. She stepped between me and the door.

"Sit down, Francis!" she said imperiously. "What would you be at?"

"What would I be at?" I cried with emotion. "I would be with my uncle. I shall take horse at once and ride Warwickshire way with all speed. It is possible that I may be in time to avert the consequences. At least I can see that my cousin comes to no harm."

"Good lad," she said placidly. "You shall start tomorrow."

"To-morrow!" I cried impatiently. "But time is everything, madam."

"You shall start to-morrow," she repeated. "Time is not everything, firebrand! If you start to-day what can you do? Nothing! No more than if the thing had happened three years ago, before you met me. But to-morrow--when you have seen the Secretary of State, as I promise you you shall, this evening if he be in London--to-morrow you shall go in a different character, and with credentials."

"You will do this for me?" I exclaimed, leaping up and taking her hand, for I saw in a moment the wisdom of the course she proposed. "You will get me----"

"I will get you something to the purpose," my lady answered roundly. "Something that shall save your uncle if there be any power in England can save him. You shall have it, Frank," she added, her color rising, and her eyes filling, as I kissed her hand, "though I have to take Master Secretary by the beard!"

CHAPTER XXII.

SIR ANTHONY'S PURPOSE.

Late, as I have heard, on the afternoon of November 20, 1558, a man riding between Oxford and Worcester, with the news of the queen's death, caught sight of the gateway tower at Coton End, which is plainly visible from the road. Though he had already drunk that day as much ale as would have sufficed him for a week when the queen was well, yet much wants more. He calculated he had time to stop and taste the Squire's brewing, which he judged, from the look of the tower, might be worth his news; and he rode through the gate and railed at his nag for stumbling.

Half way across the Chase he met Sir Anthony. The old gentleman was walking out, with his staff in his hand and his dogs behind him, to take the air before supper. The man, while he was still a hundred paces off, began to wave his hat and shout something, which ale and excitement rendered unintelligible.

"What is the matter?" said Sir Anthony to himself. And he stood still.

"The queen is dead!" shouted the messenger, swaying in his saddle.

The knight stared.

"Ay, sure!" he ejaculated after a while. And he took off his hat. "Is it true, man?"

"As true as that I left London yesterday afternoon and have never drawn rein since!" swore the knave, who had been three days on the road, and had drunk at every hostel and at half the manor-houses between London and Oxford.

"God rest her soul!" said Sir Anthony piously, still in somewhat of a maze. "And do you come in! Come in, man, and take something."

But the messenger had got his formula by heart, and was not to be defrauded of any part of it.

"God save the queen!" he shouted. And out of respect for the knight, he slipped from his saddle and promptly fell on his back in the road.

"Ay, to be sure, God save the queen!" echoed Sir Anthony, taking off his hat again. "You are right, man!" Then he hurried on, not noticing the messenger's mishap. The tidings he had heard seemed of such importance, and he was so anxious to tell them to his household--for the greatest men have weaknesses, and news such as this comes seldom in a lifetime--that he strode on to the house, and over the drawbridge into the courtyard, without once looking behind him.

He loved order and decent observance. But there are times when a cat, to get to the cream-pan, will wet its feet. He stood now in the middle of the courtyard, and raising his voice, shouted for his daughter. "Ho, Petronilla! do you hear, girl! Father! Father Carey! Martin Luther! Baldwin!" and so on, until half the household were collected. "Do you hear, all of you? The queen is dead! God rest her soul!"

"Amen!" said Father Carey, as became him, putting in his word amid the wondering silence which followed; while Martin Luther and Baldwin, who were washing themselves at the pump, stood with their heads dripping and their mouths agape.

"Amen!" echoed the knight. "And long live the queen! Long live Queen Elizabeth!" he continued, having now got his formula by heart. And he swung his hat.

There was a cheer, a fairly loud cheer. But there was one who did not join in it, and that was Petronilla. She, listening at her lattice upstairs, began at once to think, as was her habit when any matter great or small fell out, whether this would affect the fortunes of a certain person far away. It might, it might not; she did not know. But the doubt so far entertained her that she came down to supper with a heightened color, not thinking in the least, poor girl, that the event might have dire consequences for others almost as dear to her, and nearer home.

Every year since his sudden departure a letter from Francis Cludde had come to Coton; a meager letter, which had passed through many hands, and reached Sir Anthony now through one channel, now through another. The knight grumbled and swore over these letters, which never contained an address to which an answer could be forwarded, nor said much, save that the writer was well and sent his love and duty, and looked to return, all being well. But, meager as they were, and loud as he swore over them, he put them religiously away in an oak-chest in his parlor; and another always put away for her share something else, which was invariably inclosed--a tiny swallow's feather. The knight never said anything about the feather; neither asked the meaning of its presence, nor commented upon its absence when Petronilla gave him back the letter. But for days after each of these arrivals he would look much at his daughter, would follow her about with his eyes, be more regular in bidding her attend him in his walk, and more particular in seeing that she had the tidbits of the joint.

For Petronilla, it cannot be said, though I think in after times she would have liked to make some one believe it, that she wasted away. But she did take a more serious and thoughtful air in these days, which she never, God bless her, lost afterward. There came from Wootton Wawen and from Henley in Arden and from Cookhill gentlemen of excellent estate, to woo her. But they all went away disconsolate after drinking very deeply of Sir Anthony's ale and strong waters. And some wondered that the good knight did not roundly take the jade to task and see her settled.

But he did not; so possibly even in these days he had other views. I have been told that, going up once to her little chamber to seek her, he found a very singular ornament suspended inside her lattice. It was no other than a common clay house-martin's nest. But it was so deftly hung in a netted bag, and so daintily swathed in moss always green, and the Christmas roses and snowdrops and violets and daffodils which decked it in turn were always so pure and fresh and bright--as the knight learned by more than one stealthy visit afterward--that, coming down the steep steps, he could not see clearly, and stumbled against a cook-boy, and beat him soundly for getting in his way.

To return, however. The news of the queen's death had scarcely been well digested at Coton, nor the mass for her soul, which Father Carey celebrated with much devotion, been properly criticised, before another surprise fell upon the household. Two strangers arrived, riding late one evening, and rang the great bell while all were at supper. Baldwin and the porter went to see what it was, and brought back a message which drew the knight from his chair, as a terrier draws a rat.

"You are drunk!" he shouted, purple in the face, and fumbling for the stick which usually leaned against his seat ready for emergencies. "How dare you bring cock-and-bull stories to me?"

"It is true enough!" muttered Baldwin sullenly: a stout, dour man, not much afraid of his master, but loving him exceedingly. "I knew him again myself."

Sir Anthony strode firmly out of the room, and in the courtyard near the great gate found a man and a woman standing in the dusk. He walked up to the former and looked him in the face. "What do you here?" he said, in a strange, hard voice.

"I want shelter for a night for myself and my wife; a meal and some words with you--no more," was the answer. "Give me this," the stranger continued, "which every idle passer-by may claim at Coton End, and you shall see no more of me, Anthony."

For a moment the knight seemed to hesitate. Then he answered, pointing sternly with his hand, "There is the hall and supper. Go and eat and drink. Or, stay!" he resumed. And he turned and gave some orders to Baldwin, who went swiftly to the hall, and in a moment came again. "Now go! What you want the servants will prepare for you."

"I want speech of you," said the newcomer.

Sir Anthony seemed about to refuse, but thought better of it. "You can come to my room when you have supped," he said, in the same ungracious tone, speaking with his eyes averted.

"And you--do you not take supper?"

"I have finished," said the knight, albeit he had eaten little. And he turned on his heel.

Very few of those who sat round the table and watched with astonishment the tall stranger's entrance knew him again. It was thirteen years since Ferdinand Cludde had last sat there; sitting there of right. And the thirteen years had worked much change in him. When he found that Petronilla, obeying her father's message, had disappeared, he said haughtily that his wife would sup in her own room; and with a flashing eye and curling lip, bade Baldwin see to it. Then, seating himself in a place next Sir Anthony's, he looked down the board at which all sat silent. His sarcastic eye, his high bearing, his manner--the manner of one who had gone long with his life in his hand--awed these simple folk. Then, too, he was a Cludde. Father Carey was absent that evening. Martin Luther had one of those turns, half-sick, half-sullen, which alternated with his moods of merriment; and kept his straw pallet in some corner or other. There was no one to come between the servants and this dark-visaged stranger, who was yet no stranger.

He had his way and his talk with Sir Anthony; the latter lasting far into the night and producing odd results. In the first place, the unbidden guest and his wife stayed on over next day, and over many days to come, and seemed gradually to grow more and more at home. The knight began to take long walks and rides with his brother, and from each walk and ride came back with a more gloomy face and a curter manner. Petronilla, his companion of old, found herself set aside for her uncle, and cast, for society, on Ferdinand's wife, the strange young woman with the brilliant eyes, whose odd changes from grave to gay rivaled Martin Luther's; and who now scared the girl by wild laughter and wilder gibes, and now moved her to pity by fits of weeping or dark moods of gloom. That Uncle Ferdinand's wife stood in dread of her husband, Petronilla soon learned, and even began to share this dread, to shrink from his presence, and to shut herself up more and more closely in her own chamber.

There was another, too, who grew to be troubled about this time, and that was Father Carey. The good-natured, easy priest received with joy and thankfulness the news that Ferdinand Cludde had seen his errors and re-entered the fold. But when he had had two or three interviews with the convert, his brow, too, grew clouded, and his mind troubled. He learned to see that the accession of the young Protestant queen must bear fruit for which he had a poor appetite. He began to spend many hours in the church--the church which he had known all his life--and wrestled much with himself--if his face were any index to his soul. Good, kindly man, he was not of the stuff of which martyrs are made; and to be forced, pushed on, and goaded into becoming a martyr against one's will--well, the Father's position was a hard one. As was that in those days of many a good and learned clergyman bred in one church, and bidden suddenly, on pain of losing his livelihood, if not his life, to migrate to another.

The visitors had been in the house a month--and in that month an observant eye might have noted much change, though all things in seeming went on as before--when the queen's orders enjoining all priests to read the service, or a great part of it, in English, came down, being forwarded by the sheriff to Father Carey. The missive arrived on a Friday, and had been indeed long expected.

"What shall you do?" Ferdinand asked Sir Anthony.

"As before!" the tall old man replied, gripping his staff more firmly. It was no new subject between them. A hundred times they had discussed it already, even as they were now discussing it on the terrace by the fish-pool, with the church which adjoins the house full in view across the garden. "I will have no mushroom faith at Coton End," the knight continued warmly. "It sprang up under King Henry, and how long did it last? A year or two. It came in again under King Edward, and how long did it last? A year or two. So it will be again. It will not last, Ferdinand."

"I am of that mind," the younger man answered, nodding his head gravely.

"Of course you are!" Sir Anthony rejoined, as he rested one hand on the sundial. "For ten generations our forefathers have worshiped in that church after the old fashion--and shall it be changed in my day? Heaven forbid! The old fashion did for my fathers; it shall do for me. Why, I would as soon expect that the river yonder should flow backward as that the church which has stood for centuries, and more years to the back of them than I can count, should be swept away by these Hot Gospelers! I will have none of them! I will have no new-fangled ways at Coton End!"

"Well, I think you are right!" the younger brother said. By what means he had brought the knight to this mind without committing himself more fully, I cannot tell. Yet so it was. Ferdinand showed himself always the cautious doubter. Father Carey even must have done him that justice. But-- and this was strange--the more doubtful he showed himself, the more stubborn grew his brother. There are men so shrewd as to pass off stones for bread; and men so simple-minded as to take something less than the word for the deed.

"Why should it come in our time?" cried Sir Anthony fractiously.

"Why indeed?" quoth the subtle one.

"I say, why should it come now? I have heard and read of the sect called Lollards who gave trouble a while ago. But they passed, and the church stood. So will these Gospelers pass, and the church will stand."

"That is our experience certainly," said Ferdinand.

"I hate change!" the old man continued, his eyes on the old church, the old timbered house--for only the gateway tower at Coton is of stone--the old yew trees in the churchyard. "I do not believe in it, and, what is more, I will not have it. As my fathers have worshiped, so will I, though it cost me every rood of land! A fig for the Order in Council!"

"If you really will not change with the younger generations----"

"I will not!" replied the old knight sharply. "There is an end of it!"

To-day the Reformed Church in England has seen many an anniversary, and grown stronger with each year; and we can afford to laugh at Sir Anthony's arguments. We know better than he did, for the proof of the pudding is in the eating. But in him and his fellows, who had only the knowledge of their own day, such arguments were natural enough. All time, all experience, all history and custom and habit, as known to them, were on their side. Only it was once again to be the battle of David and the Giant of Gath.

Sir Anthony had said, "There is an end of it!" But his companion, as he presently strolled up to the house with a smile on his saturnine face, well knew that this was only the beginning of it. This was Friday.

On the Sunday, a rumor of the order having gone abroad, a larger congregation than usual streamed across the Chase to church, prepared to hear some new thing. They were disappointed. Sir Anthony stalked in as of old, through the double ranks of people waiting at the door to receive him; and after him Ferdinand and his wife, and Petronilla and Baldwin, and every servant from the house save a cook or two and the porter. The church was full. Seldom had such a congregation been seen in it. But all passed as of old. Father Carey's hand shook, indeed, and his voice quavered; but he went through the ceremony of the mass, and all was done in Latin. A little change would have been pleasant, some thought. But no one in this country place on the borders of the forest held very strong views. No bishop had come heretic-hunting to Coton End. No abbey existed to excite dislike by its extravagance or by its license or by the swarm of ragged idlers it supported. Father Carey was the most harmless and kindest of men. The villagers did not care one way or the other. To them Sir Anthony was king. And if any one felt tempted to interfere, the old knight's face, as he gazed steadfastly at the brass effigy of a Cludde, who had fallen in Spain fighting against the Moors, warned the meddler to be silent.

And so on that Sunday all went well. But some one must have told tales, for early in the week there came a strong letter of remonstrance from the sheriff, who was an old friend of Sir Anthony, and of his own free will, I fancy, would have winked. But he was committed to the Protestants, and bound to stand or fall with them. The choleric knight sent back an answer by the same messenger. The sheriff replied, the knight rejoined--having his brother always at his elbow. The upshot of the correspondence was an announcement on the part of the sheriff that he should send his officers to the next service, to see that the queen's order was obeyed; and a reply on the part of Sir Anthony that he should as certainly put the men in the duck-pond. Some inkling of this state of things got abroad, and spread as a September fire flies through a wood; so that there was like to be such a congregation at the next service to witness the trial of strength, as would throw the last Sunday's gathering altogether into the shade.

It was clear at last that Sir Anthony himself did not think that here was the end of it. For on that Saturday afternoon he took a remarkable walk. He called Petronilla after dinner, and bade her get her hood and come with him. And the girl, who had seen so little of her father in the last month, and who, what with rumors and fears and surmises, was eating her heart out, obeyed him with joy. It was a fine frosty day near the close of December. Sir Anthony led the way over the plank-bridge which crossed the moat in the rear of the house, and tramped steadily through the home farm toward a hill called the Woodman's View, which marked the border of the forest. He did not talk, but neither was he sunk in reverie. As he entered each field he stood and scanned it, at times merely nodding, at times smiling, or again muttering a few words such as, "The three-acre piece! My father inclosed it!" or, "That is where Ferdinand killed the old mare!" or, "The best land for wheat on this side of the house!" The hill climbed, he stood a long time gazing over the landscape, eying first the fields and meadows which stretched away from his feet toward the house; the latter, as seen from this point, losing all its stateliness in the mass of stacks and ricks and barns and granaries which surrounded it. Then his eyes traveled farther in the same line to the broad expanse of woodland--Coton Chase--through which the road passed along a ridge as straight as an arrow. To the right were more fields, and here and there amid them a homestead with its smaller ring of stacks and barns. When he turned to the left, his eyes, passing over the shoulders of Barnt Hill and Mill Head Copse and Beacon Hill, all bulwarks of the forest, followed the streak of river as it wound away toward Stratford through luscious flood meadows, here growing wide, and there narrow, as the woodland advanced or retreated.

"It is all mine," he said, as much to himself as to the girl. "It is all Cludde land as far as you can see."

There were tears in her eyes, and she had to turn away to conceal them. Why, she hardly knew. For he said nothing more, and he walked down the hill dry-eyed. But all the way home he still looked sharply about, noting this or that, as if he were bidding farewell to the old familiar objects, the spinneys and copses--ay, and the very gates and gaps and the hollow trees where the owls built. It was the saddest and most pathetic walk the girl had ever taken. Yet there was nothing said.

CHAPTER XXIII.

THE LAST MASS.

The north wall of the church at Coton End is only four paces from the house, the church standing within the moat. Isolated as the sacred building, therefore, is from the outer world by the wide-spreading Chase, and close-massed with the homestead, Sir Anthony had some excuse for considering it as much a part of his demesne as the mill or the smithy. In words he would have been willing to admit a distinction; but in thought I fancy he lumped it with the rest of his possessions.

It was with a lowering eye that on this Sunday morning he watched from his room over the gateway the unusual stream of people making for the church. Perchance he had in his mind other Sundays--Sundays when he had walked out at this hour, light of heart and kind of eye, with his staff in his fist and his glove dangling, and his dog at his heels; and, free from care, had taken pleasure in each bonnet doffed and each old wife's "God bless ye, Sir Anthony!" Well, those days were gone. Now the rain dripped from the eaves--for a thaw had come in the night--and the bells, that could on occasion ring so cheerily, sounded sad and forlorn. His daughter, when she came, according to custom, bringing his great service-book, could scarcely look him in the face. I know not whether even then his resolution to dare all might not, at sound of a word from her, or at sight of her face, have melted like yesterday's ice. But before the word could be spoken, or the eyes meet, another step rang on the stone staircase and brother Ferdinand entered.

"They are here!" he said in a low voice. "Six of them, Anthony, and sturdy fellows, as all Clopton's men are. If you do not think your people will stand by you----"

The knight fired at this suggestion. "What!" he burst out, turning from the window, "if Cludde men cannot meet Clopton men the times are indeed gone mad! Make way and let me come! Though the mass be never said again in Coton church, it shall be said to-day!" And he swore a great oath.

He strode down the stairs and under the gateway, where were arranged, according to the custom of the house on wet days, all the servants, with Baldwin and Martin Luther at their head. The knight stalked through them with a gloomy brow. His brother followed him, a faint smile flickering about the corners of his mouth. Then came Ferdinand's wife and Petronilla, the latter with her hood drawn close about her face, Anne with her chin in the air and her eyes aglow. "It is not a bit of a bustle will scare her!" Baldwin muttered, as he fell in behind her, and eyed her back with no great favor.

"No--so long as it does not touch her," Martin replied in a cynical whisper. "She is well mated! Well mated and ill fated! Ha! ha!"

"Silence, fool," growled his companion angrily. "Is this a time for antics?"

"Ay, it is!" Martin retorted swiftly, though with the same caution. "For when wise men turn fools, fools are put to it to act up to their profession! You see, brother?" And he deliberately cut a caper. His eyes were glittering, and the nerves on one side of his face twitched oddly. Baldwin looked at him, and muttered that Martin was going to have one of his mad fits. What had grown on the fool of late?

The knight reached the church porch and passed through the crowd which awaited him there. Save for its unusual size and some strange faces to be seen on its skirts, there was no indication of trouble. He walked, tapping his stick on the pavement a little more loudly than usual, to his place in the front pew. The household, the villagers, the strangers, pressed in behind him until every seat was filled. Even the table monument of Sir Piers Cludde, which stood lengthwise in the aisle, was seized upon, and if the two similar monuments which stood to right and left below the chancel steps had not been under the knight's eyes, they too would have been invaded. Yet all was done decently and in order, with a clattering of rustic boots indeed, but no scrambling or ill words. The Clopton men were there. Baldwin had marked them well, and so had a dozen stout fellows, sons of Sir Anthony's tenants. But they behaved, discreetly, and amid such a silence as Father Carey never remembered to have faced, he began the Roman service.

The December light fell faintly through the east window on the Father at his ministrations, on his small acolytes, on the four Cludde brasses before the altar. It fell everywhere--on gray dusty walls buttressed by gray tombs which left but a narrow space in the middle of the chancel. The marble crusader to the left matched the canopied bed of Sir Anthony's parents on the right; the Abbess's tomb in the next row faced the plainer monument of Sir Anthony's wife, a vacant place by her side awaiting his own effigy. And there were others. The chancel was so small--nay, the church too--so small and old and gray and solid, and the tombs were so massive, that they elbowed one another. The very dust which rose as men stirred was the dust of Cluddes. Sir Anthony's brow relaxed. He listened gravely and sadly.

And then the interruption came. "I protest!" a rough voice in rear of the crowd cried suddenly, ringing harshly and strangely above the Father's accents and the solemn hush. "I protest against this service!"

A thrill of astonishment ran through the crowd, and all rose. Every man in the church turned round, Sir Anthony among the first, and looked in the direction of the voice. Then it was seen that the Clopton men had massed themselves about the door in the southwest corner--a strong position, whence retreat was easy. Father Carey, after a momentary glance, went on as if he had not heard; but his voice shook, and all still waited with their faces turned toward the west end.

"I protest in the name of the Queen!" the same man cried sharply, while his fellows raised a murmur so that the priest's voice was drowned.

Sir Anthony stepped into the aisle, his face inflamed with anger. The interruption taking place there, in that place, seemed to him a double profanation.

"Who is that brawler?" he said, his hand trembling on his staff; and all the old dames trembled too. "Let him stand out."

The sheriff's spokesman was so concealed by his fellows that he could not be seen; but he answered civilly enough.

"I am no brawler," he said. "I only require the law to be observed; and that you know, sir. I am here on behalf of the sheriff; and I warn all present that a continuation of this service will expose them to grievous pains and penalties. If you desire it, I will read the royal order to prove that I do not speak without warrant."

"Begone, knave, you and your fellows!" Sir Anthony cried. A loyal man in all else, and the last to deny the queen's right or title, he had no reasonable answer to give, and could only bluster. "Begone, do you hear?" he repeated; and he rapped his staff on the pavement, and then, raising it, pointed to the door.

All Coton thought the men must go; but the men, perhaps, because they were Clopton, did not go. And Sir Anthony had not so completely lost his head as to proceed to extremities except in the last resort. Affecting to consider the incident at an end, he stepped back into his pew without waiting to see whether the man obeyed him or no, and resumed his devotions. Father Carey, at a nod from him, went on with the interrupted service.

But again the priest had barely read a dozen lines before the same man made the congregation start by crying loudly, "Stop!"

"Go on!" shouted Sir Anthony in a voice of thunder.

"At your peril!" retorted the intervener.

"Go on!" from Sir Anthony again.

Father Carey stood silent, trembling and looking from one to the other. Many a priest of his faith would have risen on the storm and in the spirit of Hildebrand hurled his church's curse at the intruder. But the Father was not of these, and he hesitated, fumbling with his surplice with his feeble white hands. He feared as much for his patron as for himself; and it was on the knight that his eyes finally rested. But Sir Anthony's brow was black; he got no comfort there. So the Father took courage and a long breath, opened his mouth and read on, amid the hush of suppressed excitement, and of such anger and stealthy defiance as surely English church had never seen before. As he read, however, he gathered courage, and his voice strength. The solemn words, so ancient, so familiar, fell on the stillness of the church, and awed even the sheriff's men. To the surprise of nearly every one, there was no further interruption; the service ended quietly.

So after all Sir Anthony had his way, and stalked out, stiff and unbending. Nor was there any falling off, but rather an increase in the respect with which his people rose, according to custom, as he passed. Yet under that increase of respect lay a something which cut the old man to the heart. He saw that his dependents pitied him while they honored him; that they thought him a fool for running his head against a stone wall--as Martin Luther put it--even while they felt that there was something grand in it too.

During the rest of the day he went about his usual employments, but probably with little zest. He had done what he had done without any very clear idea how he was going to proceed. Between his loyalty in all else and his treason in this, it would not have been easy for a Solomon to choose a consistent path. And Sir Anthony was no Solomon. He chose at last to carry himself as if there were no danger--as if the thing which had happened were unimportant. He ordered no change and took no precautions. He shut his ears to the whispering which went on among the servants, and his eyes to the watch which by some secret order of Baldwin was kept upon the Ridgeway.

It was something of a shock to him, therefore, when his daughter came to him after breakfast next morning, looking pale and heavy-eyed, and, breaking through the respect which had hitherto kept her silent, begged him to go away.

"To go away?" he cried. He rose from his oak chair and glared at her. Then his feelings found their easiest vent in anger. "What do you mean, girl?" he blustered, "Go away? Go where?"

But she did not quail. Indeed she had her suggestion ready.

"To the Mere Farm in the Forest, sir," she answered earnestly. "They will not look for you there; and Martin says----"

"Martin? The fool!"

His face grew redder and redder. This was too much. He loved order and discipline; and to be advised in such matters by a woman and a fool! It was intolerable!

"Go to, girl!" he cried, fuming. "I wondered where you had got your tale so pat. So you and the fool have been putting your heads together! Go! Go and spin, and leave these maters to men! Do you think that my brother, after traveling the world over, has not got a head on his shoulders? Do you think, if there were danger, he and I would not have foreseen it?"

He waved his hand and turned away expecting her to go. But Petronilla did not go. She had something else to say and though the task was painful she was resolved to say it.

"Father, one word," she murmured. "About my uncle."

"Well, well! What about him?"

"I distrust him, sir," she ventured, in a low tone, her color rising. "The servants do not like him. They fear him, and suspect him of I know not what."

"The servants!" Sir Anthony answered in an awful tone.

Indeed it was not the wisest thing she could have said; but the consequences were averted by a sudden alarm and shouting outside. Half a dozen voices, shrill or threatening, seemed to rise at once. The knight strode to the window, but the noise appeared to come, not from the Chase upon which it looked, but from the courtyard or the rear of the house. Sir Anthony caught up his stick, and, followed by the girl, ran down the steps. He pushed aside half a dozen women who had likewise been attracted by the noise, and hastened through the narrow passage which led to the wooden bridge in the rear of the buildings.

Here, in the close on the far side of the moat, a strange scene was passing. A dozen horsemen were grouped in the middle of the field about a couple of prisoners, while round the gate by which they had entered stood as many stout men on foot, headed by Baldwin and armed with pikes and staves. These seemed to be taunting the cavaliers and daring them to come on. On the wooden bridge by which the knight stood were half a dozen of the servants, also armed. Sir Anthony recognized in the leading horseman

Sir Philip Clopton, and in the prisoners Father Carey and one of the woodmen; and in a moment he comprehended what had happened.

The sheriff, in the most unneighborly manner, instead of challenging his front door, had stolen up to the rear of the house, and, without saying with your leave or by your leave, had snapped up the poor priest, who happened to be wandering in that direction. Probably he had intended to force an entrance; but he had laid aside the plan when he saw his only retreat menaced by the watchful Baldwin, who was not to be caught napping. The knight took all this in at a glance, and his gorge rose as much at the Clopton men's trick as at the danger in which Father Carey stood. So he lost his head, and made matters worse. "Who are these villains," he cried in a rage, his face aflame, "who come attacking men's houses in time of peace? Begone, or I will have at ye!"

"Sir Anthony!" Clopton cried, interrupting him, "in Heaven's name do not carry the thing farther! Give me way in the Queen's name, and I will----"

What he would do was never known, for at that last word, away at the house, behind Sir Anthony, there was a puff of smoke, and down went the sheriff headlong, horse and man, while the report of an arquebuse rang dully round the buildings. The knight gazed horrified; but the damage was done and could not be undone. Nay, more, the Coton men took the sound for a signal. With a shout, before Sir Anthony could interfere, they made a dash for the group of horsemen. The latter, uncertain and hampered by the fall of their leader, who was not hit, but was stunned beyond giving orders, did the best they could. They let their prisoners go with a curse, and then, raising Sir Philip and forming a rough line, they charged toward the gate by which they had entered.

The footmen stood the brunt gallantly, and for a moment the sharp ringing of quarter-staves and the shivering of steel told of as pretty a combat as ever took place on level sward in full view of an English home. The spectators could see Baldwin doing wonders. His men backed him up bravely. But in the end the impetus of the horses told, the footmen gave way and fled aside, and the strangers passed them. A little more skirmishing took place at the gateway, Sir Anthony's men being deaf to all his attempts to call them off; and then the Clopton horse got clear, and, shaking their fists and vowing vengeance, rode off toward the forest. They left two of their men on the field, however, one with a broken arm and one with a shattered knee-cap; while the house party, on their side, beside sundry knocks and bruises, could show one deep sword-cut, a broken wrist, and half a dozen nasty wounds.

"My poor little girl!" Sir Anthony whispered to himself, as he gazed with scared eyes at the prostrate men and the dead horse, and comprehended what had happened. "This is a hanging business! In arms against the Queen! What am I to do?" And as he went back to the house in a kind of stupor, he muttered again, "My little girl! my poor little girl!"

I fancy that in this terrible crisis he looked to get support and comfort from his brother--that old campaigner, who had seen so many vicissitudes and knew by heart so many shifts. But Ferdinand, though he thought the event unlucky, had little to say and less to suggest; and seemed, indeed, to have become on a sudden flaccid and lukewarm. Sir Anthony felt himself thrown on his own resources. "Who fired the shot?" he asked, looking about the room in a dazed fashion. "It was that which did the mischief," he continued, forgetting his own hasty challenge.

"I think it must have been Martin Luther," Ferdinand answered.

But Martin Luther, when he was accused, denied this stoutly. He had been so far along the Ridgeway, he said, that though he had returned at once on hearing the shot fired, he had arrived too late for the fight. The fool's stomach for a fight was so well known that this seemed probable enough, and though some still suspected him, the origin of the unfortunate signal was never clearly determined, though in after days shrewd guesses were made by some.

For a few hours it seemed as if Sir Anthony had sunk into his former state of indecision. But when Petronilla came again to him soon after noon to beg him to go into hiding, she found his mood had altered. "Go to the Mere Farm?" he said, not angrily now, but firmly and quietly. "No, girl, I cannot. I have been in fault, and I must stay and pay for it. If I left these poor fellows to bear the brunt, I could never hold up my head again. But do you go now and tell Baldwin to come to me."

She went and told the stern, down-looking steward, and he came up.

"Baldwin," said the knight when the door was shut, and the two were alone, "you are to dismiss to their homes all the tenants--who have indeed been called out without my orders. Bid them go and keep the peace, and I hope they will not be molested. For you and Father Carey, you must go into hiding. The Mere Farm will be best."

"And what of you, Sir Anthony?" the steward asked, amazed at this act of folly.

"I shall remain here," the knight replied with dignity.

"You will be taken," said Baldwin, after a pause.

"Very well," said the knight.

The man shrugged his shoulders, and was silent.

"What do you mean?" asked Sir Anthony in anger.

"Why, just that I cannot do it," Baldwin answered, glowering at him with a flush on his dark cheek. "That is what I mean. Let the priest go. I cannot go, and will not."

"Then you will be hanged!" quoth the knight warmly. "You have been in arms against the Queen, you fool! You will be hanged as sure as you stay here!"

"Then I shall be hanged," replied the steward sullenly. "There never was a Cludde hanged yet without one to keep him company. To hear of it would make my grandsire turn in his grave out there. I dare not do it, Sir Anthony, and that is the fact. But for the rest I will do as you bid me."

And he had his way. But never had evening fallen more strangely and sadly at Coton before. The rain pattered drearily in the courtyard. The drawbridge, by Baldwin's order, had been pulled up, and the planks over the moat in the rear removed.

"They shall not steal upon us again!" he muttered. "And if we must surrender, they shall see we do it willingly."

The tenants had gone to their homes and their wives. Only the servants remained. They clustered, solemn and sorrowful, about the hearth in the great hall, starting if a dog howled without or a coal flew from the fire within. Sir Anthony remained brooding in his own room, Petronilla sitting beside him silent and fearful, while Ferdinand and his wife moved restlessly about, listening to the wind. But the evening and the night wore peacefully away, and so, to the surprise of everybody, did the next day and the next. Could the sheriff be going to overlook the matter? Alas! on the third day the doubt was resolved. Two or three boys, who had been sent out as scouts, came in with news that there was a strong watch set on the Ridgeway, that the paths through the forest were guarded, that bodies of armed men were arriving in the neighboring villages, and that soldiers had been demanded--or so it was said--from Warwick and Worcester, and even from a place as far away as Oxford. Probably it was only the sheriff's prudence which had postponed the crisis; and now it had come. The net was drawn all round. As the day closed in on Coton and the sun set angrily among the forest trees, the boys' tale, which grew no doubt in the telling, passed from one to another, and men swore and looked out of window, and women wept in corners. In the Tower-room Sir Anthony sat awaiting the summons, and wondered what he could to save his daughter from possible rudeness, or even hurt, at the hands of these strangers.

There was one man missing from hall and kitchen, but few in the suspense noticed his absence. The fool had heard the boys' story, and, unable to remain inactive under such excitement, he presently stole off in the dusk to the rear of the house. Here he managed to cross the moat by means of a plank, which he then drew over and hid in the grass. This quietly managed--Baldwin, be it said, had strictly forbidden any one to leave the house--Martin made off with a grim chuckle toward the forest, and following the main track leading toward Wootton Wawen, presently came among the trees upon a couple of sentinels. They heard him, saw him indistinctly, and made a rush for him. But this was just the sport Martin liked, and the fun he had come for. His quick ear apprised him of the danger, and in a second he was lost in the underwood, his mocking laugh and shrill taunts keeping the poor men on the shudder for the next ten minutes. Then the uncanny accents died away, and, satisfied with his sport and the knowledge he had gained, the fool made for home. As he sped quickly across the last field, however, he was astonished by the sight of a dark figure in the very act of launching his--Martin's--plank across the moat.

"Ho, ho!" the fool muttered in a fierce undertone. "That is it, is it? And only one! If they will come one by one, like the plums in the kitchen porridge, I shall make a fine meal!"

He stood back, crouching down on the grass, and watched the unknown, his eyes glittering. The stranger was a tall, big fellow, a formidable antagonist. But Martin cared nothing for that. Had he not his long knife, as keen as his wits--when they were at home, which was not always. He drew it out now, and under cover of the darkness crept nearer and nearer, his blood glowing pleasantly, though the night was cold. How lucky it was he had come out! He could hardly restrain the "Ho, ho!" which rose to his lips. He meant to leap upon the man on this side of the water, that there might be no tell-tale traces on the farther bank.

But the stranger was too quick for him in this. He got his bridge fixed, and began to cross before Martin could crawl near enough. As he crossed, however, his feet made a slight noise on the plank, and under cover of it the fool rose and ran forward, then followed him over with the stealthiness of a cat. And like a cat too, the moment the stranger's foot touched the bank, Martin sprang on him with his knife raised--sprang on him silently, with his teeth grinning and his eyes aflame.

CHAPTER XXIV.

AWAITING THE BLOW.

A moment later the servants in the hall heard a scream--a scream of such horror and fear that they scarcely recognized a human voice in the sound. They sprang to their feet scared and trembling, and for a few seconds looked into one another's faces. Then, as curiosity got the upper hand, the boldest took the lead and all hurried pell-mell to the door, issuing in a mob into the courtyard, where Ferdinand Cludde, who happened to be near and had also heard the cry, joined them. "Where was it, Baldwin?" he exclaimed.

"At the back, I think," the steward answered. He alone had had the coolness to bring out a lantern, and he now led the way toward the rear of the house. Sure enough, close to the edge of the moat, they found Martin, stooping with his hands on his knees, a great wound, half bruise, half cut, upon his forehead. "What is it?" Ferdinand cried sharply. "Who did it, man?"

Baldwin had already thrown his light on the fool's face, and Martin, seeming to become conscious of their presence, looked at them, but in a dazed fashion. "What?" he muttered, "what is what?"

By this time nearly every one in the house had hurried to the spot; among them not only Petronilla, clinging to her father's arm, but Mistress Anne, her face pale and gloomy, and half a dozen womenfolk who clutched one another tightly, and screamed at regular intervals.

"What is it?" Baldwin repeated roughly, laying his hand on Martin's arm and slightly shaking him. "Come, who struck you, man?"

"I think," the fool answered slowly, gulping down something and turning a dull eye on the group; "a--a swallow flew by--and hit me!"

They shrank away from him instinctively and some crossed themselves. "He is in one of his mad fits," Baldwin muttered. Still the steward showed no fear. "A swallow, man!" he cried aloud. "Come, talk sense. There are no swallows flying at this time of year. And if there were, they do not fly by night, nor give men wounds like that. What was it? Out with it, now. Do you not see, man," he added, giving Martin an impatient shake, "that Sir Anthony is waiting?"

The fool nodded stupidly. "A swallow," he muttered. "Ay, 'twas a swallow, a great big swallow. I--I nearly put my foot on him."

"And he flew up and hit you in the face?" Baldwin said, with huge contempt in his tone.

Martin accepted the suggestion placidly. "Ay, 'twas so. A great big swallow, and he flew in my face," he repeated.

Sir Anthony looked at him compassionately. "Poor fellow!" he said; "Baldwin, see to him. He has had one of his fits and hurt himself."

"I never knew him hurt *himself*," Baldwin muttered darkly.

"Let somebody see to him," the knight said, disregarding the interruption. "And now come, Petronilla. Why--where has the girl gone?"

Not far. Only round to the other side of him, that she might be a little nearer to Martin. The curiosity in the other women's faces was a small thing in comparison with the startled, earnest look in hers. She gazed at the man with eyes not of affright, but of eager, avid questioning, while through her parted lips her breath came in gasps. Her cheek was red and white by turns, and, for her heart--well, it had seemed to stand still a moment, and now was beating like the heart of some poor captured bird held in the hand. She did not seem to hear her father speak to her, and he had to touch her sleeve. Then she started as though she were awakening from a dream, and followed him sadly into the house.

Sadly, and yet there was a light in her eyes which had not been there five minutes before. A swallow? A great big swallow? And this was December, when the swallows were at the bottom of the horse-ponds. She only knew of one swallow whose return was possible in winter. But then that one swallow--ay, though the snow should lie inches deep in the chase, and the water should freeze in her room--would make a summer for her. Could it be that one? Could it be? Petronilla's heart was beating so loudly as she went upstairs after her father, that she wondered he did not hear it.

The group left round Martin gradually melted away. Baldwin was the only man who could deal with him in his mad fits, and the other servants, with a shudder and a backward glance, gladly left him to the steward. Mistress Anne had gone in some time. Only Ferdinand Cludde remained, and he stood a little apart, and seemed more deeply engaged in listening for any sound which might betoken the sheriff's approach than in hearkening to their conversation. Listen as he might he would have gained little from the latter, for it was made up entirely of scolding on one side and stupid reiteration on the other. Yet Ferdinand, ever suspicious and on his guard, must have felt some interest in it, for he presently called the steward to him. "Is he more fool or knave?" he muttered, pointing under hand at Martin, who stood in the gloom a few paces away.

Baldwin shrugged his shoulders, but remained silent. "What happened? What is the meaning of it all?" Ferdinand persisted, his keen eyes on the steward's face. "Did he do it himself? Or who did it?"

Baldwin turned slowly and nodded toward the moat. "I expect you will find him who did it there," he said grimly. "I never knew a man save Sir Anthony or Master Francis hit Martin yet, but he paid for it. And when his temper is up, he is mad, or as good as mad; and better than two sane men!"

"He is a dangerous fellow," Ferdinand said thoughtfully, shivering a little. It was unlike him to shiver and shake. But the bravest have their moods.

"Dangerous?" the steward answered. "Ay, he is to some, and sometimes."

Ferdinand Cludde looked sharply at the speaker, as if he suspected him of a covert sneer. But Baldwin's gloomy face betrayed no glint of intelligence or amusement, and the knight's brother, reassured and yet uneasy, turned on his heel and went into the house, meeting at the door a servant who came to tell him that Sir Anthony was calling for him. Baldwin Moor, left alone, stood a moment thinking, and then turned to speak to Martin. But Martin was gone, and was nowhere to be seen.

The lights in the hall windows twinkled cheerily, and the great fire cast its glow half way across the courtyard, as lights and fire had twinkled and glowed at Coton End on many a night before. But neither in hall nor chamber was there any answering merriment. Baldwin, coming in, cursed the servants who were in his way, and the men moved meekly and without retort, taking his oaths for what they were--a man's tears. The women folk sat listening pale and frightened, and one or two of the grooms, those who had done least in the skirmish, had visions of a tree and a rope, and looked sickly. The rest scowled and blinked at the fire, or kicked up a dog if it barked in its sleep.

"Hasn't Martin come in?" Baldwin growled presently, setting his heavy wet boot on a glowing log, which hissed and sputtered under it. "Where is he?"

"Don't know!" one of the men took on himself to answer. "He did not come in here."

"I wonder what he is up to now?" Baldwin exclaimed, with gloomy irritation; for which, under the circumstances, he had ample excuse. He knew that resistance was utterly hopeless, and could only make matters worse, and twist the rope more tightly about his neck, to put the thought as he framed it. The suspicion, therefore, that this madman--for such in his worst fits the fool became--might be hanging round the place in dark corners, doing what deadly mischief he could to the attacking party, was not a pleasant one.

A gray-haired man in the warmest nook by the fire seemed to read his thoughts. "There is one in the house," he said slowly and oracularly, his eyes on Baldwin's boot, "whom he has just as good a mind to hurt, has our Martin, as any of them Clopton men. Ay, that has he, Master Baldwin."

"And who is that, gaffer?" Baldwin asked contemptuously.

But the old fellow turned shy. "Well, it is not Sir Anthony," he answered, nodding his head, and stooping forward to caress his toasting shins. "Be you very sure of that. Nor the young mistress, nor the young master as was, nor the new lady that came a month ago. No, nor it is not you, Master Baldwin."

"Then who is it?" cried the steward impatiently.

"He is shrewd, is Martin--when the saints have not got their backs to him," said the old fellow slyly.

"Who is it?" thundered the steward, well used to this rustic method of evasion. "Answer, you dolt!"

But no answer came, and Baldwin never got one; for at this moment a man who had been watching in front of the house ran in.

"They are here!" he cried, "a good hundred of them, and torches enough for St. Anthony's Eve. Get you to the gate, porter, Sir Anthony is calling for you. Do you hear?"

There was a great uprising, a great clattering of feet and barking of dogs, and some wailing among the women. As the messenger finished speaking, a harsh challenge which penetrated even the courtyard arose from many voices without, and was followed by the winding of a horn. This sufficed. All hurried with one accord into the court, where the porter looked to Baldwin for instructions.

"Hold a minute!" cried the steward, silencing the loudest hound by a sound kick, and disregarding Sir Anthony's voice, which came from the direction of the gateway. "Let us see if they are at the back too."

He ran through the passage and, emerging on the edge of the moat, was at once saluted by a dozen voices warning him back. There were a score of dark figures standing in the little close where the fight had taken place. "Right," said Baldwin to himself. "Needs must when the old gentleman drives! Only I thought I would make sure."

He ran back at once, nearly knocking down Martin, who with a companion was making, but at a slower pace, for the front of the house.

"Well, old comrade!" cried the steward, smiting the fool on the back as he passed, "you are here, are you? I never thought that you and I would be in at our own deaths!"

He did not notice, in the wild humor which had seized him, who Martin's companion was, though probably at another time it would have struck him that there was no one in the house quite so tall. He sped on with scarcely a glance, and in a moment was under the gateway, where Sir Anthony was soundly rating everybody, and particularly the porter, who with his key in the door found or affected to find the task of turning it a difficult one. As the steward came up, however, the big doors at some sign from him creaked on their hinges, and the knight, his staff in his hand, and the servants clustering behind him with lanterns, walked forward a pace or two to the end of the bridge, bearing himself with some dignity.

"Who disturbs us at this hour?" he cried, peering across the moat, and signing to Baldwin to hold up his large lantern, since the others, uncertain of their reception, had put out their torches. By its light he and those behind him could make out a group of half a dozen figures a score of yards away, while in support of these there appeared a bowshot off, and still in the open ground, a clump of, it might be, a hundred men. Beyond all lay the dark line of trees, above which the moon, new-risen, was sailing through a watery wrack of clouds. "Who are ye?" the knight repeated.

"Are you Sir Anthony Cludde?" came the answer.

"I am."

"Then in the Queen's name, Sir Anthony," the leader of the troop cried solemnly, "I call on you to surrender. I hold a warrant for your arrest, and also for the arrest of James Carey, a priest, and Baldwin Moor, who, I am told, is your steward. I am backed by forces which it will be vain to resist."

"Are you Sir Philip Clopton?" the knight asked. For at that distance and in that light it was impossible to be sure.

"I am," the sheriff answered earnestly. "And, as a friend, I beg you, Sir Anthony, to avoid useless bloodshed and further cause for offense. Sir Thomas Greville, the governor of Warwick Castle, and Colonel Bridgewater are with me. I implore you, my friend, to surrender, and I will do you what good offices I may."

The knight, as we know, had made up his mind. And yet for a second he hesitated. There were stern, grim faces round him, changed by the stress of the moment into the semblance of dark Baldwin's; the faces of men, who though they numbered but a dozen were his men, bound to him by every tie of instinct, and breeding, and custom. And he had been a soldier, and knew the fierce joy of a desperate struggle against odds. Might it not be better after all?

But then he remembered his womenkind; and after all, why endanger these faithful men? He raised his voice and cried clearly, "I accept your good offices, Sir Philip, and I take your advice. I will have the drawbridge lowered, only I beg you will keep your men well in hand, and do my poor house as little damage as may be."

Giving Baldwin the order, and bidding him as soon as it was performed come to him, the knight walked steadily back into the courtyard and took his stand there. He dispatched the women and some of the servants to lay out a meal in the hall. But it was noticeable that the men went reluctantly, and that all who could find any excuse to do so lingered round Sir Anthony as if they could not bear to abandon him; as if, even at the last moment, they had some vague notion of protecting their master at all hazards. A score of lanterns shed a gloomy, uncertain light--only in places reinforced by the glow, from the hall windows--upon the group. Seldom had a Coton moon peeped over the gables at a scene stranger than that which met the sheriff's eyes, as with his two backers he passed under the gateway.

"I surrender to you, Sir Philip," the knight said with dignity, stepping forward a pace or two, "and call you to witness that I might have made resistance and have not. My tenants are quiet in their homes, and only my servants are present. Father Carey is not here, nor in the house. This is Baldwin Moor, my steward, but I beg for him your especial offices, since he has done nothing save by my command."

"Sir Anthony, believe me that I will do all I can," the sheriff responded gravely, "but----"

"But to set at naught the Queen's proclamation and order!" struck in a third voice harshly--it was Sir Thomas Greville's--"and she but a month on the throne! For shame, Sir Anthony! It smacks to me of high treason. And many a man has suffered for less, let me tell you."

"Had she been longer on the throne," the sheriff put in more gently, "and were the times quiet, the matter would have been of less moment, Sir Anthony, and might not have become a state matter. But just now----"

"Things are in a perilous condition," Greville said bluntly, "and you have done your little to make them worse!"

The knight by a great effort swallowed his rage and humiliation. "What will you do with me, gentlemen?" he asked, speaking with at least the appearance of calmness.

"That is to be seen," Greville said, roughly over-riding his companion. "For to-night we must make ourselves and our men comfortable here."

"Certainly--with Sir Anthony's leave, Sir Thomas Greville," quoth a voice from behind. "But only so!"

More than one started violently, while the Cludde servants almost to a man spun round at the sound of the voice--my voice, Francis Cludde's, though in the darknesss no one knew me. How shall I ever forget the joy and lively gratitude which filled my heart as I spoke; which turned the night into day, and that fantastic scene of shadows into a festival, as I felt that the ambition of the last four years was about to be gratified. Sir Anthony, who was one of the first to turn, peered among the servants. "Who spoke?" he cried, a sudden discomposure in his voice and manner. "Who spoke there?"

"Ay, Sir Anthony, who did?" Greville said haughtily. "Some one apparently who does not quite understand his place or the state of affairs here. Stand back, my men, and let me see him. Perhaps we may teach him a useful lesson."

The challenge was welcome, for I feared a scene, and to be left face to face with my uncle more than anything. Now, as the servants with a loud murmur of surprise and recognition fell back and disclosed me standing by Martin's side, I turned a little from Sir Anthony and faced Greville. "Not this time, I think, Sir Thomas," I said, giving him back glance for glance. "I have learned my lesson from some who have fared farther and seen more than you, from men who have stood by their cause in foul weather as well as fair; and were not for mass one day and a sermon the next."

"What is this?" he cried angrily. "Who are you?"

"Sir Anthony Cludde's dutiful and loving nephew," I answered, with a courteous bow. "Come back, I thank Heaven, in time to do him a service, Sir Thomas."

"Master Francis! Master Francis!" Clopton exclaimed in remonstrance. He had known me in old days. My uncle, meanwhile, gazed at me in the utmost astonishment, and into the servants' faces there flashed a strange light, while many of them hailed me in a tone which told me that I had but to give the word, and they would fall on the very sheriff himself. "Master Francis," Sir Philip Clopton repeated gravely, "if you would do your uncle a service, this is not the way to go about it. He has surrendered and is our prisoner. Brawling will not mend matters."

I laughed out loudly and merrily. "Do you know, Sir Philip," I said, with something of the old boyish ring in my voice, "I have been, since I saw you last, to Belgium and Germany, ay, and Poland and Hamburg! Do you think I have come back a fool?"

"I do not know what to think of you," he replied dryly, "but you had best----"

"Keep a civil tongue in your head, my friend!" said Greville with harshness, "and yourself out of this business."

"It is just this business I have come to get into, Sir Thomas," I answered, with increasing good humor. "Sir Anthony, show them that!" I continued, and I drew out a little packet of parchment with a great red seal hanging from it by a green ribbon; just such a packet as that which I had stolen from the Bishop's apparitor nearly four years back. "A lantern here!" I cried. "Hold it steady, Martin, that Sir Anthony may read. Master Sheriff wants his rere-supper."

I gave the packet into the knight's hand, my own shaking. Ay, shaking, for was not this the fulfillment of that boyish vow I had made in my little room in the gable yonder, so many years ago? A fulfillment strange and timely, such as none but a boy in his teens could have hoped for, nor any but a man who had tried the chances and mishaps of the world could fully enjoy as I was enjoying it. I tingled with the rush through my veins of triumph and gratitude. Up to the last moment I had feared lest anything should go wrong, lest this crowning happiness should be withheld from me. Now I stood there smiling, watching Sir Anthony, as with trembling fingers he fumbled with the paper. And there was only one thing, only one person, wanting to my joy. I looked, and looked again, but I could not anywhere see Petronilla.

"What is it?" Sir Anthony said feebly, turning the packet over and over. "It is for the sheriff; for the sheriff, is it not?"

"He had better open it then, sir," I answered gayly.

Sir Philip took the packet and after a glance at the address tore it open. "It is an order from Sir William Cecil," he muttered. Then he ran his eye down the brief contents, while all save myself pricked their ears and pressed closer, and I looked swiftly from face to face, as the wavering light lit up now one and now another. Old familiar faces for the most part.

"Well, Sir Philip, will you stop to supper?" I cried with a laugh, when he had had time, as I judged, to reach the signature.

"Go to!" he grunted, looking at me. "Nice fools you have made of us, young man!" He passed the letter to Greville. "Sir Anthony," he continued, a mixture of pleasure and chagrin in his voice, "you are free! I congratulate you on your luck. Your nephew has brought an amnesty for all things done up to the present time save for any life taken, in which case the matter is to be referred to the Secretary. Fortunately my dead horse is the worst of the mischief, so free you are, and amnestied, though nicely Master Cecil has befooled us!"

"We will give you another horse, Sir Philip," I answered.

But the words were wasted on the air. They were drowned in a great shout of joy and triumph which rang from a score of Cludde throats the moment the purport of the paper was understood; a shout which made the old house shake again, and scared the dogs so that they fled away into corners and gazed askance at us, their tails between their legs; a shout that was plainly heard a mile away in half a dozen homesteads where Cludde men lay gloomy in their beds.

By this time my uncle's hand was in mine. With his other he took off his hat. "Lads!" he cried huskily, rearing his tall form in our midst; "a cheer for the Queen! God keep her safe, and long may she reign!"

This was universally regarded as the end of what they still proudly call in those parts "the Coton Insurrection!" When silence came again, every dog, even the oldest and wisest, had bayed himself hoarse and fled to kennel, thinking the end of the world was come. My heart, as I joined roundly in, swelled high with pride, and there were tears in my eyes as well as in my uncle's. But there is no triumph after all without its drawback, no fruition equal to the anticipation. Where was Petronilla? I could see her nowhere. I looked from window to window, but she was at none. I scanned the knot of maids, but could not find her. Even the cheering had not brought her out.

It was wonderful, though, how the cheers cleared the air. Even Sir Thomas Greville regained good humor, and deigned to shake me by the hand and express himself pleased that the matter had ended so happily. Then the sheriff drew him and Bridgewater away, to look to their men's arrangements, seeing, I think, that my uncle and I would fain be alone awhile; and at last I asked with a trembling voice after Petronilla.

"To be sure," Sir Anthony answered, furtively wiping his eyes. "I had forgotten her, dear lad. I wish now that she had stayed. But tell me, Francis, how came you back to-night, and how did you manage this?"

Something of what he asked I told him hurriedly. But then--be sure I took advantage of the first opening--I asked again after Petronilla. "Where has she gone, sir?" I said, trying to conceal my impatience. "I thought that Martin told me she was here; indeed, that he had seen her after I arrived."

"I am not sure, do you know," Sir Anthony answered, eying me absently, "that I was wise, but I considered she was safer away, Francis. And she can be fetched back in the morning. I feared there might be some disturbance in the house--as indeed there well might have been--and though she begged very hard to stay with me, I sent her off."

"This evening, sir?" I stammered, suddenly chilled.

"Yes, an hour ago."

"But an hour ago every approach was guarded, Sir Anthony," I cried in surprise. "I had the greatest difficulty in slipping through from the outside myself, well as I know every field and tree. To escape from within, even for a man, much less a woman, would have been impossible. She will have been stopped."

"I think not," he said, with a smile at once sage and indulgent--which seemed to add, "You think yourself a clever lad, but you do not know everything yet."

"I sent her out by the secret passage to the mill-house, you see," he explained, "as soon as I heard the sheriff's party outside. I could have given them the slip myself, had I pleased."

"The mill house?" I answered. The mill stood nearly a quarter of a mile from Coton End, beyond the gardens, and in the direction of the village. I remembered vaguely that I had heard from the servants in old days some talk of a secret outlet leading from the house to it. But they knew no particulars, and its existence was only darkly rumored among them.

"You did not know of the passage," Sir Anthony said, chuckling at my astonishment. "No, I remember. But the girl did. Your father and his wife went with her. He quite agreed in the wisdom of sending her away, and indeed advised it. On reaching the mill, if they found all quiet they were to walk across to Watney's farm. There they could get horses and might ride at their leisure to Stratford and wait the event. I thought it best for her; and Ferdinand agreed."

"And my father--went with her?" I muttered hoarsely, feeling myself growing chill to the heart. Hardly could I restrain my indignation at Sir Anthony's folly, or my own anger and disappointment--and fear. For though my head seemed on fire and there was a tumult in my brain, I was cool enough to trace clearly my father's motives, and discern with what a deliberate purpose he had acted. "He went with her?"

"Yes, he and his wife," the knight answered, noticing nothing in his obtuseness.

"You have been fooled, sir," I said bitterly. "My father you should have known, and for his wife, she is a bad, unscrupulous woman! Oh, the madness of it, to put my cousin into their hands!"

"What do you mean?" the knight cried, beginning to tremble. "Your father is a changed man, lad. He has come back to the old faith and in a dark hour too. He----"

"He is a hypocrite and a villain!" I retorted, stung almost to madness by this wound in my tenderest place; stung indeed beyond endurance. Why should I spare him, when to spare him was to sacrifice the innocent? Why should I pick my words, when my love was in danger? He had had no mercy and no pity. Why should I shrink from exposing him? Heaven had dealt with him patiently and given him life; and he did but abuse it. I could keep silence no longer, and told Sir Anthony all with a stinging tongue and in gibing words; even, at last, how my father had given me a hint of the very plan he had now carried out, of coming down to Coton, and goading his brother into some offense which might leave his estate at the mercy of the authorities.

"I did not think he meant it," I said bitterly. "But I might have known that the leopard does not change its spots. How you, who knew him years ago, and knew that he had plotted against you since, came to trust him again--to trust your daughter to him--passes my fancy!"

"He was my brother," the knight murmured, leaning white and stricken on my shoulder.

"And my father--heaven help us!" I rejoined.

CHAPTER XXV.

IN HARBOR AT LAST.

"We must first help ourselves," Sir Anthony answered sharply; rousing himself with wonderful energy from the prostration into which my story had thrown him. "I will send after her. She shall be brought back. Ho! Baldwin! Martin!" he cried loudly. "Send Baldwin hither! Be quick there!"

Out of the ruck of servants in and about the hall, Baldwin came rushing presently, wiping his lips as he approached. A single glance at our faces sobered him. "Send Martin down to the mill!" Sir Anthony ordered curtly. "Bid him tell my daughter if she be there to come back. And do you saddle a couple of horses, and be ready to ride with Master Francis to Watney's farm, and on to Stratford, if it be necessary. Lose not a minute; my daughter is with Master Ferdinand. My order is that she return."

The fool had come up only a pace or two behind the steward. "Do you hear, Martin?" I added eagerly, turning to him. My thoughts, busy with the misery which might befall her in their hands, maddened me. "You will bring her back if you find her, mind you."

He did not answer, but his eyes glittered as they met mine, and I knew that he understood. As he flitted silently across the court and disappeared under the gateway, I knew that no hound could be more sure, I knew that he would not leave the trail until he had found Petronilla, though he had to follow her for many a mile. We might have to pursue the fugitives to Stratford, but I felt sure that Martin's lean figure and keen dark face would be there to meet us.

Us? No. Sir Anthony indeed said to me, "You will go of course?" speaking as if only one answer were possible.

But it was not to be so. "No," I said, "you had better go, sir. Or Baldwin can be trusted. He can take two or three of the grooms. They should be armed," I added, in a lower tone.

My uncle looked hard at me, and then gave his assent, no longer wondering why I did not go. Instead he bade Baldwin do as I had suggested. In truth my heart was so hot with wrath and indignation that I dared not follow, lest my father, in his stern, mocking way, should refuse to let her go, and harm should happen between us. If I were right in my suspicions, and he had capped his intrigue by deliberately getting the girl I loved into his hands as a hostage, either as a surety that I would share with him if I succeeded to the estates, or as a means of extorting money from his brother, then I dared not trust myself face to face with him. If I could have mounted and ridden after my love, I could have borne it better. But the curse seemed to cling to me still. My worst foe was one against whom I could not lift my hand.

"But what," my uncle asked, his voice quavering, though his words seemed intended to combat my fears, "what can he do, lad? She is his niece."

"What?" I answered, with a shudder. "I do not know, but I fear everything. If he should elude us and take her abroad with him--heaven help her, sir! He will use her somehow to gain his ends--or kill her."

Sir Anthony wiped his brow with a trembling hand. "Baldwin will overtake them," he said.

"Let us hope so," I answered. Alas, how far fell fruition short of anticipation. This was my time of triumph! "You had better go in, sir," I said presently, gaining a little mastery over myself. "I see Sir Philip has returned; from settling his men for the night. He and Greville will be wondering what has happened."

"And you?" he said.

"I cannot," I answered, shaking my head.

After he had gone I stood a while in the shadow on the far side of the court, listening to the clatter of knives and dishes, the cheerful hum of the servants as they called to one another, the hurrying footsteps of the maids. A dog crept out, and licked my hand as it hung nerveless by my side. Surely Martin or Baldwin would overtake them. Or if not, it still was not so easy to take a girl abroad against her will.

But would that be his plan? He must have hiding-places in England to which he might take her, telling her any wild story of her father's death or flight, or even perhaps of her own danger if her whereabouts were known. I had had experience of his daring, his cunning, his plausibility. Had he not taken in all with whom he had come into contact, except, by some strange fate, myself. To be sure Anne was not altogether without feeling or conscience. But she was his--his entirely, body and soul. Yes, if I could have followed, I could have borne it better. It was this dreadful inaction which was killing me.

The bustle and voices of the servants, who were in high spirits, so irritated me at last that I wandered away, going first to the dark, silent gardens, where I walked up and down in a fever of doubt and fear, much as I had done on the last evening I had spent at Coton. Then a fancy seized me, and turning from the fish-pond I walked toward the house. Crossing the moat I made for the church door and tried it. It was unlocked. I went in. Here at least in the sacred place I should find quietness; and unable to help myself in this terrible crisis, might get help from One to whom my extremity was but an opportunity.

I walked up the aisle and, finding all in darkness, the moon at the moment being obscured, felt my way as far as Sir Piers' flat monument, and sat down upon it. I had been there scarcely a minute when a faint sound, which seemed rather a sigh or an audible shudder than any articulate word, came out of the darkness in front of me. My great trouble had seemed to make superstitious fears for the time impossible, but at this sound I started and trembled; and holding my breath felt a cold shiver run down my back. Motionless I peered before me, and yet could see nothing. All was gloom, the only distinguishable feature being the east window.

What was that? A soft rustle as of ghostly garments moving in the aisle was succeeded by another sigh which made me rise from my seat, my hair stiffening. Then I saw the outline of the east window growing brighter and brighter, and I knew that the moon was about to shine clear of the clouds, and longed to turn and fly, yet did not dare to move.

Suddenly the light fell on the altar steps and disclosed a kneeling form which seemed to be partly turned toward me as though watching me. The face I could not see--it was in shadow--and I stood transfixed, gazing at the figure, half in superstitious terror and half in wonder; until a voice I had not heard for years, and yet should have known among a thousand, said softly, "Francis!"

"Who calls me?" I muttered hoarsely, knowing and yet disbelieving, hoping and yet with a terrible fear at heart.

"It is I, Petronilla!" said the same voice gently. And then the form rose and glided toward me through the moonlight. "It is I, Petronilla. Do you not know me?" said my love again; and fell upon my breast.

*   *   *   *   *

She had been firmly resolved all the time not to quit her father, and on the first opportunity had given the slip to her company, while the horses were being saddled at Watney's farm. Stealing back through the darkness she had found the house full of uproar, and apparently occupied by strange troopers. Aghast and not knowing what to do, she had bethought herself of the church and there taken refuge. On my first entrance she was horribly alarmed. But as I walked up the aisle, she recognized--so she has since told me a thousand times with pride--my footstep, though it had long been a stranger to her ear, and she had no thought at the moment of seeing me, or hearing the joyful news I brought.

And so my story is told. For what passed then between Petronilla and me lies between my wife and myself. And it is an old, old story, and one which our children have no need to learn, for they have told it, many of them for themselves, and their children are growing up to tell it. I think in some odd corner of the house there may still be found a very ancient swallow's nest, which young girls bring out and look at tenderly; but for my sword-knot I fear it has been worn out these thirty years. What matter, even though it was velvet of Genoa? He that has the substance, lacks not the shadow.

I never saw my father again, nor learned accurately what passed at Watney's farm after Petronilla was missed by her two companions. But one man, whom I could ill spare, was also missing on that night, whose fate is still something of a mystery. That was Martin Luther. I have always believed that he fell in a desperate encounter with my father, but no traces of the struggle, or his body were ever found. The track between Watney's farm and Stratford, however, runs for a certain distance by the river; and at some point on this road I think Martin must have come up with the refugees, and failing either to find Petronilla with them, or to get any satisfactory account of her, must have flung himself on my father and been foiled and killed. The exact truth I have said was never known, though Baldwin and I talked over it again and again; and there were even some who said that a servant much resembling Martin Luther was seen with my father in the Low Countries not a month before his death. I put no credence in this, however, having good reason to think that the poor fool--who was wiser in his sane moments than most men--would never have left my service while the breath remained in his body.

I have heard it said that blood washes out shame. My father was killed in a skirmish in the Netherlands shortly before the peace of Chateau Cambrésis, and about three months after the events here related. I have no doubt that he died as a brave man should; for he had that virtue. He held no communication with me or with any at Coton End later than that which I have here described; but would appear to have entered the service of Cardinal Granvelle, the governor of the Netherlands, for after his death word came to the Duchess of Suffolk that Mistress Anne Cludde had entered a nunnery at Bruges under the Cardinal's auspices. Doubtless she is long since dead.

And so are many others of whom I have spoken--Sir Anthony, the Duchess, Master Bertie, and Master Lindstrom. For forty years have passed since these things happened--years of peaceful, happy life, which have gone by more swiftly, as it seems to me in the retrospect, than the four years of my wanderings. The Lindstroms sought refuge in England in the second year of the Queen, and settled in Lowestoft under the Duchess of Suffolk's protection, and did well and flourished as became them; nor indeed did they find, I trust, others ungrateful, though I experienced some difficulty in inducing Sir Anthony to treat the Dutch burgher as on an equality with himself. Lord Willoughby de Eresby, the Peregrine to whom I stood godfather in St. Willibrod's church at Wesel, is now a middle-aged man and my very good friend, the affection which his mother felt for me having descended to him in full measure. She was indeed such a woman as Her Majesty; large-hearted and free-tongued, of masculine courage and a wonderful tenderness. And of her husband what can I say save that he was a brave Christian--and in peaceful times--a studious gentleman.

But it is not only in vacant seats and gray hairs that I trace the progress of forty years. They have done for England almost all that men hoped they might do in the first dawn of the reign. We have seen great foes defeated, and strong friends gained. We have seen the coinage amended, trade doubled, the Exchequer filled, the roads made good, the poor provided for in a Christian manner, the Church grown strong; all this in these years. We have seen Holland rise and Spain decline, and well may say in the words of the old text, which my grandfather set up over the hall door at Coton, "*Frustra, nisi Dominus.*"

THE END

Milton Keynes UK
Ingram Content Group UK Ltd.
UKHW032232011124
450424UK00008B/911